MW01711425

PENGUIN BOOKS

Peter Snell

From Olympian to Scientist

The legendary Peter Snell, born in Opunake in 1938, is one of the greatest athletes of all time. He won three Olympic gold medals at 800 and 1500 metres in sensational fashion in the 1960s, displaying a powerful finishing burst that has perhaps never been matched by anyone. He has held eight world records and was voted New Zealand's Sports Champion of the 20th Century. Snell left New Zealand in his early 30s to study in the US and is now an associate professor at the Department of Internal Medicine at the University of Texas Southwestern Medical Center and director of the UT Southwestern Human Performance Center. He lives in Dallas with his wife Miki.

Garth Gilmour was born in Dunedin in 1925, and from 1941 until 1986 worked as a journalist on various newspapers throughout the country and in advertising and public relations. He began writing books in the 1960s. His first book was with Arthur Lydiard, the leading coach and inventor of jogging. Under his influence Garth gave up smoking and took up jogging. He has run five marathons and is an occasional golfer and recreational cyclist. He lives in Auckland with his wife Kay.

Peter Snell

From Olympian to Scientist

Peter Snell and Garth Gilmour

PENGUIN BOOKS

PENGUIN BOOKS
Published by the Penguin Group
Penguin Group (NZ), 67 Apollo Drive, Rosedale
North Shore 0632, New Zealand (a division of Pearson New Zealand Ltd)
Penguin Group (USA) Inc., 375 Hudson Street,
New York, New York 10014, USA
Penguin Group (Canada), 90 Eglinton Avenue East, Suite 700, Toronto,
Ontario, M4P 2Y3, Canada (a division of Pearson Penguin Canada Inc.)
Penguin Books Ltd, 80 Strand, London, WC2R 0RL, England
Penguin Ireland, 25 St Stephen's Green,
Dublin 2, Ireland (a division of Penguin Books Ltd)
Penguin Group (Australia), 250 Camberwell Road, Camberwell,
Victoria 3124, Australia (a division of Pearson Australia Group Pty Ltd)
Penguin Books India Pvt Ltd, 11, Community Centre,
Panchsheel Park, New Delhi – 110 017, India
Penguin Books (South Africa) (Pty) Ltd, 24 Sturdee Avenue,
Rosebank, Johannesburg 2196, South Africa

Penguin Books Ltd, Registered Offices: 80 Strand, London, WC2R 0RL, England

First published by Penguin Group (NZ), 2007
1 3 5 7 9 10 8 6 4 2

Copyright © Peter Snell and Garth Gilmour, 2007

The right of Peter Snell and Garth Gilmour to be identified as the authors of this work
in terms of section 96 of the Copyright Act 1994 is hereby asserted.

Designed by Mary Egan
Typeset by Egan Reid
Printed in Australia by McPherson's Printing Group

All rights reserved. Without limiting the rights under copyright reserved above,
no part of this publication may be reproduced, stored in or introduced into a retrieval
system, or transmitted, in any form or by any means (electronic, mechanical,
photocopying, recording or otherwise), without the prior written permission of
both the copyright owner and the above publisher of this book.

ISBN: 978 0 14 302086 8

A catalogue record for this book is available
from the National Library of New Zealand.

www.penguin.co.nz

CONTENTS

PART TWO

Introduction

I was 40 when I had both the pleasure and the privilege of co-authoring the story of the first half of Peter Snell's life, *No Bugles No Drums*. Now, 40 years on, I have renewed the experience and the enjoyment by co-authoring the story of the totally different second slice of his life. Both halves have been remarkable. Together, they are inspirational evidence of the truth that, if you set your mind to it, you can do anything you want to.

During the first half of his career, Peter propelled himself to the heights of athletic success by winning three Olympic gold medals and setting two Olympic records and eight world records over distances from 800 metres to the mile with displays of raw power-running strength which had journalists scrabbling for words to adequately describe him.

Some of these descriptions were imaginative and creative gems: the power and build of a Percheron; the style of a Sherman tank with overdrive; a modern Pegasus with the ability to run as fast as 29-cent nylons; the lungs of a Metropolitan Opera star. The epithets were ingenious if somewhat exaggerated because they give an impression of immense size. But Snell was just over 170 pounds (77 kg) although he was more heavily muscled than your average middle-distance runner. What he did have, however, was power, the ability to suddenly unleash booming nine-foot strides that totally shattered the aspirations of his rivals — and they included all the other international stars of his time.

Several characteristics shone through Peter Snell's athletics career:

an ability to overcome the many setbacks he encountered, even the self-inflicted ones; the determination to produce some of his finest moments at times when he felt least like making the effort, because he could not contemplate defeat; and the mental strength to switch race tactics instantly when danger threatened.

The second half of Peter's life began after his retirement from running. He faced an uncertain and not particularly promising future until he decided to gamble everything on a completely new direction. His academic background was undistinguished but, at 34 years old, he resolved to become an academic. His subsequent success is virtually a mirror image of his running career — in his tenacity in mastering the setbacks, in his determination to succeed, and in his choice of the right tactics at the right time. He told me once that in whatever he chose to do he wanted to be the best. Why else would he have become US orienteering champion in his age group when he finally turned to that sport?

Peter Snell arrived on the world athletics scene almost unannounced. When he made his Olympic and international debut in Rome in 1960, he was 21 years old and ranked 25th among international 800-metre runners. When he left Rome, he was ranked first. And, for a number of reasons, he might never have been ranked as a champion runner at all — or even a runner. In 1944, when Peter was just six years old, he came close to being killed beneath the wheels of a truck driven by a man employed by his father, George Snell, who was then the engineer for the Opunake Electric Power Board in south Taranaki, where the young Snell grew up.

Relating the incident, which had been kept secret for nearly 60 years, the driver, Gordon Keats, said he saw Peter riding his mini two-wheeled bicycle along Opunake's main street. As he passed the boy, Keats tooted his horn, Peter looked towards him, wobbled, hit the side of the truck and fell in a heap on the roadside. He could just as easily have gone under the truck's wheels. Keats took boy and bike home to his mother. He was later medically checked and x-rayed, found to be merely bruised, and went on in later years to do more damage to his body — fractures of both left and right collarbones and a shoulder separation from cycling mishaps — as well as develop a passion for and expertise in several sports, except running, and, in time, become New Zealand's most memorable athlete.

So, 40 years ago, Peter Snell retired from competition with an international reputation as the greatest and most dramatic middle-distance runner the world had yet seen. Forty years on, he remains on that pinnacle. And, although he left New Zealand to build a new life, with startling success, more than 30 years ago, his level of recognition remains so high here that he was rated New Zealand's Sportsman of the 20th Century and, in 2005, was ranked 12th in a list of 100 New Zealand history-makers, even though many of the judges may have been only vaguely aware of what he has been achieving in the past three decades. By comparison, his fellow Olympic gold medallist, Sir Murray Halberg, was ranked 40th; his coach, the incomparable Arthur Lydiard, 53rd; and John Walker, who ran more than 100 sub-four-minute miles, won Olympic gold over 1500 metres, and was the first to run under 3:50 for the mile, 55th.

When the New Zealand Sports Hall of Fame was established, the first person to be inducted as a member was Peter Snell. He was also twice New Zealand Sportsman of the Year during his all-too-brief running career. He has since been inducted into the International Scholar-Athlete Hall of Fame in recognition of the fact that his illustrious running career has been followed by an equally brilliant scientific life. Snell now has a postdoctoral fellowship at the University of Texas Southwestern Medical Center, where he is an Assistant Professor and Director of the Human Performance Laboratory. He has also written or been co-author of 60 published papers and abstracts on exercise-related research and served as President of the Dallas division of the American Heart Association. He is currently Race Director of a major road race in Dallas and active in that city's bid for the 2012 Olympic Games. Maintaining his contact with New Zealand, he has served as a Governor of the Sports Foundation and returns most years to lend his name and reputation to various sporting events.

Perhaps a most significant occurrence took place in 1994 when Peter Snell became a citizen of the United States. But he retained his New Zealand citizenship as well, because, although America does not officially recognise dual citizenship, staying a New Zealander is important to him. And this year, Massey University finally did what he had to leave to attain three decades ago — it honoured his scientific expertise with an honorary doctorate in Science. Subsequently, Snell has embarked on a series of research studies in New Zealand in collaboration with the university's Institute of Food, Nutrition and Human Health. He is recognised as the Massey University Foundation Fellow in Health and Exercise Science, in association with Telecom's ICT (Information and Communications Technology) subsidiary Gen-i.

Peter Snell has achieved an international reputation for innovative scientific research and practice through his diverse approach to tackling the issue of human health. Asked to summarise his life, he subdivided it into smaller segments. This is how he encapsulated it:

> As I look back over my life, various milestones can be neatly packaged into decades. The first two represent the *first age* of dependence, the third to fifth decades are the *second age* of the career builder and provider, to, finally, beyond 50 years (aka the *third age*), which is the subject of my second book with co-author Garth Gilmour, *Use It or Lose It*, published last year [2006].
>
> For me, the *first decade* involved the innocence of growing up in the beach resort town of Opunake. The *second decade* saw the family move to the bigger, but still small, town of Te Aroha, which, though inland, was nestled at the foot of a 3000-foot mountain that provided ample opportunity for teenage adventure. These were the years when the foundation of sporting skills was laid, including rugby, tennis, badminton, golf, cricket, hockey, gymnastics and even running.
>
> The *third decade* was dominated by athletic achievement and was also most notable for family — my marriage to first wife Sally and the birth of two daughters, Amanda and Jacqueline.
>
> I see the *fourth decade* as one of maturity and reaching a critical decision

point — a 'midlife crisis' at the age of 34 when I decided that the only way to lift myself into a satisfying career was to acquire academic qualifications. The *fifth decade* challenge to translate seven years of formal education into a satisfying career saw the end of my marriage to Sally and took me to meet my second wife, Miki.

During the *sixth decade*, health and fitness issues were important and, as I approach the end of the *seventh*, I am following my own advice by keeping busy at work but not so busy that I do not have time to spend with Miki travelling, cycling and working out together.

There you have it: Peter Snell's short, sweet and succinct skeletal summary of his extraordinary life. Now let us put the flesh on those bones and infuse the lot with the blood of a remarkable athlete, scholar and life scientist.

Garth Gilmour
Auckland, 2007

PART ONE

CHAPTER ONE

Right is left

It may have been an early indication of Peter Snell's mindset for doing things he wanted to do that, when he was at primary school in Opunake, his teacher (whose name he has forgotten) encouraged him, without success, to change his writing hand. He was a natural left-hander and still is but, when he was 16, he forced himself to make the switch to using his right hand for written work. Those were the days of inkwells and nib pens and he was smudging his work writing left-handed from the top — as lefties nearly always do — and having to use a blotter all the time. He recalls deciding, 'Geez, I'm going to write right-handed.' And he did.

These days, if he goes to a whiteboard during a lecture, he uses his left hand — and he's left-handed and left-footed in everything else.

For the first decade from his birth on 17 December 1938, the young Snell lived in Opunake. He was an active lad. He figured that the faster he got to an activity the longer he would have to do it, so he either ran or cycled everywhere around the town. His life was all about freedom and hanging out with his best friend, John Harvey, who lived on a farm up towards Mt Taranaki, the almost perfect volcanic cone which dominates Taranaki province, and in those days was known as Mt Egmont. It helped that his mother and father were sports-active, he at cricket, she at tennis, and that Opunake's location close to a beach sheltered by a horseshoe of cliffs provided an ideal background in which to develop the strength and co-ordination which led him to excel in a variety of sports.

Tennis was Peter's first love. He practised diligently on the local club's volley-board but he also became his father's shadow when the local cricket team played. At ten, he was led, as were most young New Zealanders, into rugby union, but later he played badminton, golf — his father was a four-handicapper — and hockey. Everything interested him, and in everything he displayed the same intensity towards improved technique and performance which later stamped his development as a runner.

In 1947 his father left his post as Opunake Power Board chief engineer and moved the family to Te Aroha, becoming assistant chief to the much larger Thames Valley board. Young Peter lost his beach, his cliffs and nearby Mt Taranaki, but the physical side of his life continued at an increased pace. Some milestones were: primary schools' tennis champion; Thames Valley primary schools' representative rugby halfback; Te Aroha High School first fifteen and first eleven; Thames Valley tennis singles and doubles champion; quarter-finalist in the New Zealand under-17 tennis championship.

And running? The beginnings of ability showed but the interest didn't. He ran when races were available to run in or when he was required to run for his school, but he was just as happy toying with the pole vault or the high jump. In fact, he scored several successes at both disciplines, even after he was established as a more-than-promising young half-miler.

The ability stemmed from his Opunake habit of running every morning for no apparent reason other than to burn off his abundance of energy or to give himself more time at other things. Then, in Te Aroha, he ran daily between home and school; he didn't then have a bike, and running gave him more time for football or cricket. At a Sunday school picnic at Waihi, he easily won a race of about a mile along the beach.

Then, at 12, Peter competed in his first primary school sports meeting. He was unplaced in the sprints but, for the first time, natural ability combined with the stamina he had unwittingly built up through his energetic lifestyle and he won both the 440 yards and 880 yards in record times. The following year, he improved his half-mile time by about 11 seconds but competed only because it was one of those meetings at which he was expected to do something. He remained convinced that tennis would be his future in sport.

Snell's perfectionist nature was demonstrated when he moved on to high school. Before the annual steeplechase — one of those 'everybody starts' events so popular with high schools of the day — he made several exploratory runs over the course. His reasoning: if a thing was worth doing it was worth doing well. He also learnt that he could run well over the rugged cross-country surfaces favoured back then. Again, this ability and his practice runs combined to win him the junior event in record time. He knocked 16 seconds off his own record the next year and was 2 minutes 21 seconds ahead of the next boy to finish.

At 14, Peter raced his first mile. He competed because he was the school steeplechase champion, he couldn't sprint, and he had to run something. His time, which he remembers as a pathetic 5 minutes 21 seconds was, nevertheless, a school record.

Meantime, his tennis was going particularly well. He played in the Auckland under-17 championship and it took Lew Gerrard, New Zealand's most outstanding post-war player, three sets to get rid of him in the quarter-finals.

As the moulding of a future champion at anything, it was an indiscriminate but thorough grounding, and Peter Snell had developed a confidence born of success — but a rude shock lay just ahead.

CHAPTER TWO

Towers of strength

In 1955, Peter Snell was sent as a boarder to Auckland's Mt Albert Grammar School, which enabled him to take science courses such as physics, chemistry and calculus, which were not available at Te Aroha. This was to help prepare him for a career in electrical engineering and thus follow in the footsteps of his father and brother. He came into almost immediate contact with one of the country's most enthusiastic sports masters, Herbie Towers, who had heard from his brother in Te Aroha that Peter was quite a good athlete and was keen to continue with this sport.

So, Peter found himself racing over a mile — and struggling home third about 150 yards behind the winner — and a half-mile — third again and this time about 80 yards back. Each time, he was headed by two Auckland junior representatives, Michael Macky and Tony Aston. As Peter recalls:

> So much for my natural talent. My reaction to these quick and overwhelming defeats was to conclude that they were vastly superior runners and I had better stick to tennis.
>
> Meantime, my father, trying to pull a fast one over my mother, had let the cricket master Daddy Weir know that I was a fairly useful left-arm slow bowler. Daddy promptly tried me out at the nets and I impressed him sufficiently to win a place in the first eleven for its first match. Perhaps I tried a bit too hard at cricket for someone who preferred to play tennis but, luckily, it turned out that cricket was played in the afternoons and I was able to play tennis for the school in the mornings.

> Not so luckily, however, I was at this stage still eligible, under tennis rules, to play for Waikato, and the second school cricket match clashed with a Waikato tennis fixture. Faced with this awkward choice, I committed the unforgivable sin, in the eyes of the school, of electing to play tennis. I didn't play cricket for the school again for two years.

As a runner, Peter's best performance in his first Mt Albert year was fourth place in the intersecondary schools cross-country, behind the formidable Macky and two King's College boys. The following year, he ran second, again behind Macky but ahead of Aston. The only event he won in that first year was the high jump, at 5 feet 2 inches (1.57 m), but he finally came under the influence of Macky, who was a fellow boarder, and was introduced to serious training for the first time. He developed his form well enough to make the 4 x 880 yards relay team for the 'intersec' relays at the end of 1955, which placed him in distinguished company: Aston was the intercollegiate mile champion, provincial two-mile champion and national two-mile runner-up; Macky held the intersec and Auckland junior 880 titles and was national runner-up. The trio, with D. E. Lynch, ran 8:28.7 to whack 7.3 seconds off the record.

Peter did not run another relay until 1961 — the world 4 x mile record against the British in Dublin, when he was teamed with Murray Halberg, Barry Magee and Gary Philpott.

So, his Mt Albert career was distinguished by excellent sporting performances and undistinguished by academic achievement. In 1956 and 1957, he was the school's tennis champion and, because Macky and Aston had both now left, he won the mile and half-mile titles in 1957 and went on to take the intersec 880 in record time.

> The record had been N. Wilson's two minutes flat, a time which both Aston and Macky could have beaten by several seconds, except that they never struck the right conditions or were in the right form at the right time. So, despite the fact that I could never top them, I won the title when all the ingredients of track, weather and fitness were right and clocked 1:59.6.

He also finished second in the broad jump and third in the mile.

These intersecs were terrific meetings. Every college turned on great blocks of supporters, with organised cheerleaders and masses of school colours, and they made a fabulous row the whole time. Running that record in those circumstances was, I think, one of my really big athletic thrills. I remember that when the time was called, the announcer got as far as 'one minute . . .' and the rest was drowned in a Mt Albert roar. It was rather like the feeling that came later with the sub-four-minute mile.

And as I listened, I recalled the comment of an experienced Te Aroha team-mate and sprinter Bob Lipsey, at the Waikato intersecs in 1953. For the second year, I'd finished second in the junior mile after leading all the way to the last 220 yards. Lipsey said, 'Pete, you'll never do any good until you learn how to sprint.'

What, I've often wondered, was Bob's reaction a handful of years later when Peter began demonstrating the most vicious finishing sprint in middle-distance running and led his friend and close rival, the late and lamented John Davies, to describe how chunks of the track were thrown up in his face when Peter streaked past him with two or three hundred yards to run?

In other engagements in this sport-mad period, I played three seasons for the first fifteen — halfback in 1955, second five-eighths in 1956 and first five and wing in 1957. This was a fairly natural promotion away from the pack, where I think I was fouling the team up a bit too much.

In his last Mt Albert year, Peter ran a 4:48.4 mile and a 2:1.6 half-mile but his addiction to tennis suffered from the demands of school team games. At the same time, he developed his golf, taught by his four-handicap father, and played in several schoolboy tournaments, scoring steadily between 80 and 90. The winter badminton he had played at Te Aroha was one omission from his Mt Albert sporting agenda, but he went back to it for a while before the 1960 Olympics because it relaxed his mind from the tensions of athletics training.

In 1957, I joined the Te Aroha Athletic Club so I could run in their New Year's carnival. I won the handicap mile and half-mile and the prospect of winning some more nice trophies lured me back the following year. But this time, the handicappers decided I wasn't going to repeat my 1957 performance so easily. I found myself back on only 15 yards in the 880 — which was only 15 yards ahead of one Bill Baillie and the former national half-mile champion Paul Penlington. My heart sank. No pretty trophies this time.

Nevertheless, I decided to run as hard as I possibly could and I concentrated on catching the runners ahead of me, while all the time expecting Baillie and Penlington to come flying past. I eventually hit the front and, not daring to look back, bashed on until I hit the tape. I was amazed to get there first. The time was 1:57.0 which, with my handicap, compared well with my previous best.

Bill and Paul eventually finished well back in the field. I was elated at the thought that I'd beaten these two outstanding athletes on my own merits. What I didn't realise until I became more conversant with athletics was that they'd been on holiday, were in the meeting for the fun of it, and weren't trying too hard.

This meeting also brought me to my second encounter with Arthur Lydiard, who won a 17-mile road race at the meeting, but I saw him only long enough to tell him I was really interested in tennis, to which he replied casually, 'Okay, it's a good game.'

Peter had met Lydiard for the first time in Auckland. The day after Murray Halberg ran his national mile record of 4:01.2, Macky had taken Peter to Lydiard's home and they'd all run 15 miles together. At least that was the intention, but Peter, now on an intensive learning curve that exposed his inexperience and deficiencies of endurance, wasn't able to finish the distance.

However, the 1:57.0, coupled with a glowing write-up in the local newspaper, was enough to turn his mind in the direction of doing a bit more training for a graded-scratch meeting at Te Aroha at which a Waikato team was to be chosen to challenge Auckland at the end of January. He pulled out his best half-mile, a 1:58.0 off the back mark, to win by 35 yards. This time, a *New Zealand Herald* reporter who had been watching his progress gave him a write-up which encouraged him to toss tennis aside in favour of a growing interest in his prospects as a runner.

> Coupled with his encouragement, of course, was the aspect of achievement. Public repute is a good feeling and, I think, a fairly natural one as it does tend to inspire a sportsman to seek a little more of the same. The *Herald*, for the record, stated that my performance 'was amazing for one who, until three weeks ago, had been training for athletics on a mixed diet of cricket and lawn tennis. It emphasised the potential of a brilliant all-round sportsman . . .' Enough to make anyone keep going at that tender, impressionable age.
>
> I was selected for the Waikato team. But my hopes of doing well against the Auckland half-milers were rudely squashed by the more experienced Waikato runners. I, they informed me, was going to be slaughtered. Probably, I was so irritatingly naïve about myself that I got under their skins. If I know me, I most likely asked them in superior tones who the good half-milers in Auckland were.

Before the Waikato–Auckland meeting, Peter shifted to Auckland to begin work in a quantity surveyors' office and went back to Mt Albert Grammar to do some training. This included a 660 which pleased him and led him to a local coach to find out what he should now do to prepare for the upcoming half-mile.

> Vaguely, he told me to keep jogging around. So to the meeting, to clash with John Hinton, Auckland record-holder at 1:52.8, and 1956 New Zealand champion Penlington. I can't recall exactly what happened during the race, except that, with the exuberance of youth and with nothing to lose, I got stuck straight in and was astounded and delighted to win in the startling time of 1:54.1 — seconds faster than anything I had hoped to do.
>
> Straight after the race, Mike Macky came out of the crowd and cornered me. He asked me if I'd seen Arthur Lydiard. Well, no, I said, since I could hardly count our two previous brief encounters as meetings in the sense Mike was obviously meaning. 'Well,' said Mike, 'after this you have to.'

> At our third meeting, Mike did all the talking, which was pretty much his custom anyway, and, at the end of it, without Arthur asking me or my asking Arthur, I'd agreed to be coached by Arthur and he'd agreed to coach me.
>
> I was an enthusiastic pupil. One of my first workouts with Arthur was with Murray and several others doing 220s. After, I think, three or four of these, I pulled out and said to Arthur, 'Well, these are fairly easy. Should I do them any faster if I feel like it?'
>
> Murray overheard this and his eyes nearly popped out. I think it irritated him more than a little. He was running them flat out . . . Murray at this stage was quite positively the fastest sprinter in the Lydiard group and I guess he must have regarded me as mighty big-headed. But, on Arthur's go-ahead, I joined back in and regularly finished several yards ahead.

Peter had great respect for Arthur, addressing him as 'Mr Lydiard', until told curtly that 'the name is Arthur', and was quickly absorbed into the running family, ready to do anything he was told to succeed. Tennis and everything else was tossed aside as Arthur talked convincingly of national championships and even Empire Games (now Commonwealth Games) possibilities.

> One embarrassing outcome of my early training with Arthur was the spasms of cramp caused by repeated speed work. Several times at movies I caused a stir by suddenly leaping to my feet with a startled shout as one leg or the other stiffened rigidly and agonisingly.

Peter's first nationals were his chance to crack the Empire Games team and he believes that, but for inexperience, he could have done it. But he let Penlington get away with a 53-second first lap; Penlington was caught at the head of the straight by Mike Earwaker, the national 440 record-holder, and they fought all the way to the tape. Earwaker won, both were clocked at a record 1:52.5, but neither went as fast as Snell did as he chased them over the last 220 yards to finish third in 1:52.9.

That was about to change.

CHAPTER THREE

'I struggled'

Now a dedicated Lydiard athlete, Peter Snell joined Arthur's Owairaka club, which, as well as the noted trio of Halberg, Baillie and Magee, included an assorted and cheerful bunch of runners who may not have had the spectacular successes of the top three but trained as hard and as determinedly and provided Peter with the training companions he needed at that stage of his career. He could not handle Lydiard's demanding schedules on his own.

His last race of that 1957–58 season showed him how much he needed the stamina build-up Arthur had mapped out for him. It was a half-mile for Waikato against the Australian Universities track and field team, which included the brilliant Tony Blue, later to become a close friend.

> I had established at least a small reputation as New Zealand's third-best half-miler and I lived up to this by taking the lead from the start and holding it comfortably — for 660 yards. Tony then made me look somewhat silly by clearing out and winning easily.
>
> Arthur urged me to get out with the boys and move into full distance training as soon as I could. I found this particularly hard and my early efforts to get into the 100-mile-a-week stride produced intermittent results. Two good 15-mile runs would be followed by a feeble four-miler as I struggled to recover . . . I was deeply conscious of my shortcomings because a certain line of Arthur's advice was in my mind . . . when I got distance running under my belt so comfortably that I could run a hard Waiatarua and still feel like going round again — *then* I would be ready

for anything in the world. Since the Waiatarua is a soul-searing 22-miler (35.4 km) through the steep and densely bushed Waitakere Ranges, it seemed a remote and improbable objective in my initial distance-running days.

After several weeks of 10- and 15-milers, Peter was persuaded to tackle the full Waiatarua circuit, for which Arthur arranged a large party of runners.

The first eight miles, out through Avondale and Glen Eden, were okay. But then we got into the hills . . . and quickly there were runners straggled out all along the road. I struggled on and actually found myself leaving Arthur and Barry Magee behind. This was nothing exceptional; Barry had just had his injections for the Cardiff Empire Games and was taking it easy and Arthur was staying with him for encouragement.

At the top of the big hill, I was reduced to a walk and feeling rather gloomy about the many miles that still lay ahead. Arthur overtook me, asked me tersely what I was walking for, and went on. Obediently, I broke into a trot again. Nearing Titirangi, 15 miles out, I was in difficulties again and I was convinced everyone else was miles in front. Then Ray Puckett came up from behind. In response to my surprised question, he said tactfully that nature had delayed him a couple of times, he was now right and would keep me company the rest of the way.

At 18 miles, Peter was positive he wasn't going to make it and turned to Keith Scott, who, as arranged by Lydiard, had been following slowly along in his car all the way, and told him to stay handy because he would be needed soon. Keith was a Lydiard ally, a wise philosopher and master masseur who soothed the minds and muscles of many athletes through those remarkable years.

Two miles later, I needed him. But when I looked back, no Keith. He'd gone. He said later that he didn't think I was going to die and that he felt if I conquered the course the first time it would never get me under again. Fine philosophy, no doubt, but the gentle incline of St Jude's hill back in Avondale seemed like the south col of Everest, and if I didn't walk up it then I must have crawled. I remember vaguely getting into

> Hendon Avenue . . . my legs were too sore to even walk and I draped myself over a fence and told myself I was going to make it at all costs. In that company, I wasn't going to let anyone down, least of all myself.
>
> Stupid, blind determination forced me on, reeling along the streets until, somehow, I made home. The rest were all inside, dressed in tracksuits. I tottered in, collapsed on a sofa and burst into tears. It was most humiliating but I just couldn't stop myself.

Keith Scott was right, of course. The Waiataruas no longer held any real fears for Peter Snell. The difficulties still presented themselves from time to time, but the fun and satisfaction became paramount. He cut his time to two and a half hours, and the benefits came quickly when he ran third-fastest time behind Murray and Barry in the Southland Centennial relays around the Avondale racecourse. Now, on the Waiatarua runs, he sought out the faster groups to get the best response out of himself. However, his first national cross-country appearance was a shocker. He finished 55th, unable then to handle the longer distance involved. He never dreamt that he would in time win the title by the best part of a minute and actually take a walk on the way.

Peter's 1959–60 track season kicked off with a 2000-metre race against Murray Halberg but he cannot remember how he got into it. Murray was running as an exhibition for his club and the public after his long overseas campaign which established him among the world's greatest middle-distance stars and saw him break four minutes for the mile in Dublin, the first by any New Zealander.

> It was a race between the all-conquering master, there to exhibit his form, and me, itching to break into the big time. So I had nothing to lose, lots to gain and got stuck in. Murray discovered with a quarter to go that I was still around and stirred up the pace. With 220 to go, he saw I was still there. This time he really stepped on it. I fought back up to his shoulder, hung there round the last bend and from somewhere found a sprint which just got me to the tape ahead of him. I really ran above myself for that one and clocked 5:15.8, which was actually a few seconds better than Murray's Australian record for the distance.

From there on, nothing could go wrong for the raw 20-year-old beginner. He won the Auckland 880 and mile titles in 1:51.6 and 4:12.4, the former actually gaining him his first New Zealand record, for the 800 metres, and giving him huge confidence for the approaching nationals. In the New Zealand mile, he sat back in the field as was his habit, and when the pace hotted up at the bell, trailed the leader, fine Wellington runner Dave Beauchamp, round the last bend and outsprinted him up the straight. Just under an hour later, he faced Beauchamp, the favoured Gerry Hack, from Canterbury, and old bête noir Tony Aston in the half. Again, he sat until the straight and sprinted Hack and Aston out of it in a record 1:52.4. This was the first of a notable series of doubles for Peter: the world's best half-mile for 1961 and a leg of the 4 x mile relay record in Dublin; the half and mile in the Perth Commonwealth Games in 1962; and the 800/1500 double at the Tokyo Olympics in 1964.

A week later came his first international, against American sub-four miler Don Bowden, at the old Olympic Stadium in Newmarket, Auckland, where a howling wind whipped sawdust across the track from a nearby rubbish tip. Peter made the mistake of racing Bowden and nobody else. He let go 300 yards out and was, he thought, comfortably ahead into the straight when Bill Baillie charged past and edged him out in a furious finish. This was Baillie's heyday as an all-rounder: he was national six-mile champion; he'd lost the three-mile title to Halberg by mere inches; he'd beaten Snell over a mile and downed Ray Puckett in a 30-mile marathon — he was close to being unbearably cocky among his friends.

Peter's form raced ahead through the next harrier season. His national cross-country performance improved from 55th to 4th, he won the Round-the-Bridges in Hamilton, ran second to Puckett in the Great Eastern road race and was to run the anchor leg for an Owairaka team in Auckland's Round-the-Harbour relay in September. Warming up to run the last lap from Avondale to Grey Lynn Park, he noticed a sharp pain in one leg but didn't worry about it, although the pain annoyed him for the first two miles. By the two-and-a-half-mile mark, he was limping, by three he was walking, and then he had to stop. He remembers Gordon Gibson, a top runner from Owairaka's arch-rival Lynndale, leaning out of a passing car window and yelling, 'Snell, you're gutless!' The day after, he was on crutches. After several days, a doctor gave him deep-heat treatment. It didn't work. A specialist x-rayed the leg and found a stressed fracture of the tibia. Verdict: three months off.

After two months of total inactivity, Peter was desperate — Olympic Games selection season was approaching. And then a friend drew his attention to the presence in Auckland of Dr Christopher Woodard, of London's Wimpole Street, on a lecture tour on faith-healing. Woodard was known, too, as a world authority on sports injuries.

> I wrote to Dr Woodard and received back a delightful letter. He gave me the impression that he knew exactly what my injury was and exactly how to fix it. The pith of his advice was: don't waste another day; get out in thick-soled shoes on springy grass and begin running and do as much salt-water swimming as possible. This was the sort of active progressive direction I'd been chafing for. I was off, and immediately I sensed that my leg was becoming stronger again.

Then he was taken in hand by good friend, athlete and later coach Don McFarquahar for a holiday at Maraetai Beach, south of Auckland, close to where Lydiard was to build his last home at Beachlands. A 10-mile jog every morning, all the way at seven-and-a-half to eight-minute miles, and a tough routine of speed work every night sent him back to Lydiard recovered and ready to run. Lydiard promptly rushed him off on a test run and he covered 17 miles before he cried enough and spent the next day in bed recovering. Lydiard later confessed that this run nearly killed him, too.

First race up, rising national junior half-mile record-holder Gary Philpott sloshed him by 15 yards in a half-mile handicap race, sending him back to Lydiard for a few sessions of morale-building talks and some strenuous speed workouts, many on a clay road at Stanmore Bay, with Bill Baillie setting a killing pace.

I set my sights now on the Auckland championships, Gary notwithstanding, and it was he who stirred the half-mile along. He streaked through the first quarter in 53 seconds and held a three-yard lead at the bell. He increased speed round the bend into the back and I had to go hard to catch him on the last turn. I think I passed him as we straightened, when I could feel that he was beginning to fade from his fierce pace-setting.

My time was something I'd never expected. I was not only under 1:50 for the first time but I broke Doug Harris's national record with 1:49.2. I felt such a terrific sense of achievement at coming right after such a trying period that I tended to show a little less sympathy than I might have when I learnt that Gary had fallen out of the race with stomach cramps after I passed him.

Snell ran the mile heats and didn't do it very easily, but Lydiard told him he expected him to win the final the following Saturday, despite the presence of Halberg in the field. Rain washed the meeting out for several days and, in heavy, wet conditions which Snell could not handle, Murray won in 4:13 and Snell straggled in much later in 4:24. The nationals followed, on an extraordinary track in Invercargill. Laid out on Rugby Park, it had four straights. In one of the roughest national half-miles ever run in New Zealand, Peter took the lead at the quarter and stayed clear as his most likely rivals bumped and shoved. Gary Philpott was almost pushed right off the track.

Thus far, all Peter's races had been virtual two-man affairs — against Halberg, against Philpott, against Baillie, and against Gerry Hack — but he now went to Melbourne's Moomba Festival to race against Tony Blue — who had just outsprinted Herb Elliott — Elliott, Hack and a lively South Islander, Mike Earwaker.

My time in winning was a relatively slow 1:51.3 but the race proved to me that I was capable of running tactically in international company and, I think, with my New Zealand record, clinched my eventual Olympic selection. But I felt in the race that once again my form was on the down grade. It was a desperate performance and I don't think I would have won if Tony hadn't run a very fast solo 880 two nights earlier.

Snell returned home close to the end of his tether after a long season on inadequate training. He dithered about with his training but finally, on 2 March, he renewed his determination to do his best should he ever get to Rome and kicked off by running 11 and a half miles. He walked some of it near the end and finished with sore stomach muscles but ran the same course the next day and covered 73 and a half miles in the first week. Two weeks later, he hit 100 miles for the first time. Then he folded up with a bad stomach upset. He managed only 50 hard-earned and painful miles the following week.

The seesaw in his condition continued into May. A good week was followed by a bad patch and, although he had the company and the encouragement of Barry Magee, the marathon club, Vern Walker and Ray Puckett, among others, he couldn't sustain the required mileage. In late May, his place in the Olympic Games A team was announced and he concluded he must have been chosen on unfulfilled promise rather than performance.

Inevitably, the selections roused antagonisms.

> I came under fire [from Val Breidis, coach of Marise Chamberlain, the national women's quarter- and half-mile star and former world 440 record-holder, who was not selected], presumably because I happened to run the same distance she did. I found the comparison hard to justify. But, asked Breidis, whose potential is the higher? And he pointed out that I had actually qualified only once and that was with competition which Marise, who had beaten the Olympic standard twice, had never had.
>
> I was still at the age to be affected by the comments of sports writers, but any criticism I received was nicely cancelled out by Charlie Jenkins, in the Wellington *Evening Post*, who made the courageous prophecy: 'He is a high athletic soul destined some day to be the hero of a hundred brilliant victories.' On my record at that stage, he was sticking his neck a long way out.

What might be interpreted as even greater encouragement came from the unlikely source of Murray Halberg, who in those days was as sparing in his praise of anyone as he was in talking about himself.

'Don't think I'm peeing in your pocket,' Halberg said as they ran the Waiatarua one day, 'but you could do bloody well.' Lydiard had five of his athletes in the team — Peter (800 metres), Murray (5000 and 10,000 metres), and marathoners Barry Magee, Ray Puckett and Jeff Julian.

Selection spurred Peter to train harder, including a bid to run the Waiatarua twice in a weekend. He did it and his second circuit was in a personal record of 2:12.45. Moving into circuit training in May, he ran a 5:09 record leg in the Southland Centennial relay and the next day carved five minutes off his Waiatarua record. Training through the New Zealand winter was tough in those primitive days — the choices were soggy grass, muddy clay or the dark, ill-lit and sometimes rain-swept roads. But, in sandshoes and running in the Domain in July, he reeled off three 440s in 51 seconds, 51.5 and 51.2. He was timed by Bill Baillie, who pressed the stopwatch button at the start, jumped in his car and raced along to press it again at the finish.

So, all was going well on the training circuit and, although officialdom tried to throw a spanner in the works, it was going to continue onto the running track.

CHAPTER FOUR

Sharp move

Unbelievably, when the Auckland Athletic Centre asked the New Zealand Association to include Lydiard in the team as official coach, the request was met with the objection that to do so would set a precedent for other sports. The request was passed on to the New Zealand Olympic and Empire Games Association but it was fairly obvious that Lydiard was going to be left behind. This despite the unchallenged assertion after the 1956 Olympics that Halberg, who performed disappointingly in the 1500 final by using the wrong tactics at the start, could have and perhaps would have won if Arthur had been there to guide him. And it ignored the truth that the five Lydiard-trained runners in the team were the pick of the crop.

Auckland harrier section chairman Frank Sharp got Arthur to Rome by launching a public appeal, which rapidly raised the money to enable him to travel as an independent, unofficial coach and virtually guaranteed that New Zealand would be among the track and marathon medals. But how the little-known Snell fitted into this picture was exemplified when he and Murray ran a three-quarter-mile time trial in Rome. Peter finished with great power and full of running in 2:57 after a 2:02 half-mile and Murray ran about 3:01. Back in New Zealand, the story was headlined: 'Halberg in great three-quarter trial' and concentrated on his prospects for the 500 and 10,000 double, adding near the end that 'Snell also registered an excellent 2:57'. Peter would never be in that position again.

About 10 days before the Games, Arthur used the excellent New Zealand quarter-miler Barry Robinson as a pace-maker for an 800-

metre trial, aiming for a first lap of about 53 seconds and a full trial around 1:50.

> Barry, with complete lack of pace judgement, scorched round the first lap in 51.5. I was forced to trail him closely to make use of the pace-making. The result was that it was a hang-on struggle for the last lap; so I was more than pleased with the final time of 1:48. I hadn't the slightest inkling then that Barry was going to pull the same tearaway stunt on me 18 months later and drag me out to a world record for the distance.
>
> I decided then and there that I would be prepared to reproduce a run of this nature to progress beyond the first round and, looking back at the qualifying times required at the previous Olympics — 1:50 and even as slow as 1:53 — I felt that my 1:48 should get me to the final . . . Had I been told that it would be necessary to break the Olympic record just to get beyond the semi-finals, I would probably have given up in despair. I wasn't *that* confident.
>
> A few days before the racing began, we saw a Canadian half-miler run about six quarters in 53 seconds. He was looking particularly impressive, but Arthur's reassuring comment was: 'The clot is leaving it all on the training track. He probably won't get past the first round.' He didn't.

Then Arthur was delighted to learn that an extra round of heats had been scheduled because of the number of entries, which meant two races on one day and four races over three days for those who went right through. He told Peter: 'This is going to be a test of stamina and you are probably the only athlete sufficiently prepared to stand four races in three days.' As usual, he knew exactly what he was talking about. There were many who didn't but could possibly be excused. One story has it that before the four-man field in Snell's heat took their marks, a BBC commentator declared: 'This is ridiculous. A four-man field and you can write down the first three names before the race starts.' He meant Ernie Cunliffe, the American ranked third in the world; Christian Waegli (Switzerland), the fifth ranked; and Istvan Rozsavoegli (Hungary), the top-ranked 1500-metre runner.

> Waegli, a renowned front runner, led most of the way. I sprinted in the straight and passed him. I didn't realise how fast we were running. I was

> carried away by the atmosphere and quite forgot that I had another race to run in the afternoon. I recorded 1:48.1 . . . I felt tremendously satisfied. I felt that at no stage had I been really extended. Among the rest of the team, my win had been a major sensation — nothing that I required was too much trouble. I had suddenly become quite precious material.
>
> The quarter-finals were set for 4.30 on the afternoon of a hot day — and we were excited to find that I was drawn against the gaunt Belgian Roger Moens, the world 800 metres record-holder and favourite for the event. Following the tactics we worked out, I was content to run the first lap towards the end of the field, where I could keep an eye on proceedings. The second and last time down the back straight, I moved up. I felt a little tiredness. With 300 to go, I jumped and hit the front. We swung round towards the straight and Roger challenged me and edged past. A glance behind showed we were clear of the rest . . . there was little point in expending excessive energy in chasing Roger and I was quite happy to run home second, clocking 1:48.6 to Roger's 1:48.5.

The real strategy for winning the gold medal now kicked in. Rumour had it that Moens had psychological problems and had never won a really big race so, since they were both drawn in the first semi-final, the plan was for Peter to try to win the race and, psychologically, put paid to the Belgian. The first quarter of the race was run fairly fast and, although the tempo quickened down the back straight, the previous day's racing was beginning to have an effect. Moens passed the pace-maker, Cunliffe, with Peter on his heels. Cunliffe called, 'Come on, Jerry', to his team-mate Siebert but he, like Ernie, had had it.

> I tracked Moens round to the straight entrance and applied the pressure. I was going hard to beat him to the tape but there was still, I felt, a slight amount in reserve and that was comforting. I clocked 1:47.2, which would have been a Games record except that the Jamaican George Kerr was forced to run 1:47.1 in the other semi to head off Waegli — and, for the first time since 1896, there were no Americans in the final.
>
> Through these three races, I'd been wearing shoes which Arthur, who was then in the shoe business, had made specially for me. After

my third success, representatives of adidas wasted no time in reaching me with samples of their latest model. Undeniably, with their world-dominating experience, it was a far superior shoe, but not for a moment did I entertain the idea of making a change . . . I'd become attached to those Lydiard shoes.

Arthur assured Peter that Moens and Kerr, when they passed his strategic position at the 200-metre mark, had shown real strain but that he, Peter, had looked easy when he went past. And they were surprised the following day by the amount of time the other finalists spent warming up — much longer than they had for the heats.

From the gun, I sprinted hard in my outside position round to the point in the back straight where we broke lanes. I looked across and found myself a hole in fourth place. The crowd noise was so overpowering I didn't hear the time or the bell. We turned into the back straight. I was quite well positioned but the runners in front now started to run wide and spread themselves across the track.

Moens came past with a burst of speed. My pre-arranged plan was to sprint at 200-to-go, but now I found that the speed of the whole field was too great to allow me to get into the challenging position from which I could let the sprint go. I almost started to lose hope. We reached the 200 mark and the field in front of me was three wide going into the last bend. I had the choice of continuing running on the inside or trying to run right round the field.

In view of the pace, I chose the easier course. I stayed inside. I felt that this meant abandoning the chance of winning, but there was the hope that the front runners would split and I could get through into a place. Roger had hit the front and Kerr was in a challenging position. We swung into the straight. The runners spread out — I discovered a gap and edged past the fading pace-maker Waegli and drew level with the others. Here was a chance for third . . .

Then only Moens and Kerr were in front of me and I had a clear run to the tape ahead. I realised I'd improved to a chance for second and put everything into a final sprint. Moens appeared to be slowing. With only 20 yards to go, I suddenly felt I could win. All I remember from

> that point is hurling every ounce of effort into the finish and flinging myself forward. The finishing line flashed past . . . I didn't know where I had finished. I was just so delighted with my own performance I didn't care whether I was first or second. I turned and walked back towards the finishing line . . . it hit me then that I'd just beaten some of the greatest half-milers in the world.
>
> Then Roger came over. His face looked tired. He congratulated me, too, and I asked, 'Who won?' Roger said, 'You did.'

Peter Snell was stunned by his double success — a gold medal and an Olympic record. So was the rest of the world interested in track and field. They all wanted a piece of the runner no one had taken any notice of four days earlier. He was suddenly hot property and his life would never be the same again.

CHAPTER FIVE

'Complete blank'

The sensation that was Peter Snell was quickly followed less than an hour later by the certainty that was Murray Halberg. Following Lydiard's crafty race plan, Murray sprinted away from the field with three laps to go and hung on grimly to win from the fast-closing Hans Grodotzki. Snell was probably the first to reach him after he hit the tape and then collapsed on the grass beside the track.

> I know as I wrung his limp hand, he didn't have the faintest idea who I was. He just lay there . . . But after he'd recovered and run half a lap round the track to where Arthur was waiting, I had a proprietary feeling that, right then, with two consecutive track wins, the stadium belonged to New Zealand. It was a moment never to be forgotten.
>
> Murray and I received our medals from New Zealander Sir Arthur Porritt. I haven't a notion what he said to me. My mind was still completely blank, unable to register permanently my reactions or what was going on around me.

Precisely what it meant to be an Olympic champion began to dawn on Peter when Lydiard arranged for him to escape, with an Australian friend, to Capri for some peace and quiet. They found a hotel which offered a cheap room for the night, signed in, handed over their passports and were then taken down to a basement room with an enchanting outlook — a blank retaining wall a few feet away.

> We returned upstairs to reclaim our passports. There was a notable change in the atmosphere up there. The receptionist was regarding

> us with new interest. Plainly, she had just connected the name and photograph in my passport with a race she'd been watching on television the day before. The result was an overwhelming welcome and one of the choicest rooms in the hotel with a magnificent view — still at the bargain price. It was very pleasant . . .

Halberg and Snell flew to London for the United States versus Commonwealth meeting. Peter was anchor man in a 4 x 880 yards relay with Tom Farrell (Britain), Tony Blue and George Kerr. He got the baton about 10 yards behind Jerry Siebert, who took off at a terrific pace in a bid to make amends for his poor showing in Rome.

> I managed to close the gap before the end of the first lap but I had to cover it in a flying 50 seconds to do so. Then some foolish instinct made me sprint past Jerry in the back straight, despite the fact that I was feeling flogged by the fierce pace of the first lap. As I went past, an American coach crouched by the side of the track shouted, 'Follow him, Jerry, and take him in the straight.'
>
> Flogged or not, I was positive I wasn't going to be taken by anyone anywhere. And here, for the first time, I looked back and began developing a habit that has stayed with me ever since. I had at least three looks back as I hit the straight. Jerry was well back and I went on to win by about 10 yards.

Peter was timed officially at a remarkable 1:44.9. Allowing for the half-second advantage of the flying start, this equalled a half-mile of 1:45.4 — 1.4 seconds inside the world record. It also confirmed a statement by Lydiard that Peter could have broken the record in Rome had he not been boxed in at a critical stage. Peter had disagreed with Arthur, but now realised that he had not appreciated his own capabilities. The insightful Lydiard had.

Next stop was Dublin's famous Santry Stadium, where Australians Herb Elliott and Alby Thomas had run world mile, two- and three-mile records. Peter's hopes of a world half-mile record were blown because no one would set a fast enough first-lap pace and he won in an Irish record 1:47.9 but 1.1 seconds outside the world mark. The following night, he had his first competitive run over a mile since his 4:10.2 in March 1959, but in the last lap he felt lifeless, clocking 4:01.5 while Elliott won in 3:57.

Back then to the equally famous White City for a sponsored meeting between London and Pan-American cities, which matched Peter against his old rival George Kerr in a half-mile which had a carefully selected rabbit to push the early pace. Peter followed the rabbit, and George followed Peter, but the first lap in 53 seconds was awkwardly slow and then George didn't attack and Peter was 15 yards clear in 1:47.5. Missed again.

Peter returned home then to busy weeks with speeches, supporting an appeal to raise money for a cinder track, sorting and dealing with the piles of telegrams and letters inviting talks, seeking his opinion on various subjects and asking for autographs, and the beginning of six months of sharing a flat with four other athletes.

> On which subject I won't say much except to advise anyone aspiring to high athletic deeds to think twice before surrounding themselves with the kind of environment that existed in our digs. We were all athletes in training, so the earliest anyone could get home to start dinner was about 7.30 p.m. By the time the washing up was done, it would be 9.30 or ten o'clock — rather late for two of us who were at the same time supposed to be studying for the betterment of our careers.

After that experience, he moved to what he could only describe as paradise, boarding with the Warren family in Pt Chevalier, a pleasant western Auckland suburb, and becoming practically a member of the family until he married in 1963.

The bloom faded, however, when he fell and injured one leg while racing at breakneck speed downhill in a King of the Mountain race on Mt Wellington to help raise cinder track funds.

This was, incidentally, the only time I took part in a race involving Snell. On a generous handicap to balance my jogging-only training against the seasoned background of 'real' athletes, I won the veterans' section and promptly retired.

Several weeks of treatment were needed before Peter could get back into training — only a month before Moens and Kerr and the American miler Dyrol Burleson were to begin a tour of New Zealand. Arthur hurled him into a crash training programme just before Christmas but he was still limping when he warmed up for a mile trial race in Nelson in January. He surprised himself by running 4:08.4 after a slow first half, and decided he was fit enough to compete against his Rome rivals.

The Agfa-backed tour gave New Zealand its first taste of sponsored athletics and launched a new, if somewhat short-lived, era in track and field entertainment. First, Snell beat his Rome rivals in Auckland over 880 yards, running a New Zealand record 1:49. But three days later, in Napier, George Kerr taught him a sharp lesson in tactics with a stratagem which Peter promptly added to his own repertoire and later used many times with devastating effect. Peter was leading comfortably along the back straight on the second lap when George passed him with such a burst of acceleration that Peter was momentarily demoralised — and five yards back. George took the race and Snell's new record by a tenth of a second.

> George showed me that this kind of lightning burst completely, if only momentarily, deflates the runner who is caught by it. Psychologically, he is trapped into a feeling of hopelessness by the impression of sheer speed which his opponent's surge gives. George tried this ruse on me again, in Dublin in 1961, but I was a wiser man then, appreciated what he was trying to do, and caught him before he could get the vital gap.

After Napier, Peter and George raced each other eight more times. George never won again.

Burleson shaped early as the star of the tour, beating Halberg and Baillie over 1500 metres and winning with a 4:04.4 mile in Napier before returning to Auckland for a meeting expected to produce the first sub-four-mile run in New Zealand. What it did produce for the 15,000 spectators was an extraordinary contest. Baillie and Neville Scott teamed for the early pace-making, ran the first half in 1:58 and had a lead of 60 yards on Burleson, Halberg, Snell and the rest. They also had a firm grasp on that sub-four time.

But then Scott caught his foot on a marker peg and fell.

> Bill looked around and behaved like a startled rabbit with no place to hide and the hawks circling overhead . . . Burleson, Murray and I reacted as if Bill really was the trapped rabbit. We knew we had him out in the open, our pace quickened, and we began the inexorable swoop in for the kill. Bill was game to the last. But with about 200 yards to go, we gathered him in.

Straightening for the tape, Burleson led. Peter, in third, made his break — but so did Murray, blocking him for a crucial moment, and the American won in 4:05.6 with Peter on his shoulder.

Then, in Christchurch, Peter, Roger and George finished another half in their Rome order. The only difference was that Burleson beat them all. Finally, in Wellington's wind, Murray beat Burleson over a mile in 4:04.2.

Peter was feeling jaded by now and skipped the nationals. He was lazily fishing off the deck of a launch in the Hauraki Gulf, off Auckland, when the radio announced that Gary Philpott had just won the New Zealand half title and beaten Peter's record with a brilliant solo run in 1:48.8. Peter was galvanised back into action and realised later that this was probably the best news he could have heard to refire his spirits when he was just beginning to enjoy the easy way out.

He cruised into 1961 on the back of determined but sometimes patchy training with the Perth Empire Games in 1962 as his goal. But, in May, Arthur was invited to lead a team of Murray, Barry Magee, Peter and a fourth runner to compete in the World Games and elsewhere in Europe. The difficulty was that Bill Baillie thought he had been named as the fourth but the decision had been left to the New Zealand selectors, who opted for Philpott. Bill's spontaneous and public expressions of his pique raised rather a bad odour for a time.

Peter was now thrown into another crash course of only six weeks to build the speed onto his undoubted endurance. He was quick to prove that it was enough as Lydiard's little team startled the world with its dominance and power from 800 metres to 10,000.

CHAPTER SIX

Cots case

First stop on the 1961 tour was California, where Peter came face to face with the burden heaped on young American runners and with the quality of the state's famous fruit. He stayed with a family whose son, at 17, had run 1:52 for the half and 4:10 for the mile. He had immediately been snapped up by Stanford University on a scholarship which required him to compete constantly in track meets, running both distances and often the 880 leg in a relay. This unremitting bid for university points — and the money that goes with them — was losing more good runners for the United States than it bred, and this lad was one of the victims.

> One of my first mistakes in California was to lose completely my sense of moderation as far as the state's apricots were concerned. The 'cots', as Californians call them, grew right to the edges of the road along which we trained, and I couldn't resist reaching up and helping myself as we ran along. Invariably, this led to my training runs finishing much faster than they began.

The tour opened with a meeting in London's White City. Halberg was to be matched against his old Polish rival Zimny and the Englishman Bruce Tulloh; but when Zimny found out that he was to face Murray over three miles, he cabled urgently that he would start in the mile, and Murray didn't start at all because he was suffering the after-effects of an anti-tetanus injection. Barry Magee ran in his place, spreadeagled the field with a Halberg-like breakaway with more than two laps to go, and won in an astonishing 13:18 — less than eight seconds outside the world record and 13 seconds faster than his previous best. Peter, with Gary setting the pace as usual, won the half comfortably in 1:48.3.

In Gateshead, feeling sluggish, Peter trailed Gary by 30 yards down the back straight on the second lap but dredged up a finishing sprint and won by four yards in 1:50.4. Murray startled everyone by winning a mile in 4:03.4 while barely recovered from his anti-tetanus reaction, which saw him swell so much it was touch and go whether he would explode.

Joined by Australian Pat Clohessy, the team crossed to Europe for the World Games in Helsinki, an athletes' paradise after the conditions they dealt with in New Zealand — comfortable quarters, 400-metre cinder track, indoor stadium, tennis courts, a gymnasium, and pleasant tracks winding through neighbouring forests. But sleep was difficult — the long, slow twilight meant only two hours of true darkness.

Peter was matched against seven elite runners, including four of the other five Rome finalists — Waegli had retired — but Gary was relegated to a B-grade 800 metres. Finnish champion Olavi Salonen led through 400 metres in 55 seconds, with Peter snuggled in behind him. Then, unchallenged, Peter sprinted home from 300 metres in comfort to win in 1:47.6. Moens and Kerr were out of the placings. Then Peter and Arthur sat through one of the most astonishing races they had ever seen.

> Murray dominated the 5000 metres tactically and, entering the last lap, was well ahead of the field, headed by Gordon Pirie. With 300 to go, he burst into his final sprint and it was all over, bar the shouting, until he ran through a tape which, at his request, had been put across at the three-mile mark in case of world record time. We were completely staggered then to see him slow, stop and begin waving happily to the crowd — 188 yards short of the finishing line.
>
> The crowd, naturally, began waving back frantically and shouting and pointing. Murray seemed to twig something was wrong, looked back and saw Gordon, grim determination all over his face, bearing down

> on him rapidly. The absence of photographers, finishing judges and other normal race-end features must also have seeped into Murray's consciousness because he abruptly took off like a startled stag. Fortunately, he had gained such an advantage he still won with room to spare . . . It was an episode none of us allowed him to forget for a long time. Arthur said later that he nearly threw his stopwatch at Murray.

Why it happened isn't clear but Halberg has said since that he frequently ran in a state of semi-coma in which he was not entirely aware of anything except the physical and mental act of running. Presumably, the feeling of the tape hitting his chest was the only significant outside influence that had any meaning for him. Barry Magee's 10,000-metre race saw him clear out from Dave Power, who won the bronze medal in the Rome 10,000, and become the second New Zealander, after Murray, to break 29 minutes — by nearly 10 seconds. Gary finished second with a lack-lustre performance in his B-grade race. Peter thought he was 'browned off by his relegation'.

Next stop: Cologne, on a 500-metre cinder track softened by heavy rain. Peter was uncertain about how to judge pace in a race which began in the back straight and got the bell first time past the finish line, and he also forgot to learn the German starter's words of command.

> I simply reasoned that the first guttural sound from him would be the instruction to get on our marks, his next would be the 'set', and then we'd get the gun. There were about 12 in the field and, again, I neglected to note that I was the only one to take a crouch start. I was on one knee waiting for the second command when the gun cracked. The big field pelted away, striving for premier positions before running into the first long bend.
>
> A bit bemused about what was going on, I found myself at the rear and tangled up with the rabbits who were dribbling into the trailing positions. I was quite unable to get clear and was 20 yards down on the leaders when we hit the bend. Taking the bend, I searched desperately for Paul Schmidt, German record-holder in 1:46.2 and fourth in the Rome final. There he was, tucked nicely behind the pace-maker with

the best of the running. Schmidt was a nice guy and we'd exchanged pleasantries while we were warming up. Now, he was 20 yards away and I didn't regard him pleasantly at all.

I was trailing the field when we got the bell. I had to get up and the only way to do it was to go several lanes wide on the big bend and battle my way through the bunch. But by the time I reached the front of the group, a select bunch of four Germans, including Schmidt, had broken away by 10 or 15 yards.

Down the back straight, I closed this deficit desperately but, as I did, Schmidt sprinted away on his own. Round the last bend and into the straight for the long 150 yards run to the tape, he was still 10 yards in front. I could hear the crowd going wild — this must have looked a sitter for the local champ — but Schmidt looked back and I knew the effort of his early sprint was beginning to affect him. I hurled everything into a final bid to catch him.

With 20 yards to go, I drew up on his shoulder. He used tactics common to many European runners, forcing me out towards the middle of the track to stop me getting past. But my momentum was so great that, somehow, I got round him and flung myself into a vital one-yard lead as we reached the tape. The result seemed to stun the crowd. There was a stony silence and the atmosphere was one of the strangest I've ever experienced. It was only when I took the victory dais that the people burst into applause.

Peter's time, 1:48.2, wasn't exceptional. He was relieved to win and thought little more of it until he met Murray and Arthur and received the full flow of praise for what Arthur later rated as the greatest race he ever saw Snell run. It was a superb demonstration of not only the unbridled power of the greatest middle-distance runner the world has seen but also of his mental resolution not to be beaten.

Looking back, I recall controlling myself firmly when I found myself so far down, telling myself not to lose my head and try sprinting to close the gap quickly. I adopted much the same attitude I would in a handicap race and, although I didn't really have time for assembled thoughts as I struggled past those tail-enders, I must have stuck pretty rigidly to this

> self-discipline to avoid panicking when I found first the bunched leaders and then Schmidt by himself keeping well out in front of me as the race ran out.

The tourists, now including more Australians, moved on to the lightning-fast Santry track in Dublin, where the only opposition for Peter appeared to be the inevitable George Kerr. Peter was inclined to discount him as a threat and decided to aim for a record. Gary couldn't set the early pace as planned because he was badly boxed at the start, but an Irishman, McLeane, shot away and Peter stayed right on his heels through a 52-second first quarter.

> Then he faded abruptly and I found myself in the lead with no desire to maintain the pace. Perhaps I was thinking of the four by one mile relay to which we'd become committed later in the meeting — anyhow, I let the pace slacken and was drifting along the back straight when George suddenly hurtled past. Thoughts of Napier sprang to mind. *Oh, no, not again!* Desperately I chased him round the last bend. I was about a yard back as we hit the straight. George was in top gear and I inched forward in an unexpectedly desperate battle. We passed the 800 metres mark locked together and, in the closest duel I've ever had with George, I finally got home by a foot. Both of us were credited with 1:47.2, the fastest half-mile time in the world for the year, and good considering the slow third 220 which ruined all chances of a world record.

Behind them, three others, including Gary, recorded their fastest times for the year.

Snell never knew exactly how the New Zealanders got roped into the 4 x mile relay but Arthur and the meeting promoter, Billy Morton, apparently organised it to give an English team a fillip in its attempt on the world record of 16:25.2, held by Hungary since 1959. Arthur's plan was that Gary would run the first leg. Because he wasn't a miler, this would force the Englishman to set the pace and drag Gary along. Murray would run second to win back the deficit Gary was expected to concede; Barry, another non-miler, would try to hold the lead Murray was expected to give him; and Peter would do his best with what was left of the race. Peter told Barry he wanted at least 20 yards' start on his leg.

The rest of us adopted a fairly patronising attitude towards Gary, telling him not to worry too much and assuring him a 4:20 mile or thereabouts would keep us in the hunt. We calculated this was the best we could expect from him . . . Murray should manage around 4:03, Barry about 4:12, and I should do approximately 4:05, rather a remote prospect after the hard half. These times added up to a 16:40 total . . . the English had already had one attempt at the record and had averaged just over 4:06 each.

Stan Taylor led off for England and Gary tucked in behind. He weakened a little in the third lap and Taylor got away by about 30 yards. We held our breaths as we waited for the inevitable in the final lap. We were obviously going to start the second mile well down. Then I suddenly thought, 'Hell, he's gaining!' He was. Only 15 yards behind going into the back straight and then we were amazed to see him starting a finishing run. I think at this moment we realised we were possibly being run back into the race so effectively that we were within reach of victory ourselves.

Gary ran on magnificently to finish only 10 yards behind Taylor in 4:12.9. Murray, matched against John Anderson, who he'd only just beaten [earlier in the tour], was able to cut the lead down to three yards. But when he failed to get into the lead, the hopes raised by Gary's run turned to despondency. Anderson ran an unexpected solo of 4:05 against Murray's 4:02.5 — this meant Barry had to run without the lead against the well-performed Alan Simpson. But suddenly Barry was striding out beautifully and had actually closed the gap in the first 220 yards. By the third lap, it looked as if he might even have the lead at the baton change until Simpson finished strongly and gained five yards before handing over to Brian Hall in 4:05 to Barry's 4:07.2.

The atmosphere was terrific. I'd completely forgotten about my half-mile, and heaved myself into the race, closing the gap immediately to get the benefit of a close trail. Hall stirred the pace along and forced me to run the first lap in 58 seconds. But then he eased and we ran the next two in 63.2 and 62.9, which gave me the breather I needed.

> Coming up to the bell, I saw Pat Clohessy performing excitedly on the inside of the track. I vaguely recall hearing some mention of a record. I felt a lot of tension. When would Hall make his sprint? Would I still be able to hang on? But I felt inspired instead of tired, intoxicated by the atmosphere. It wasn't the trouble holding Hall that it should have been. Just before the last curve, I flung everything into the finish. Wrestling up the straight, I wasn't aware of anything except that tape. I was nearly unconscious and I apparently fell straight through the tape into the arms of the others. I don't remember that.
>
> My time was 4:01.2, Hall's 4:04.8. It was my fastest mile and just enough to give us the record by 1.6 seconds. I couldn't help feeling the irony of the situation. After trying so hard for the 800 and 880 records, the one I'd got was one I'd never at any stage thought about.

Peter still regards that relay as one of the great moments of his life. Among the many individual triumphs for all of them, it was a true team effort in which everyone had performed to a remarkable level. Gary, for instance, had never before competed over a mile but ran magnificently only 75 minutes after recording his career-fastest half-mile. Murray, whose objective after Rome was to run world records for three miles and 5000 metres, took his place knowing his greatest chance for the first of those records would probably be on the same track the following evening. Yet he still hammered out 4:02.5 for New Zealand. Barry, despite his earlier three-mile and 10,000-metre runs in London and Helsinki, still had a reputation as a marathon runner, and what he did was as unexpected and out of character as his remarkable run in Murray's place in London.

For Snell, his performance proved what an athlete could do in an inspired moment and for the first time steered his thoughts towards more concentration on the mile.

The following night, Peter struggled to finish third, on tired legs, in the Santry mile, clocking 4:10, but Murray turned on another of his astonishing performances.

> He was running to approximately world time for the first two miles, looking good, and then Dave Power took over. The pace slackened off,

> but Murray was content to sit behind. Then, just as we were thinking that perhaps the mile had taken too much out of him and he was running just to win, he came up the straight to get the bell and, to our astonishment, stepped out a lane and took off like an unleashed greyhound. Never have I seen the final lap of a three-mile run as fast as Murray ran it that night. He hurtled through in 53.4 seconds — about a second faster than the second lap of my half-mile — and finished only 0.8 seconds outside the world record in 13:11.6.
>
> In the two or three laps before the last, he'd obviously thrown away a wonderful chance . . . he said he'd struck a little flat patch and had decided Power could possibly beat him. But, with a lap left, he felt so good again he just threw caution to the winds.

Off to Sweden and Peter's first race over the European distance of 1000 metres, in which he was matched against the local hero, Dan Waern, on a loose track which did not encourage fast times. Peter followed Waern until the last 200 metres and sprinted home 10 yards clear in 2:20.4, which he rated not particularly good but was the third-fastest time for the year. The record, 2:16.7, stood until 1965, when Peter broke it in Auckland.

Peter met Waern again over the half in Stockholm a few days later but the life had gone out of his running and he sat back in the field before kicking home from the back straight to win in about 1:48. Then he sat back again to watch Murray's 5000-metre bid.

> It was one of the tensest 5000-metre races I've ever seen. Barry and Murray got well clear of the field and Barry was running the race of his life. He didn't look anything like the athlete who had for so long been mesmerised by the Halberg reputation and ability. But even though he was running so strongly, he made no incisive effort to break away. Even at the point where Murray went through his usual bad patch, Barry didn't try to open up a gap . . . So they stayed together and with a lap to go Murray placed the issue beyond doubt, winding up a sprint which took him away from Barry and through the three-mile mark in the world record time of 13:10. From there, Murray finished with a terrific sprint but he was a bare fifth of a second outside Vladimir Kuts's coveted 13:35 record.

> Barry finished in 13:39.2, a marathon man's effort which went on the record as the fifth-best all-time performance, behind Kuts, Halberg, Pirie and Bolotnikov — but ahead of such illustrious runners as Iharos, Janke, Zimny, Grodotski, Chataway and Zatopek.

The race ended the most successful tour yet undertaken by any New Zealand athletics team, large or small, before or since. When they returned to Auckland, a local newspaper decided to run pictures of them back at their normal activities. Barry was back at his grocery counter, Murray was in his brewery laboratory, Gary was at the drawing board in his office — and Peter was in bed with a newspaper and a cup of tea. He was back home, trained out, and concerned about pending quantity surveying examinations rather than running.

But one thought nagged. This was the summer of Empire Games selection and the possibility was that he would run against the world-dominating mile/1500 metre Australian, Herb Elliott.

CHAPTER SEVEN

Bright idea

The urge to run again arrived on 17 September. Peter marked it as the day he ran from Pt Chevalier to the Avondale racecourse, covered six laps of the course, ran home again and for the first time felt quite good. He also had a bright idea to save himself a lot of time: he would run to work, so he could sleep in until 7 a.m., employ the time normally wasted on a morning bus trip, begin evening training half an hour earlier and, more importantly for a cadet on a meagre 13 pounds a week, save a lot of money. Every Monday morning, he took the bus to work with four changes of clothing; every Friday he took the bus home again with four sets of shirts, socks and underwear to be laundered.

> The only disadvantage was that at times, perhaps subconsciously adding merit to the money-saving aspect of this system, I tended to become competitive by attempting to race the bus into the city.

Regular commuters on the route followed his progress with fascination and many testified to the fact that there were times when the bus came a distant second. The bus fares Peter saved were not recorded but his progress was. In mid-October, he won a mile against Murray and Bill Baillie in 4:13 and trained 100 miles in one week. But it was November before he managed to get around Waiatarua. He ran four miles to Arthur's home first and then padded round in 2:11, his best since before Rome.

> The following day I began my circuit training but I did only two weeks of this, missing out Wednesdays because I competed in club events that

night. During the first week, Alan McKnight, Johnny Robinson, sprinter John Trathen and I took off by rental car to run in a scratch meeting at Ohakune. None of us bothered to consult a road map and Alan was driving when we shot past the turn-off just south of Te Kuiti. We drove on blithely until, eventually, water appeared on our right. What was the sea doing down in the middle of the North Island?

Alan insisted it was a big lake; one existed, he said confidently, around these parts. He had to change his opinion when we rounded another bend and it became obviously the rolling Tasman. We were in Awakino. We drove on to Mokau, stopped to think about our predicament, and finally hailed a local motorist. He told us it was possible to cut inland rather than double all the way back, which led us to a nightmarish trip over a twisting metal road. I find that driving myself is a successful antidote to car sickness but not this time. Four times, I had to stop and get out from behind the wheel to be ill.

Eventually, they reached Ohakune, and Peter's 4:14.7 on the rough school track was, in the circumstances, hard running. The following weekend, he ran his first — and last — marathon, the Owairaka annual round a circuit of Mt Albert streets. He was keen to do a respectable time but had never run more than 22 miles before and wondered whether this had conditioned him against running any farther.

I felt fine for 15 miles and at 20 was fourth behind Ivan Keats [a future Olympic marathoner], Halberg and Merv Hellier. I remember lapping Murray's father, Jock, who, at the age of 58, was running his first marathon, too. Half a mile later, my legs gave in and I was forced to slow to a walk. Jock came sailing past me this time. He had a gleeful expression on his face. He said later it was one of the highlights of his belated athletics participation to pass an Olympic champion.

I had four miles to go. I managed to break into a run again until I got to the next feeding station. I stopped there for a long drink. I continued pathetically, drifting farther back in the field and, at 24 miles, felt that my legs would not carry me any more. I stopped and sat down on the side of the road. Somehow, as I sat there, I managed to dredge up extra

> reserves. I was determined not to allow this marathon thing to beat me. So, eventually, I finished and, in the circumstances, I consider my time of 2:41 was quite good.
>
> In a burst of enthusiasm, I'd agreed to turn out for the Owairaka cricket team that afternoon, which committed me to spend a rather harrowing few hours limping around on blistered feet and aching legs. I lasted three balls before being clean-bowled. My vision was still obscured and there was no co-ordination at all. On top of this, I had also accepted an invitation to a small party that night. I was in no condition to take along a partner and turned up alone, intending to flake quietly in a chair for the rest of the evening. In these delightful circumstances, I first met Sally Turner, who 18 months later was to become my wife.

Plans for a sponsored tour by American and English athletes threatened Peter's intention, for the first time, to do Arthur's complete three months' half-mile speed schedule, but Arthur convinced him to stay with the programme and take the tour competitions as they came. The training just couldn't go wrong. Within the first week, he ran his fastest two miles — 9:18.5 — and three days later ran what was supposed to be a half-effort three-quarter mile in 3:04.5. For the little effort involved, these were unbelievable times.

Over Christmas, on tour with Murray, sprinter Doreen Porter and all-rounder Dave Norris, Peter ran 1:52 for 880 and 4:15 for a mile within two hours in Waimate; a lethargic 9:16 for two miles; and then, in Timaru, discovered a disused, overgrown cinder track which had been laid down years earlier for the famous Ces Matthews [a dominant three- and six-miler just before World War II] and then neglected. He used it for the best flock of half-miles he had yet run, averaging 2:10 for each with half-mile rests between.

Later that day, he was pipped by inches in a handicap race, but his 4:01.3 was his fastest mile and he tore through the last lap in 56.3 seconds. The following day, he ran 20 miles with local harriers over the steeply pitched Cashmere Hills of Christchurch. His ability to absorb hard work astonished him and so did the consistency with which he continued to race and train while moving round the country before the first of the internationals, which were looming as vital stepping stones to his future.

What never entered his head was that the races coming up would be run so confusedly that he would have to adjust his race tactics dramatically after the starter's gun had sounded.

CHAPTER EIGHT

'What I needed'

These were the glory days of New Zealand track and field. The first of the international meets catered for athletes from 10-year-olds to seniors, with 68 races in the morning and eight finals in the first 15 minutes of the afternoon session at Eden Park, jammed with 30,000 spectators as well as hundreds of competitors. But it was humid and the track wasn't a full quarter and was crumbly under its matting of grass.

Peter faced a field of seven, including at least four — Americans Ernie Cunliffe and Jim Dupree, Gary Philpott and Bob Hamilton — all capable of bettering 1:50. Peter's best time in New Zealand was only 1:49.0 from the previous international tour, and that had been wiped out as a record by George Kerr's 1:48.9 and then Gary's 1:48.8.

> I expected that either Gary or Ernie Cunliffe, or both, would set the race alight by following their usual front-running practice and was rather surprised when neither did. But a willing pace-maker appeared anyway. Barry Cossar, a Western Suburbs runner whose best half at that time was about 1:56, got off to the front at a smart pace. Even so, the first 440 yards was run at a relatively easy speed. I heard 55 seconds called as I passed the timekeepers. I didn't feel prepared to let fly with a finishing drive, and as the pace slackened I slackened with it, running second behind the flagging Cossar.
>
> Then Cunliffe snatched the initiative and whipped round the bottom curve past the pair of us. This was what I needed to stimulate me into

> action. I swung out, passed Barry and closed the gap opened by Ernie's initial break. With 250 yards to go, I sprinted, rocked past Ernie and, even though I was trying to get the best out of myself, finished feeling comparatively fresh.

Peter's winning margin was about 15 yards in 1:48.2, so he got his name back in the record books; his 800 metres time of 1:47.7 was also accepted.

The next meeting was four days later in Hamilton, but the half-mile programmed there was less on Peter's mind than the mile race scheduled for Wanganui's Cook's Gardens three days after that. The prospect of running New Zealand's first sub-four mile at home loomed large — but he had little idea of just how large it was going to loom in the rest of the world.

Hamilton's Seddon Park had a 500-seat grandstand, but 6000 were packed around the track as Peter trailed off after the field at a leisurely pace, planning to conserve his energy reserves as much as possible and counting on a repetition of the slow start in Auckland.

> Suddenly, I realised that Philpott had gone off like a bullet and taken three others with him. I woke up rapidly and snapped into action. The race had started on a curve so I waited till we reached the straight before attempting to improve my position. I was surprised at the ease with which I was able to pass the other runners and settle into the trail immediately behind Gary.
>
> The time at the bell was 52 seconds, far from the easy pace I'd expected. And, entering the back straight, Gary accelerated into a three-yard lead. I decided that, if I wanted to win — and I did — I would have to ignore all hopes of an easy run. Just before the final curve, I threw in my challenge, raced up to Gary's shoulder and then moved past. As I did, he suddenly sprawled on the turf.
>
> My thoughts flashed back to that similar incident in the Auckland championships and immediately the keenness and competition of the race left me. I must have eased off, because when I glanced back entering the straight there was John Bork closing up on me at a fast pace.

I hurriedly stretched out — it wasn't a sprint — and concentrated over the last 80 yards.

My time was a shock: 1:47.1 for the 880 and an intermediate time of 1:46.3 for the 800 metres, exactly equalling my Olympic record. Bork ran 1:48.5 and a newcomer, John Davies, was third in 1:50.7. John's reputation at that stage was such that in Auckland he'd been given a mark of 30 yards in a handicap mile with 4:14 performers — I'd seen him use the handicap to win the race. I'd thought how good he looked but hadn't realised I was watching the man who was to be my main mile opposition in the very near future.

It must have looked to many as if I had tripped or interfered with Gary in some way and been the cause of his fall. At least one person said to me afterwards: 'What did you do to him?' When I replied, 'Nothing, I didn't even touch him,' he said, unbelievingly, 'Oh, come off it. It looked from here as if you tripped him.'

Gary's nose-dive must have looked somewhat suspicious and may have accounted for the rather lukewarm reception I was given. A lot of people must have attributed caddish behaviour to me and been disinclined to give me too much credit for what were two very good times.

The meeting was also enlivened by Murray's two-miler against Bruce Tulloh and the two tough Aussies, Dave Power and Alby Thomas. After a languid 4:20 first mile, Murray accelerated, then Power attacked with a lap and a half to run. Murray pulled him in at the bell and then Tulloh launched his attack, closed to within a yard, and he and Murray flew the last lap, locked together, to finish in 8:33.8.

Then the circus moved on to Wanganui and the New Zealand fans' attention focused on the possibility that, at last, someone was going to run a sub-four mile in New Zealand. Murray's ground-breaking 3:57.5 had been run in Dublin in 1958.

Peter played it close to his chest. He realised he was virtually certain to run under four for the first time, might get close to or beat Murray's record but, when asked about his chances of worrying Herb Elliott's world mark of 3:54.5, shrugged it off as ridiculous.

These were the days before pace-making became accepted practice in major races, but Peter went to considerable lengths to ensure the pace would be taken care of for at least the first three laps, leaving the rest up to him. Cunliffe indicated he would be willing to force the pace along, and Barry Cossar agreed to travel down from Auckland to take the field through a fast first quarter. Murray said he thought he could hit the three-quarter in three minutes flat. Alby Thomas, who made Elliott's record possible, was also in the field and still running well.

> I ignored the presence of little Bruce Tulloh, who was relatively unperformed over the distance . . . at all events, it seemed that I was the only one likely on current form to break four minutes whatever the speed was for the first three laps.

On race morning, Snell jogged for half an hour in the morning in Auckland and caught the afternoon plane to Wanganui, kept a low profile and munched through a packet of barley sugars while he mulled over the race in his darkened hotel bedroom. His concern had intensified when he found out that Arthur was quoted in a local newpaper as saying Peter was going to run 3:55.

> This kind of advance publicity irritated me because, although it was Arthur who made the statement, it was naturally going to be assumed that this time was also my particular intention. It committed me and I didn't like being in the position possibly of going out, running just under four minutes and then having it suggested that I'd overrated my own ability.
>
> The difference between Arthur and me is that he tends, with his knowledge and insight, to evaluate the maximum of an athlete's capabilities when everything else is in his favour — track, training, weather and so on. I knew in my own mind that I could and would beat four minutes but I wanted to leave it at that. If I did end up running well inside four minutes, I preferred it to be something better than expected. This habit of publicly committing their charges to highly demanding performances seems to be an unfortunate trait of most prominent coaches.
>
> I took a look at the track at six o'clock. There had been some adverse publicity about it because the grass was bare in patches. It didn't look

particularly beautiful, but as a running surface in the conditions that prevailed it was excellent. The inside lane was being carefully preserved, so it would be virtually untouched when the mile began at 9.30 p.m.

The weather was looming and still as I began my warm-up about 35 minutes before the scheduled start. The ground was jammed with people, more than half the population of the city. At 9.30 p.m. it was apparent that the programme was hopelessly behind schedule so we asked the meeting manager if he would break into the order of events to allow us to get away on time. After consultation, he agreed.

The track wasn't quite the full 440 yards so we started halfway down the back straight with four laps to run when we passed the finish the first time. When the gun shattered the tense silence, I didn't leap away with my usual keenness. Normally, I would have run and jockeyed for a suitable position fairly near the front, from which I could watch developments. But this time, taking the view that there were plenty of others in the race to help me, I decided to sit well back.

The expected didn't happen. There was some shuffling around and, to avoid running too wide round the first curve, I was forced to drift back to the rear of the field. Tension probably caused this mix-up and it also affected my pace judgement because when we passed the first quarter mark I heard 61 seconds called. This was still reasonably within the four-minute schedule so I wasn't unduly disturbed. The field was now in fairly close Indian file and I was content to stay where I was, 15 yards back from the leader, Barry Cossar.

Midway through the second lap, I sensed the thinning of the field and surged forward to the middle and then again into a gap between Murray and Bruce. This put me third. Then Murray, my hope for the third lap, dropped two yards on Cossar. I had to leave him and go past to get a close trail on Cossar. He was doing a tremendous job and two minutes was called as we passed the half-mile. I moved up to his shoulder and glanced back to see who was coming through for the third lap. All I saw was a large gap.

Impatience got the best of me, and I moved into the lead myself, determined that I would make the three-quarter mark in three minutes. It wasn't going the way it was planned, but all was not necessarily lost.

> I concentrated purely on the time and on keeping my running as relaxed as possible, and I was still moving comfortably as I came up to the three-quarter timekeeper and heard him calling '. . . 59 . . . 60 . . .'
>
> Then, a surprise. Tulloh drew level as we approached the bell; the bell clanged and Bruce was out in front, sprinting like a rocket and obviously intent on stealing the race. Even though it came from the runner I'd discounted, this was the stimulus I needed. Rather than fight him round the bend, I stepped up pace only enough to poise myself on his shoulder. As we swung into the back straight with 300 yards to run, I had him covered. I wasn't worrying about him. I was racing time, not Tulloh.
>
> At that point, I abandoned the studied relaxation of my running and let go with my finishing drive. This is the moment when you stop consciously controlling what you are doing and pour everything into driving out the utmost speed. I found myself running in complete freedom from restraint. I was holding nothing back and I don't think I've ever felt such a glorious feeling of strength and speed without strain as I did during that final exhilarating 300 yards. I knew I must be well within four minutes as I raced the last curve. I straightened, heard for the first time the rising roar of the crowd and kept on driving. Still there was no conscious effort.

This was probably the first real demonstration of the stunning finishing power which became Peter's trademark, and it hurtled him straight into chaos. That was virtually the end of the meeting. People were everywhere and din and confusion reigned. Someone shoved a stopwatch at Peter but he saw only that he'd beaten four minutes. The meeting announcer was trying to say something but his voice was drowned by the clamour of the crowd.

Then, 3:54.4 was announced as Peter's official time. He'd equalled Elliott's world record — according to the printed programme. Peter had already run a victory lap and the noise was dying until it was announced that Tulloh had broken four minutes for the first time too, and the crowd went nuts again — and became even noisier when the programme error was corrected and Peter's world record was announced.

Peter learnt later that Halberg hadn't been able to contribute as much to the race as he might have liked because he had just been told of the death by drowning of a popular Owairaka clubmate who had been on his way to the meeting. The news had been kept from Peter.

> My quarters were 60.7, 59.9, 59.0 and 54.8 — rather an unusual sequence because each one was faster than the preceding one. Bruce ran 3:59.3, Alby Thomas was third in 4:03.5 and Murray finished fourth. A comparison with Herb's Dublin time shows that my first quarter was 4.3 seconds slower, closing to 0.4 seconds behind with a quarter to go. At 1500 metres, I was timed at 3:39.3, compared with Murray's best time, run overseas, of 3:38.8.
>
> After I knew I had broken the record, I recalled a moment in Stockholm the winter before when Murray got his three-mile record. I was standing in the infield when Murray came wandering past me with a glazed look in his eyes. He didn't even see me. I was a little put out that he apparently ignored me, but Arthur, who was with me and similarly unseen, said, 'Don't worry. That will be you in a year or so.'

Peter didn't think he was quite as dazed as Murray, but he was a week later in Christchurch. And among the first to congratulate him on his record was Herb Elliott.

Peter raced again on Wednesday, in Invercargill, but, knowing he was practically certain to crack the world half-mile record in Christchurch, he lolloped along with a field in which no one was prepared to go hard, with the local wits among the spectators shouting, 'How slow can you go?' and 'Get a move on', as they plodded up the straight. Peter won with a sprint in 1:52.2. Tulloh ran a dazzling 8:44.9 two-mile but Peter got all the headlines.

He then careered off with friends for a hectic two-day car tour of the beautiful Southern Lakes. Hardly a suitable prelude to a world record attempt. Their coverage of Manapouri, Milford Sound, Queenstown and Dunedin was almost a record in itself. They flew to Christchurch on the Friday, and the following morning, race day, an enterprising American *Sports Illustrated* photographer, David Moore, who had chased vainly to Milford Sound in a chartered plane, finally located Peter and persuaded him to go into the Cashmere Hills to pose for some training photos.

> Having chased me over large chunks of the South Island, David wasn't particularly interested in photographs of me merely running up a steep piece of roadway, similar to Waiatarua conditions. He drove right to the top, overlooking Lyttelton Harbour, stopped the car and said, 'Now, that's terrific. I'd just like to get one of you with that background.'
>
> I pointed out that while it would doubtless make a nice picture, the rough piece of ground he wanted me to run over would hardly represent a true picture of my training. But I was inexperienced in the persuasive ways and means of this guy and I eventually submitted 'just for the record'. Of course, it was the picture *Sports Illustrated* used and it drew letters from kids all over the world who thought I trained 20 miles a day like a mountain goat. I often wonder why I was soft enough to agree.

Despite the fine weather and the prospect of another epic clash between Halberg and Tulloh and the almost certain promise of a world half-mile record, only 12,000 were in Lancaster Park for the meeting, which Peter thought adequately summed up the athletics attitude of the Christchurch public. When he went outside the park to warm up, cricketers a stone's throw away carried on playing, completely ignoring the likelihood that history was about to be made close by.

CHAPTER NINE

'Wait!'

Peter was feeling particularly confident. Barry Robinson, the national quarter-mile champion, had come down from Auckland to run the half, which removed the worry that there would no one to stir up the first lap.

> My approach differed from my pre-race attitude in Wanganui. This time, I was definitely going for a world record — I wanted to complement my Olympic title with the 800 metres record. I was so confident of the outcome that I think Barry was really far more concerned than I was.
>
> It's an interesting aspect of half-miling that the fast times have always been gained when the first lap has been fast — the runners have belted through the first quarter and then concentrated on hanging on for the second. Nine times out of ten, the runner will fold, but the tenth always manages to hang on — and up goes another good time. I think this hinges largely on the problem of the oxygen debt, the factor which causes runners to peter out, and this is why, even though it's virtually a sprint event, it's the stamina man who is dominant.

The Christchurch officials still followed the old practice of setting the field in a curve across the track rather than in lanes, and Peter was placed on the inside with Barry on the outside of the eight-strong field.

> When the gun cracked, Barry leapt away just as if he were running a 440. Bearing in mind what happened in Wanganui, I was pinning my hopes on one pace-maker only, so I took off, too, at what I thought was a

sensibly fast pace, only to find that John Bork, another 440-type runner, had also sprinted hard to get the inside advantage on the first curve. He was probably better geared to the curve start than I was and that sprint for position was the sensible thing to do. But it wasn't good for me, because after his fast start, Bork eased and let Robbie [Robinson] go. Almost in the first 10 to 20 yards, I had lost contact with my pace-maker.

I whipped hurriedly round Bork as soon as possible but Barry was still going away. In less than 50 yards, I realised we were travelling at a suicidal pace and that the pace-making was going to be of no benefit to me at all. In desperation, I yelled after Barry, 'Wait!', but it was futile, he didn't hear me.

The track was hard and fast and I was able to stretch out and keep him within five yards down the back straight, without actually sprinting, although I was not far from it. I drew on a little more effort round the bottom curve to trail him coming up the straight. I completely lost track of my pace judgement and I listened hard to pick up the threads as we came up to the bell. I expected to hear the timekeeper chanting seconds beginning with 'fifty . . .' but the first call I heard was 'forty . . .' The fifty came up as I went past him.

Now, for some unaccountable reason, Barry moved out a lane. I was thinking with particular clarity now — probably stimulated by that fantastic time — and instead of being shocked into easing back or coasting, I realised I was feeling as good as or better than I had in many of my other races when I'd passed through the quarter two or three seconds slower. So, through some crazy impulse, I threw away all textbook procedure and sprinted. This was pure effort against the stopwatch now. Into the back straight, I felt myself travelling fast and I was sharply aware I was well inside both world records — it was only a matter of being able to continue.

This particular problem didn't present itself until the beginning of the bottom curve. Then, like a wave, the effect of that first 660 — run in 1:16.9 — hit me. This was the moment when the real effort of the race was needed. I felt myself slowing. I felt that I had come to the end of my run — and I was only just swinging into the straight. In a frantic effort to keep my legs going, to maintain drive, I wobbled and I was fighting to regain control, to squeeze out the extra ounce of speed as I struggled up the straight on dying legs.

But after going through the tapes, I didn't need anyone to tell me the times. I knew I must have gone inside the records . . . In a semi-detached way, I watched the other runners come in. The most remarkable feature of the race was the speed and ease with which I recovered. I've experienced this before after good performances, which suggests the ability to recover really stems from the mind. When you know you've really achieved something, the body seems to relax into a nerveless state in which it's apparently unaware of any distress and in which functions effortlessly return to normal.

Peter ran 24.8 seconds for that first crazy 220 yards, 26.2 for the second, 25.9 for the third, and a struggling 28.2 to get to the finish. His 1:45.1 slashed 1.7 seconds off the 880 record and 1.4 off the 800. His best 220 yards time was 22.4 seconds and he believed his 440 best would be around 48 seconds, so this race in Christchurch confirmed the truth of one of the first statements Arthur Lydiard had made to him: that the main requirement of the top half-miler was endurance.

The rest of the tour was far from an anticlimax. In Wellington, Halberg had to fight every inch of the way to a 4:02.7 mile win ahead of a young newcomer, John Davies; the barefooted Tulloh ran the fastest two-mile recorded in the country; and Bork made another frantic sprint effort to beat Peter in the half — but Peter discovered enough reserve strength to head the challenge off by six yards with another whirlwind finish in 1:49.9.

I discovered later that I'd been wearing Murray's shoes in this race. They were identical to mine, only a size smaller. I'd wondered why they felt a little bit tight.

One of the more hilarious sequels to Peter's record-breaking feats came from Sydney's *Sunday Mirror*, whose front page carried a full-length, two-column photo under the bold headline: 'He's the New Wonderman'. The caption read: 'Peter Snell . . . shows the smooth style which helped him break three world records in eight days.' Inside, a dramatic profile shot was used in a story about Herb Elliott's hopes of reclaiming his record. The problem was that both photos, first used in *Run to the Top*, which Arthur Lydiard and I wrote after the 1960 Olympics, were not of young Peter but of the weather-beaten, 44-year-old Arthur. The *Mirror*'s man in New Zealand, the late Bob Gilmore, who worked with me at the *Auckland Star*, had trawled the paper's files and uplifted what he mistakenly thought were pictures of Peter.

Bob, an inveterate snooper, also went through Peter's room at the Warrens, in his absence and without his permission, and drew some erroneous impressions from what he found there. And he was the man who, after seeing a photo of Peter with Sally Turner at a reception, quizzed her at the bank where she worked about her age and how long she had known Peter, and then supplied the picture to London's *Daily Telegraph* with a caption saying that Peter was expected to announce their engagement soon. Peter and Sally had not even discussed an engagement, and five months elapsed before he eventually popped the question.

And the grip the Lydiard team held on the sport was going to close even tighter before then.

CHAPTER TEN

Centrifugal force

Following the New Zealand tour, Arthur, Murray and Peter were immediately invited to the United States. Peter was to run his first race, over 1000 metres indoors, on the day of the Auckland championship mile race. The ever-co-operative Frank Sharp, now Auckland Athletic Centre president, waived the right to insist that Auckland should have Peter before the Americans by a compromise that Peter would run a special mile when he returned home. Peter, incidentally, had won the Auckland half-mile title from Gary Philpott the previous weekend.

The 160-yard banked wooden track at the Los Angeles Sports Arena posed a problem for Peter because of his stride length and weight, as well as because of the difficulty in passing anyone in the short flat straights.

> I tried hugging the pole line, taking the curve about halfway up and running right round the top, and finally decided it was best to follow the course set by my own natural centrifugal force. This took me about halfway up the banking by the middle of the curve and I could then accelerate down to the pole line into the straight. I was somewhat surprised to find that on the straights the board track, being laid direct on concrete, was quite dead. But the give and bounce on the curves was a delightful sensation.
>
> The strategy in the 1000 yards would be to try to lead from start to finish regardless of what anyone else did. Murray managed the track much better than I did and looked completely at home on the boards.

The meeting was a revelation. The 13,500-seat arena had been transformed into a one-ring circus, with everyone dressed up, the officials in white tuxedos and black bow ties, bare patches of grass in the centre covered and dyed green, pot plants and bunting everywhere, and an organist on a balcony pouring out mood music in keeping with whatever events were taking place. A fan kept the Stars and Stripes fluttering.

> My race started at the top of the finishing straight. We were to run to the finish and then have six to go. I was given the courtesy of the No. 1 starting position. The gun precipitated a mad scramble as all five of us tried to get to the first bend first. I managed to be the fastest and the race was on.
>
> On boards, you completely lose any sense of pace judgement — I found myself hurtling around completely unaware of the distance I'd travelled or how fast I was running. The only thing I knew was that I was near my top half-mile speed. After about two and three-quarter laps, a group of officials loomed up and I heard the call for the first quarter-mile. Fifty-three seconds — a crazy pace for an indoor 1000 yards. It hit me that I must have expended a great deal of energy in the excitement of the supercharged atmosphere. It also hit me that my legs were beginning to feel the combined effects of the pace and the difficult cornering.
>
> With still two laps to go, I felt I was coming to the end of my run. I glanced back. I was clear by about 15 yards. I was slowing down considerably as I battled on through the half. The time was 1:50.3 — a second quarter of 56.3 seconds. I raised a feeble sprint for the last 110 yards. A mounting roar from the crowd told me someone was not too far behind. I plugged on and hit the tape.

Peter ran a world record of 2:06. Canadian Bill Crothers, second 10 or 12 yards back in 2:07.4, also broke the old mark, which showed how amazing Peter's time was for a board track novice.

Murray was up against another of the young new breed of runner, Canada's 1961 Athlete of the Year, Bruce Kidd, so it became a needle match between the old master and the young pretender. Murray spread-eagled the field for a meet record 8:41.5.

> Murray looked the perfect board runner. He took the bends naturally

and happily, his withered inside arm giving him a compensating balance and poise on the corners. Where my legs seem to go bandy, he seemed to flow . . .

It was at this meeting that Peter began to work up a thing about America's top miler, Jim Beatty. Jim was supposed to face Peter in the 1000 but chose to contest the mile instead. He implied that Peter would have an unfair advantage over him because the New Zealanders were coming off their summer season and would be at peak whereas the Americans would not be peaking for some weeks.

Said Beatty: He *might* look forward to competing against me over a mile later in the season — presumably when he'd be at peak and I wouldn't. So he ran a mile . . . and ran a fabulous finish for 3:58.9 — the first sub-four mile indoors and 2.5 seconds inside Ronny Delaney's world indoor record. It was as I watched Beatty cavorting about afterwards that I first framed a desire to beat him. It wasn't merely that he'd pulled off a better performance than I had. It was the way in which he showed it. I found his acting somewhat sickening. If, I told myself, I ever meet him on the track, it will be my pleasure to beat him.

Three days later, Peter was back in Auckland to run the mile he'd promised as compensation for missing the Auckland champs. He let it be known he'd set a fairly fast target of under four minutes, hope to make the three-quarter mark and the 1500 faster than in Wanganui, and would hang on from there. About 30,000 Aucklanders, long denied a sub-four mile even during the great Halberg–Scott clashes, packed into Western Springs, a speedway cinder track, designed for 20,000.

Parking outside was chaotic. One athlete, caught in the crush, missed his event, which was fifth on the programme. The chairman of the city traffic committee nearly missed the mile because he had to park two miles away. Three thousand got in free when someone opened a side gate, but many hopefuls missed the mile altogether. Peter was okay. He jogged to the ground from his home less than a mile away.

An unfortunate feature was the lack of co-operation I got from the rest of the field. All day, on the radio, the build-up had been: 'Come along and see Snell break four minutes tonight.' I had to do it, and to do it I obviously needed some pace-making help. But the field was studded with runners whose main concern seemed to be their own personal best performances. Finally, to my delight, Gary Philpott said he would start to give me some early assistance.

I couldn't help thinking how bad the reaction would be if I failed. The public are notably fickle and quick to condemn.

To prove the sincerity of my intentions, I ran the first lap spot on 59 seconds. Gary then moved alongside, swung to the front and handed over with a perfect 1:58 at the half. Meantime, the event was developing behind me into a fantastic race for second. Dave Karl was the only one who bothered to chase Gary and me, and even he gave up early in the second lap and was gathered in by the bunch prowling along behind with no concern for the exhibition the race was supposed to be.

The gap was widening behind us to about 40 yards when I took over for the third lap. The crowd was catching the mood of the pace and beginning to roar. Their racket encouraged me as I concentrated on that 1500-metre mark. I barely rested the third lap with a 60-second circuit and went on round the bottom bend into the back straight.

I could see the 1500-metre timekeepers clustered in the distance but I found that, after pushing the pace for three laps and running the third on my own, I couldn't whip up a sprint. I could only force myself on as hard as possible, a desperate feeling which I was to experience again when I broke my mile record on the same track.

Peter ran the 1500 in 3:39.6, slower than in Wanganui, and the mile in 3:56.8, while Halberg, Davies, Baillie and Karl sprinted for second. Murray got it in 4:02.2, Baillie had the same time, John 4:02.4 and Dave 4:02.9 in a blanket finish. Murray's time was his fastest since 1958; the other three ran personal bests. The depth of the performance immediately triggered talk of another 4 x mile relay. Peter's reaction: 'Some people are never satisfied.'

He was exhausted from weeks of hard training, racing and travelling; the momentum of excitement had gone and the tiredness poured in. But there wasn't much time for relaxation.

CHAPTER ELEVEN

Immense courage

After winning the national half-mile championship, slushing through pouring rain in 1:53.9 — the accident-prone Gary Philpott again falling over entering the straight — Peter, Murray and coach Arthur were off to Tokyo to run an indoor mile together one night and a separate half and two-miler the second night on a 16-yard track. Peter found it difficult but managed to win the mile from Murray by four seconds in just under 4:07.

After the meeting, the New Zealanders were taken to a Chinese restaurant and then a bathhouse, where Murray plunged his foot into a scalding pool. Peter 'laughed like mad', but Murray was in agony for the rest of the trip. Peter ran his half the following night in 1:49.9 for a world indoor record, the first in Japan. Murray, with huge blisters on his foot, which made it pure agony for him to squash into his running shoe, nevertheless ran a winning two-miler in an excellent 8:50, once more demonstrating his immense courage and determination neither to give in nor disappoint the race promoters and the massed fans.

> Back home, I allowed myself four days' recovery, and on Monday, 16 March, in anticipation of further trips to the United States for their outdoor season, headed my diary 'Commence training for Beatty clash'.

Invitations were flowing in from Europe for another New Zealand team tour along 1961 lines, and a tentative but tough itinerary was drawn up for Murray, Peter, Barry, John Davies and sprinter-jumper Dave Norris. Peter was aware that the trip for the others depended solely on his acceptance of the tour, but the Empire Games in Perth were close and the talk was that Herb Elliott would make a comeback to run in his home town so Peter's decision was to make training for Perth his priority. The European tour, as he expected, fell through.

But meetings in America were part of the schedule and Peter and Barry Magee went to the Coliseum Relays. Peter had four weeks of speed work and a 4:00.5 handicap mile in Hastings under his belt and he looked forward to meeting — and beating — Beatty. The American had wanted to race Peter over a mile when he was last in the States but now, with Peter entered for the Relays mile, he switched to the 880. His coach said this was what his training schedule called for.

In a race in Hawaii on the way over, Peter ripped through a first lap in 52 seconds for a half of 1:47.8, winning from the next runner by 8.2 seconds and breaking the Hawaiian record by 2.2 seconds. Barry ran a guest record over two miles, which Halberg slaughtered when he passed through less than a month later. In Hawaii, the New Zealanders learnt that their 4 x mile record had been smashed by a University team from Eugene, Oregon, and that Dyrol Burleson had run the fourth leg solo in 3:57.9.

> 'I was pleased to think that I wouldn't be meeting him in Los Angeles . . . but we arrived to the stunning news that Burleson was a late Coliseum Relays entry. What, the press asked, did I think? They knew that Arthur rated him better than the great Beatty and as one of the men most likely to run 3:50 for the mile. I still had vivid memories of my defeats by him the year before. Burleson was quoted as saying that he felt in the greatest form of his life.
>
> The race was billed as 'the miracle mile' — the first of several to come — and drew about 40,000 people to the 103,000-seat Coliseum. Even though Barry was with me, I felt very much on my own. This was the first time I'd been away from New Zealand without Murray's company and, apart from the Moomba Festival [in Australia], my first trip away without Arthur. This aspect made me even more determined to do well.
>
> The early pace was taken by a 'rabbit', who ran us through the first lap

in 59 seconds. I was lying third at the half in 2:01.8 and still felt relaxed when the three-quarters came up in 3:02. There had been a great deal of talk about Burleson's terrific sprint ability in the last lap and I was planning to make a long sprint from about 300-to-go to nullify any advantage he might possibly have.

The pace lifted as we entered the last lap but it was still quite comfortable. I was now lying second behind Weisiger and could sense Burleson close on my heels, where he had been right through the race. I now decided that I wouldn't move until I could be certain of maintaining full pressure all the way but reasoned that, as I was in front of Burleson, the move, when I made it, would have to be swift and sudden to catch him napping.

The moment came just before the last curve. I gave no more indication of my intention than a sudden dipping of my head — something I automatically do as I gather strength for a break. I tore past Weisiger, planning to get him between Burleson and myself as quickly as possible so that Burleson would have to run wide round the bend to stay with me. This was one of the few races in which I haven't looked back entering the home straight. I just kept going hard right through the tape. I won by a clear 10 yards in 3:56.1, an American record. Burleson ran second in 3:57.8 and Jim Grelle was third in 3:58.9. After all my doubts and worries, it was as clear-cut and simple as that.

Later, Peter watched Barry Magee score a miraculous win in the 5000 metres. With 220 yards to go, the Australian Pat Clohessy shot past him and was 10 yards ahead into the home straight. Then Pat faltered and, without change of pace, Barry sneaked past for a Relays record of 14:10.2.

On top of his strenuous season, Peter began training for Perth on 5 June. Two weeks of 103-mile training were followed by calf muscle soreness which reduced him to 60 miles. He was also in demand as a guest speaker and, because he was unable to say 'no' gracefully and successfully, this cut into the valuable training and resting time. But he enjoyed his most successful cross-country season, winning the Auckland title from Bill Baillie by a mere three yards and then the national title in Napier by 41 seconds. The course included a dangerously steep plunge into a gully. Peter inspected it the day before and decided he was going to descend it very gingerly to avoid injury before Perth.

> But the next day, I was first to the top of the hill and, with all thoughts of Perth banished by the exhilaration of running, I plummeted down into the gully at breakneck speed to establish a long lead. The terrain didn't bother me. I sprinted up the hills and raced down them flat out to my most rewarding New Zealand title win.

But he'd now been competing at high pressure for six months and knew he was reaching a point in his physiological pattern from which he would enter a natural depression in training performance.

> I was on the brink of the inevitable abyss. This is both mental and physical. Mentally, it's very hard to continue the pressure and, if you ignore the warning signs, it's very easy to go down with flu or some similar upset which forces you to have the lay-off you need. Heeding the warnings, I continued my training carefully, not strenuously, and at the end of August I began my hill work for Perth without the backlog of several weeks of 100-mile running.

But, lacking transport, it was difficult for Peter to get to Arthur's hill circuit in the west, where Magee and Baillie worked out, or the area in the east where Halberg and Julian trained.

> So I picked out what I thought would be a good substitute — the Western Springs Bullock Track. It was shorter and much steeper than the other hills but I'd used it before quite successfully. After one and a half weeks on this hill, I developed acute pain in the arch of one foot. I managed to hobble home but next day could barely walk.

An x-ray revealed a cracked metatarsal bone, probably caused by the intense strain of springing up the steep hill. It was a severe blow — a month out of training with nothing to do but get all the massage and heat treatment he could and count off the days to the Empire Games. The only bright spot in his September was his engagement to Sally Turner and planning for their marriage in 1963.

Training resumed on 1 October, the day the doctor gave the all-clear, but all in short sessions three times a day on grass as he battled sore thighs, tender knees, and a tendency to overwork his other foot to protect the injured one. After a week, he tested himself with a mile round the Western Springs track and was shocked by the time it took — 4:41.5. Other trials over other distances in the next days were no more encouraging and he was seriously doubting his ability to run two events in Perth as planned. Perth was by now only a month away.

On 10 October he ran a handicap half, off scratch with Gary Philpott, who was also in the Games team and had been training well.

> He provided a good competitive stimulus. But Gary made absolutely no race of it. I was fighting to stay with him through the first lap, run in 53 seconds, and completely foundered round the next curve . . . The race, however, was a necessary and important stepping stone in my bid to regain racing fitness, and the fact that it was my first defeat of the year was scarcely a consideration compared to the value it had in telling me exactly where I stood.

There were some bright spots. At the end of October, Peter peeled off ten 440s, each with a 440 recovery jog, in an average of 59.5 seconds. It convinced him he could still come right. But the road ahead contained another great stumbling block to upset his comeback.

CHAPTER TWELVE

Death shock

Just before the 1962 Empire Games, Peter Snell's father died after an illness which had begun in 1957 when Peter was a boarder at Mt Albert Grammar. He was shocked then and he was shocked now, because he had always shared the family belief that his father would get better.

> Over the years, I had more or less accepted his condition and I think a great deal of my determination to succeed may well have stemmed from it. He became ill at what was probably a crucial point in my life. I know a lot of fellows have gone through youth and early manhood without having their dads around but this was just the time when I was wanting to ask a lot of questions and he just wasn't able to help me much. Probably, this was why I reacted so strongly to Arthur and was prepared to do what he said and lean heavily on him during the first year or so of our partnership.

Peter and his brother Jack also felt increased responsibility for their mother and spent a lot of time building a house at Pukekohe so the whole family could be much closer if anything went wrong. Friday nights, Peter took the bus to Runciman, changed in a garage there and ran out to Pukekohe. After a hard-working weekend, he ran back to Runciman to change and catch the bus back to Auckland.

> Probably, too, Dad's illness made me grow up a lot faster . . . He had been my best friend; I got on particularly well with him . . . He was in my eyes a great bloke and it affected me deeply to see him robbed of the

> power of speech, paralysed down one side and obviously suffering at the premature close of an active life. His illness bred in me a determination to look after myself.

Peter and I have since collaborated on a book, *Use It or Lose It*, published last year by Penguin New Zealand, designed to help everyone declare the same determination to look after themselves.

On 3 November, another meeting was held at Western Springs, which Peter saw as a vital guide to the form he was in. In the half-mile field were the confident Gary Philpott and John Davies. As usual, Gary careered off to a 10-yard lead by the first bend but Peter was content to run an even-paced race between 1:50 and 1:52 and followed through the first quarter in 56 seconds, two seconds behind.

> I was delighted with how I felt. I ran on strongly, closed to within striking distance of Gary as we entered the straight, passed him there and went on to win in 1:50.9. John came through for second in 1:51.8 and Gary clocked 1:52. Murray looked in terrific form, winning handsomely over three miles in 13:18.6, a world-class time. He looked the biggest certainty in the New Zealand team.

In Perth, Murray and Peter were hounded by the press as the pre-Games ballyhoo built up, but found an unknown grass track at a nearby school and chose to train there instead of on the crowded cinder training track near the stadium. Inevitably, they were accused of using secrecy tactics as Brasher, Bannister and Chataway had done in Vancouver in 1954.

> Fantastic rumours and speculation developed. After I ran a 1:20.6 660 yards trial, the word raced around that I had done a fantastic time in the region of 1:16 and no one seemed prepared to believe anything else, least of all the truth.

And when Peter told a reporter that he thought 1:47 and 3:57 might be needed to win the half and the mile, this became his forecast of the times he intended to run.

Major interest centred on the clash between Peter and George Kerr, with George's coach Herb McKenley predicting the Jamaican's new killer instinct made him more dangerous. And then Canadian Bruce Kidd, overflowing with confidence, announced he would also contest the mile. Since he already planned to run the three miles, six miles and marathon, the intention seemed crazy. In the end, Bruce ran three races and, although he won one, ended up what Peter called 'a pathetic wreck'.

Peter won the first half-mile heat in 1:50.7, but Gary Philpott was up against two strong British runners in his heat and, with only two to qualify, faced the problem of wanting to dictate from the front as usual but also needing to conserve his strength for the next round later in the day.

> As a result, he found himself outmarshalled by the two experienced internationals and failed to qualify. This showed the futility of the front-running methods to which Gary was addicted.

At the end of the heats, George, Tony Blue and Peter were the only runners left with a truly international reputation, setting the stage for a three-way battle for the medals.

> As in Rome, I drew the outside lane for the final of the half. This meant that, until we broke lanes, I would have difficulty in seeing what the others were doing — particularly George in the No. 3 lane. The pre-race publicity was that he would set a scorching pacer, so I reasoned I would have to adopt the same tactics, as I couldn't afford to take the risk of letting him get away. I took off at pistol crack and, as we broke lanes, was surprised to find myself in the lead. I eased back a little and let Peter Francis, an unknown from Kenya who had run the fastest qualifying heat, through on the inside with Fleet, of Britain, after him.
>
> I continued to run wide so I could see where George was and was astonished to discover him at the back of the field. I managed to wedge into third place before the next curve. Approaching the bell, in 54 seconds, I shifted to Fleet's shoulder to duck any chance of boxing and ran wide round the curve, thinking I had to do something pretty smartly.

This slowish pace was made to order for George.

I didn't really want to go at this point. My frame of mind wasn't as it had been in other races when I managed to really explode. It was a matter now of forcing myself to crack it on or risking trouble. As I drove myself into top gear, George just moved easily with me.

We swung round the bend into the straight and I turned to my left to survey the results of my break. The well-built, dark figure of George was nowhere to be seen. Then I whipped my head back to the right — just in time to see him challenging at my outside shoulder. We hit the straight almost together and I gave it everything I had.

The stab of horror inspired by George's sudden appearance was immediately eased. He wasn't able to go past and, instantly, I realised he must be tying up and that I must have the edge. He didn't crack until we were only 20 yards from the tape, but from there I went away to win by two yards in 1:47.6, beating Herb Elliott's Games record and scoring the first half-mile Games win for New Zealand since Pat Boot's 1938 victory in Sydney.

This had been my hardest race, a fitting addition to the great rivalry which George and I had built up over eight previous clashes and another striking example of the difference between the basically fast sprinter and the relatively slow stamina-trained athlete.

Again, in Perth, Murray Halberg demonstrated his three-mile mastery by destroying the cocky Kidd and everyone else. Meantime, Peter had drawn a relatively tough heat for the mile three days later. He let Aussie Albie Thomas win by a fifth of a second in 4:02.2, with Bruce Tulloh close behind. Peter found it easy and felt it would have required little more effort to run under four minutes, despite the heat of the day. Other top qualifiers ran 4:06.6 (Terry Sullivan), 4:06.7 (John Davies), and 4:09.5 (Tony Blue).

The final was to be run the following day, and in the morning, after a considerable amount of thought, I agreed to run the final leg for the New Zealand 4 x 440 yards relay team. The theory was that if we were in a position to qualify, I would run hard; if we weren't, I would save my energy for the mile. This decision to take on an extra race on the morning of the final was construed in some quarters as belittling the mile opposition.

The relay team was in third position when I took over the baton, just a few yards ahead of Crothers, so I was forced to sprint. I ran a very hard 220 before Crothers whipped past me. So I had my hard run and we still failed to qualify.

The mile final was labelled by many as the most disappointing race of the Games. The tradition established by Bannister in Vancouver with his sub-four win over John Landy and continued by Elliott in Cardiff in 1958, and the high hopes of a new Games record, were rudely shattered when I, as world record-holder, won the title in 4:04.6.

But I'd summed up the conditions and my own physical being and decided to run a waiting race. The Empire Games is scarcely the place for foolhardy solo exhibitions or virtuoso performances. 45,000 people and the Duke of Edinburgh might be watching and waiting for fireworks, but my concern was to win, not entertain them at the risk of failure. I knew what John's tactics were to be and decided that when he made his move I'd stay handy to him.

The first lap was run in 66 seconds with no one prepared to sacrifice his chances by leading forcefully into the strong wind. Tulloh, shocked by this crawl, dived into the lead and scuttled round a 60-second second lap. He was to pay dearly for this. The pace dwindled again and at the bell the field was bunched and shuffling at 3:09. John moved up as planned, went wide round the bend and tried to get a break down the back straight. Incredibly, Terry Sullivan and I were the only ones who chased him — or were capable of chasing him.

John had two yards on Terry, and I ran past to get to John's shoulder. I stayed there right round the last bend to make it difficult for anyone to challenge. This was scarcely necessary as no one challenged. I went past John for a two-yard lead and held the margin. John, Terry and I were the only runners who finished under 60 seconds for the last lap. Tulloh, who had been idiot enough to do what everyone wanted me to do, finished with a time of over 4:20 after running 4:02.5 in his heat.

An irritating aftermath was the manner in which several New Zealand sports writers felt they must make excuses for me, particularly one

> Aucklander who specialised in delving deep into background history and coming up with psychological solutions for these apparent but non-existent mysteries. There was nothing puzzling about the Perth mile as far as I could see.

So ended a great year for Peter Snell, in which various authoritative sections of the sporting press, including Reuters, *World Sports* and *American Track and Field News*, ranked him top of their sporting polls. Even bigger greatness lay ahead.

CHAPTER THIRTEEN

Fizzing with fitness

With New Zealanders fizzing with fitness after the Perth Games, it was logical that the national authorities would advance the summer season to take advantage of the possibilities. They didn't. But Arthur Lydiard did. While the bureaucrats dithered, he found a sponsor, Rothmans, to bring Bill Bowerman's 4 x mile relay team, which now had the world record, over before Christmas. Faced with a fait accompli, the administrators could hardly veto it.

Peter, meantime, had another of his intense clashes with the remarkable Bill Baillie, who he often underestimated as an opponent over his specialty distances. An invitation mile in Auckland, which Peter treated as an exhibition, turned into a fight to the death as Bill hung on tenaciously and in the last lap suddenly whipped into the lead. Peter managed to get the lead back but both were timed at an exceptional 4:03 on a grass track at Ellerslie. It reminded Peter that their rivalry had become so intense that many of their training runs together turned into races, possibly stemming from the needling Bill subjected Peter to in his early development years. But then, Bill needled *everybody*.

On 14 December, Peter had to be in Wellington to receive his MBE.

> In a crafty move to defray the personal cost this would involve, I let the Wellington Centre know I would be prepared to run the day after the investiture. They agreed and I was able to go down with my fare paid both ways. In return, I astonished myself by running the unbelievable time of 1:47.8 for a half-mile in Upper Hutt.

Peter was then confronted by one of those decisions which beset the top ranks of amateurs in those days: Your running or your job — which comes first? Peter had been in a small quantity surveying office, learning the skills, for four years, but it had been pointed out to him that the firm was too small to afford having one member of the staff away for five or six weeks a year. What crystallised the decision was an offer from Rothmans, the Oregon tour sponsors, to join them. The cigarette company had already gathered up Arthur Lydiard. Peter was offered a thorough background and training in the marketing field with a view to future executive status.

> I weighed this long and carefully and finally accepted their offer. Naturally, it immediately became public property and, naturally, it offended some pious people who felt that the action of a clean-living athlete in joining the ranks of a cigarette firm smacked of a form of art prostitution which could adversely affect the future lives of many youngsters. In many respects, this unwarranted intrusion into my private affairs showed remarkable ignorance.

Such as not knowing how much Peter Snell enjoyed smoking a pipe.

Arthur, travelling the country in Rothmans colours and talking coaching and other athletics subjects, had no qualms about criticising smoking and Rothmans had no qualms about him doing so. Bear in mind, too, that these were days when, without the largesse of cigarette companies, many sports would have struggled financially.

The Oregon team excited terrific interest. Some 20,000 people ignored the wet weather and crowded Western Springs for the first relay meeting, and Rothmans enhanced the spirit of the event by outfitting the international runners in pure white tracksuits with their names emblazoned in royal blue across their backs. It was an instant hit with the spectators, but the athletics hierarchy in Wellington decided that linking those names with the sponsor, whose insignia was on the front of the suits, was a dastardly breach of the rules and ordered the removal of either the names or the insignia.

The names came off before the next meeting at Rotorua, but their clean outlines remained where the blue colouring had run into the white material during the rain at Western Springs.

Oregon ran Vic Reeves, Archie San Romani, Dyrol Burleson and Keith Foreman in that order against Bill Baillie, Murray, John and me. The first leg clash between Bill and Vic had all the excitement and tension of the thrilling duel that had been anticipated. The crowd kept up a continual roar, which swirled to fever pitch on the last curve as Bill overtook Vic, who had set the pace all the way.

Swinging round to the home straight, they were neck and neck. But, so suddenly that more then 20,000 people were shocked into total silence, Vic was down in the mud and Bill was going on alone. The race, in a split second, was ruined. Vic got up and ran on but, with a big gap between the teams, it became a dreary procession with no chance left of a decent time. All the excitement was gone. As Vic remarked wryly, 'I guess two athletes can't run in the same spot at once.'

The second meeting was set for Boxing Day in Rotorua, which was another administrative blunder, given the custom of New Zealanders, including athletes, to let their hair down at Christmas and use Boxing Day for recovery.

I did attempt an early-morning jog on Boxing Day but after 300 yards was violently ill in a hedge. I staggered home and continued to be ill at half-hour intervals. A doctor recommended milk to settle me down and, in my saddened state, I forgot that milk is one of the foods to which my stomach objects. So I was sick again. This continued during the car journey to Rotorua. It taught me a lesson in moderation which I have not forgotten.

Peter's state of mind was such that he packed the wrong gear for the meeting and had to run in the strip he'd worn in Auckland instead of his club colours, for which he was ticked off by the national president, Geoff Jackman, for an apparent breach of the vague policy about the right to wear national uniform.

The race was run in the coldest conditions Peter had experienced.

A strong wind meant no one was prepared to get out and pace-make, and Burleson, still believing in his sprinting ability — even after Los Angeles — tagged along behind Peter and was still there when Peter sprinted for the win.

The third meeting was held in Waimate, a small South Canterbury township chosen by Arthur for its huge athletics enthusiasm and its excellent track. Here, as elsewhere, the New Zealanders and Americans were booked into separate hotels, which gave them small chance of getting to know each other. Even the hospitality arrangements were separate. The Americans were partly responsible, turning down an invitation to join Peter, Doreen Porter, John Davies and Dave Norris on a trip to Lake Tekapo, where hapless attempts to water-ski left Peter so stiff in the shoulders and thighs the following day that he wondered whether he would be able to finish his race, let alone win it.

> A crowd several times the population of Waimate crowded every vantage point of the ground. I struggled through the first quarter of my half in 54 seconds and, at the point where the pressure normally goes on, felt nothing but dire need of a rest. The pace eased considerably round the bottom bend, then a figure came hurtling past me on the start of the back straight. It wasn't Burleson, as I expected, but Archie San Romani.
>
> This unexpected challenge shook me back into awareness of the task in which I was supposed to be involved. I struggled to close the few yards that Archie had opened up and, at the top of the straight, he, Burleson and I were all together. In the battle to the tape, Archie faded and I barely inched ahead of Burleson. He was apparently so frustrated in his desperation to beat me that, as we crossed the line, he grabbed my right elbow with his left hand, an action nicely caught by a press photographer. The final time was 1:48.

The circus moved to Nelson for a re-run of the 4 x mile, which Peter considered a better venue than Wellington, just across Cook Strait, on which he commented:

> Wellington is an athletically dead centre where, strangely, athletes don't seem to like running. I've often wondered why. Wellington, because it's the place where all the progressive decisions are supposed to be made, ought to be the pulsing heart of the sport in this country but it's more often regarded as the place where the progressive decisions are unmade.

Peter was now feeling the shallowness of his condition, but the New Zealand team decided they didn't want to risk another flop and would hustle the pace along regardless, an attitude which seemed to be shared by the Americans, except for Burleson.

> Bill, running our first leg again, led all the way from Reeves, holding off a late challenge to hand over to Murray with a slender one-and-a-half-yard lead. In the wind, Bill's 4:07.4 was a little slow and it was obvious this race could turn into a tactical battle with victory as the only consideration. Archie took the American baton and immediately attacked aggressively, eventually handing Burleson a two-yard lead over John. Right after this changeover, the crowd was shocked by an incredible display of negative running. Burleson, with a best time of 3:56.8 to his credit, actually slowed down to a near-walk to force John, who had yet to break four minutes, into the role of pace-maker.
>
> We all knew Burleson liked running from behind, but this deliberate go-slow was a ridiculous waste of the lead his team-mate had struggled to give him. It was impossible to see what his thinking was. Did he believe he could open up a race-winning lead on John in in the last lap or was his interest only in preserving his own prestige?
>
> John, probably incensed by this move, ran through the three-quarters quietly in 3:17 and on round to the back straight before Burleson struck. His big effort gained him only about two yards — he added exactly nothing to the advantage Archie had given him — and I was delighted to be handed a comfortable trail as I took off after Keith Foreman. Keith took up the challenge but I managed to edge past in the sprint and won by three yards. So New Zealand still wasn't sure which was the best team.

Peter should have stopped his season's running then, but was lured by the prospect of a mile race in front of the Queen on Dunedin's new all-weather track, where John had recently run 4:00.9. It was an obvious chance to break four minutes, though he knew he was badly out of form.

So it was not surprising that this race turned out to be the hardest I'd yet run and forced me to call up reserves of strength I didn't know I had. John and I agreed that, whatever happened, we'd try to make it a good one. The Queen had seen Bannister run but she had never seen a sub-four-minute mile and we felt we'd like to manage one.

We were taken through the first lap but the pace-maker got away to a 10-yard lead and we had to go hard to make contact. The first quarter time was 59 seconds. At the start of the back straight, the pace slowed. I decided to abandon winning tactics and ran into the lead to keep us within the four-minute schedule. The half-mile was brought up in exactly two minutes. I was having extreme difficulty in maintaining the tempo and was grateful when John moved to the front at the beginning of the back straight where I had taken over a lap earlier.

At this point, a decisive move by John would have won him the race but he just strode on evenly, apparently unaware of the struggle I was having. Around the top bend, I felt I was going to fade and lose contact. I had never before felt so tired this early in a mile and I was still too far away from the finish to pull out that little extra effort which can last over the final 200 yards or so.

Into the front straight, I had lost four yards. I grimly made them up and John and I were together as we reached the bell in 3:02. The pace began to lift and, going into the back straight, John looked round twice and then increased speed even more. I'm sure that if he'd realised just how slender was the thread by which I was mentally connected to him, he would not have stayed and waited for my sprint. But he did.

I drove myself along, telling myself that if I could last out the agony of the back straight I might possibly have a chance in the finish. I dragged myself up to John's shoulder and worried him round the bend. The straight opened out and, in a semi-conscious effort, I ignored the screaming of my legs, which were being tortured by the hard surface of the track, and with clenched hands thrashed my body into a two-feet

> lead. It was all I needed in that final desperate lunge through the tape. The time just had to be under four minutes. My racked body told me that and it was right. But, at 3:58.6, it was the slowest of the four sub-four miles I'd run.

John Davies, in cracking the barrier with 3:58.8, shared the fine achievements of the meeting with 19-year-old Geoff Pyne, from Canterbury, who outraced Neville Scott in the three miles in a world-class 13:30.9.

Peter later won back his Auckland half-mile title but skipped the nationals. He needed to bank some serious training to get rid of the overdraft on which he had been operating. In February, he settled into long, slow, gentle running until May, when his pace quickened as the chance came finally, for a crack at America's elusive little hero, Jim Beatty. The scene was being set for one of the most important races of Snell's career, a race which would make or break his reputation.

CHAPTER FOURTEEN

Champagne days

Peter ran a 1:50 half and 4:00.8 mile in Hastings at Easter 1963, proving it was possible to recover speed quickly if the basic condition was there, but it didn't convince him he had the background to support an international tour. As it turned out, his races in America, though successful, were oncers. They put his energy bank straight back into overdraft.

The chance to tackle Beatty coincided happily with Peter's marriage to Sally Turner and gave them the means for a wonderful honeymoon. They flew out of Auckland the day after the wedding, with Peter worrying about his race fitness but able to enjoy most of the contents of a bottle of champagne with which the airline presented them as they flew to a stopover in Hawaii. They were joined there a couple of days later by Murray, Arthur, and a manager, Ossie Melville.

They flew into Los Angeles and the middle of a fight between Beatty's LA Track Club and promoters over the use of the Coliseum Stadium for the meeting at which the club hoped to cash in through the Snell–Beatty clash. The uncooperative stadium promoters had booked the race for another date so the club coach, Mihaly Igloi, had pulled Beatty and his other runners out of the other tour meetings.

> Pressmen, LATC officials, promoters and the AAU members thrust Sally aside with a bouquet of roses and a vodka and ganged up on me. I'm not sure what everyone or anyone expected me to do, but Beatty was making it quite clear he wasn't going to meet me unless it was at a meeting run

by and for his club. Since he was America's top miler and, conveniently, had not run against me before, he was holding a whiphand. I gathered that matters hinged largely on my agreeing to run on June 16, which involved an addition to the tour programme.

Anyway, with the arguments boiling on, Beatty announced that, in the first tour meeting, at the Coliseum the following Friday, he would run 5000 metres against Murray, leaving me with Burleson and Tom O'Hara, the second man in the world to run under four minutes indoors.

Sally and I stayed with Glenn Davis in his North Hollywood home, which rather upset manager Melville. Murray and Arthur were quite capable of looking after themselves and had plenty of contacts to keep them occupied, and Ossie, we gathered, found it rather lonely managing a team that wasn't really there.

It looked like the LA Track Club was boycotting this race, because Jim Grelle withdrew at the last minute with a migraine headache. His wife later said with unchallengeable confidence, 'I am sure Jim would have won.'

I felt fairly lethargic in training and during the race itself. We got past the three-quarters in a slow 3:06. O'Hara did the leading and Burleson as usual was right behind me all the way, letting me run the same tactics I'd used the year before. Just before the bottom curve, I sprinted round O'Hara. Burleson evidently got some interference from Bobby Seaman about then and gave me a substantial gap in the back straight. He closed it with typical efficiency in the home straight, but I got there quite comfortably in a fraction over four minutes.

Peter was unhappy about his form. He wasn't running easily and the final sprint was an effort. His mood wasn't helped when Beatty cleared out from Murray in the final 300 yards of the 5000 metres and won by two seconds — the first time Peter had seen Murray beaten in one of his specialty events. And when Beatty announced he would run the mile at the Modesto Relays a week later, Peter thought, 'Well, it had to come. But why can't I go home now?'

In the week before the race, Peter and Sally tried to escape the heat of the pre-race build-up but could not elude the media. Particularly when one reporter timed a two-mile trial for him and the watch was stopped 20 seconds after the 9:10 he said he needed to run if he wanted to beat Beatty. Then, when he arrived in Modesto on the Friday, he learnt that the race was to be only the second in the world to be telecast live.

> It didn't help my peace of mind to reflect that now 40 million Yanks were going to be gloating simultaneously over Beatty's impending triumph. I was so worked up that I quite vividly saw this race as a high-speed shredding by Beatty of all the reputation I had battled to establish since Rome. If he won, I felt, I was done.

On the Saturday morning, Peter jogged with Murray for 20 minutes, felt 'quite good' after it and then played tenpins with Sally. After lunch came 'an afternoon stewing prematurely in my own juice in the hotel room'.

> This is the rotten part of athletics. You can't help it because so much is at stake. It's fine to say it's just a game, but when you're tied up to the extent that the race is an event of personal and national honour, this intent attitude of mind is inevitable and painful.
>
> So I stewed. I recalled a story in an American magazine, stating that Beatty in the 1963 season was going to break the world mile record and then beat me. Looked like he might be doing both jobs at once, said my boiling mind. I stewed more. Beatty would be running as one of a team. I would be running alone. I was on my honeymoon, on which some of the papers had conjectured with interest. Cary Weisiger had been quoted as saying, 'If we can't beat this guy on his honeymoon, we never will.'
>
> I stewed on. My condition, I was convinced, still wasn't what it should be. Beatty was dominant. I didn't consider greatly that his 5000 might have sapped any of his power. I didn't consider that he wouldn't necessarily be assisted by his clubmates or that Jim Grelle, for one, would be as keen to top Beatty as I was.

On his way to the track, Peter tuned in on the car radio in time to hear the beginning of the meeting and was intensely stirred to hear the playing of the New Zealand national anthem. For him. But, at the track, he was still nervous, and couldn't find much energy for his normal vigorous warm-up.

> I found myself watching the others stride out, looking confident and relaxed. Normally, I take an interest in events around me, greet familiar faces as they pass. Today, I indulged in a straight-ahead look when I passed Beatty [a moment brilliantly captured by *Life* magazine photographer Larry Schiller and printed in the original *No Bugles No Drums*].

Peter had the courtesy No 1 lane, with 'the posturing' Beatty beside him, and they were held there for long minutes because the preceding TV programme was running over schedule and their cameraman was told to hold everything up until the station was ready.

> None of this helped my comfort. But immediately the gun went, I became really geared. In that noisy split second, I came right on it. The tiredness flowed out, the adrenalin flowed in. For the first time, I felt good about this race. I've often said that in running a mile the first three laps are formalities. The race begins in the fourth. That's the way this one was.
>
> The race had a rabbit, George Jessop, who found himself in the lead by about 10 yards. And even though Beatty headed the bunch and seemed to be forcing the pace along, Jessop stayed there until the half-mile in 1:59. At the three-quarters, the leaders were just under three minutes and I was 3:02. I was lying fourth and well out of trouble behind Weisiger, Grelle and Beatty.
>
> Going into the bottom bend, I saw a chance to box Beatty and prevent his famed 300 yards kick. I ran wide up to his shoulder and hung there. Into the back straight, Grelle challenged Weisiger. They began to move away a little. I checked back left and right to check that Beatty was not planning to move outside and followed the other two. I covered them to the beginning of the last curve. Then all the emotion, tension and worry poured out of me in a terrific final effort. Never had I sprinted like this in a race before. I lunged and tore round the final curve in total abandonment.
>
> Straightening up, I risked a look back. I was amazed to see a gap of about 10 yards. The others seemed to be walking. I continued to dig

> it in all the way up the straight, although perhaps I eased over the last few yards. The race was won then. But, in the refreshing flush of total victory, I ran through the tape almost fresh. This must be a mental thing. I know that if a run like that had ended with a hard struggle to win or in defeat, I'd have been near exhaustion. Now, I felt like a crisp apple right off a tree.

In the confusion that followed Peter's sensational win, he saw Beatty go past, head down, felt the fleeting touch of his hand and did not see him again until the following day. And he heard his own time: 3:54.9 — an American record and only 0.5 seconds from his world mark. Weisiger ran 3:57.3, Beatty and Grelle 3:58.0.

After a week of high living on lavish American hospitality, tourist excursions, media interviews and other distractions, the tour ended with the Compton mile, another clash with the top Americans and another chance that Beatty would come right, top Peter off and claim the last say in the drama.

> Weisiger dictated the terms. The tempo was on all the way and he took off with 500 or 600 yards to go. I followed but, with 220 to go, I couldn't sprint as I wanted to. Somehow, I struggled past him just after the 1500 metres mark, where Cary clocked an American record, and held on down the straight for a surprising 3:55, with Beatty second in 3:55.5. For the first time, six men were inside four minutes in one race.

More lavish living followed for Peter and Sally, but the euphoria of such a triumphant demonstration of his miling mastery was to evaporate rapidly when Peter returned to Auckland.

CHAPTER FIFTEEN

Arthur's outburst

I arrived back in Auckland to have thrust in my face a newspaper carrying the headline that Arthur intended to be associated with me no longer. This state of affairs was, I feel, largely due to a troublemaking journalist, who had carefully drawn Arthur's attention to a quote from an American sports magazine article which made it sound as though I had played around with Arthur's training methods and now knew more about middle-distance training than he did. Confronted with this, Arthur, being Arthur, saw red and point-blank announced that he would have nothing more to do with me.

Odd little incidents of independent thinking on my part which had already affected our relationship doubtless contributed to this outburst, which risked the ending of a fairly successful partnership. It is a fact that Arthur had changed in the last few years. I, too, had changed. Therefore, our relationship couldn't go on as it was originally. I had become a personality in my own right and resented at times not being able to express my own individuality. Arthur, perhaps, had not accepted or understood that.

What I said in the American interview was that I was very grateful to Arthur for giving me the background of distance running which is the basis of the Lydiard system. I also said that, through doing speed work myself, I knew the effects it had on me and consequently as far as my own training was concerned I knew a little bit more about it than he did. One of my reasons for saying this is that Arthur used to incorporate in his schedules three months of track work. This, as a result of the experiences of his athletes, was reduced to two months.

Arthur and I got on well together until we grew out of the exact master–pupil relationship with which we began. Our natures were not complementary, even to begin with, but that friction had been subjugated because of my need to learn from him all that he could teach me. My own knowledge then was non-existent. But I think Arthur still regarded me simply as a pupil. He failed to see that I had gained independence or accept that I could become independent. I'm certain we had always been incompatible in many ways. Murray said we were complete opposites and this could be right.

In the early days of our partnership, I hurt myself to extremes because Arthur told me to; but when I found my own feet, my own independence, I hurt myself to extremes because I said so.

Anyway, after this public airing of grievances, Arthur and I did a two-week tour of New Zealand together and people were amazed to see that we did not step together onto the platform with gloves on. This mutual tour did a lot to clarify the position in people's minds and make them realise that the incident had been distorted out of proportion by the press. Disharmony did exist but not in the intensity that most people believed.

The internal tour disrupted Peter's training drastically, underscored his lack of in-depth fitness during the American tour, and was demonstrated when he finished 30th in the annual 10-man teams cross-country race he had won the year before. His 1964 season actually began on 21 October 1963, when he ran a mile in Masterton in the middle of his hill training. He was lined up against the Australian Ron Clarke and John Davies, with John winning in a fine early-season time of 4:06, 10 yards ahead of Ron (4:09) and another 20 yards ahead of Peter (4:12). Peter had wisely given himself some insurance against criticism by announcing beforehand that, since he would treat the race as part of his training programme, he would be happy with 4:15 or better. He demonstrated the sincerity of this by going for a solid 15-mile run immediately afterward. Ron, who followed his mile run soon after with a three-mile race in 13:48, later that season ran world records for 10,000 metres, six miles, three miles and 5000 metres.

Next up was a meeting John Davies organised in Tokoroa, with the Aussie steeplechaser/miler Trevor Vincent in the field.

> The weather was right against the meeting but even more against me. My ability comes from the thrust I can get off the turf, which gives me my long stride. I can really bounce off a hard surface but the power comes from the top, and in the wet I bog down. So John won by the length of the straight. This defeat, on top of the one at Masterton, gave me a difficult period. Arthur's supporters, harking back to our estrangement, were already saying meaningfully, 'Ah . . .'
>
> Ten days later, I lined up again against a now-confident John at a Western Springs meeting but, this time, the cards were stacked a little more on my side because we were racing over 1000 metres. We passed the half in 1:50, running well up to the time required for the world record. John was in the lead and we were sprinting flat out. I was working myself into a position near his outside shoulder when, in a split second, my left hand touched his trailing leg and he was down on the ground.
>
> My momentum carried me past but I compulsively slowed and swung to the side of the track, knowing that I had actually tripped him. John was able to get up, continue on and win, and I jogged in third. Naturally, the time was nothing.

A 1:52 half-mile in Nelson showed Peter still wasn't going too well, but he had little time to worry about that because an American team arrived for a tour starting in Wanganui. Here, Peter ran a virtual solo mile in 3:57.6, with Bill Baillie hanging on and finishing under four minutes for the first time in his long and remarkable running career. Weisiger's third showed he was in need of a race or two to hit his peak — but Peter had suddenly hit his.

He had promised an exhibition run at a club night in Gisborne, when he went there to talk at a Rotary Club luncheon, but instead found Gisborne had promoted a full-on meeting with a crowd of more than 5000.

> This meant I couldn't hope to get away with an easy exhibition half in, say, 1:56. I ran in a handicap race and whipped through the first lap in

Above: Spot the star — Snell's class photo at Opunake Primary School.

Below: All Owairaka Club members, all New Zealand representatives and all Lydiard trained. From left, back row: Puckett, Magee, Halberg, Snell, Julian, Hellier; front row: Baillie, Ernie Haskell, Lydiard, Colin Lousich, Lawrie King.

Above: Lydiard (top) with his record-breaking 1961 world tour team: Magee, Halberg, Philpott and Snell.

Below: Lydiard with some of his New Zealand champions and world-beaters. From left: Halberg, Puckett, Magee, Lydiard, Snell, Julian. Early 1960s.

Above: Snell wins the 1500m Olympic Games final, Tokyo, 1964. CENTRAL PRESS/GETTY IMAGES

Right: Acknowledging the crowd after the Olympic 800m final, 1964. CENTRAL PRESS/GETTY IMAGES

Above: Snell wins the 1962 Commonwealth Games 800m in Perth from George Kerr and Tony Blue. ALLSPORT HULTON/ARCHIVE/GETTY IMAGES

Left: Snell greets the well-wishers on his arrival home at Whenuapai Airport from the 1960 Olympic Games.

Above: Last lap of the New Zealand half-mile championships. Snell powers round the field into the straight, while Gary Philpott recovers after falling on the bend.

Below: Pre-Olympics meeting in 1964 for a cup of tea at Arthur's place before training. From left: hurdles champion Avid McIntosh, Lydiard, Bill Baillie, Snell, Barry Magee and marathoner Ivan Keats.

Above: Snell and John Davies (right), New Zealand's 1500m medal winners in Tokyo, with Czech silver medalist Josef Odlozil on the left. STAFF/AFP/GETTY IMAGES

Below: Alan McKnight, Murray Halberg, Snell and Barry Magee on a Sunday run in the 1960s over Arthur Lydiard's famous Waiatarua course in Auckland.

Above: Snell discusses a point with Lydiard.

Below: Snell on one of his orienteering jaunts.

Above: Snell runs the last leg of the Queen's Baton relay into QEII Park, Christchurch, in 1974.

54 seconds to pick up the leaders. I eased back until 220-to-go and then finished on strongly for 1:50.8. I was pleased with the ease of the run.

The next day, in Wairoa, another 'exhibition run' turned into a race meeting at which Peter first ran a 10.2-second 100 yards, equalling his best for the distance, and a 1:54 half, feeling off-colour in the second lap. Moving on to Napier, where he was to race Weisiger and John over half a mile, he had all the symptoms of dysentery. He decided, after warming up, that he was too ill to start, but the meeting manager called the meeting doctor.

The doctor felt my pulse. Since I had just warmed up, I can't imagine what good that would have done. I explained my feelings and symptoms and was totally flabbergasted when he suggested that my condition was probably the result of nervousness and there could be absolutely no harm done if I started and then withdrew if I felt any ill effects. Since the verdict was given in the hearing of the meeting manager, I had no option but to start. I managed to survive the first quarter and then completely folded, putting on a pathetic display in the last lap.

Back in Auckland, Peter was told by his own doctor that running the race was the worst thing he could have done — the total opposite of the complete rest he needed. He was a week and a half away from the next important race of the tour, a mile in Auckland, but agreed to run it, though he could only jog lightly, avoid hard training, and hope desperately that he would come right.

I didn't. This was another race I shouldn't have started, yet in a sense it was a good thing. Aucklanders had never seen me beaten in a big race and this time about 25,000 of them saw me go under. It brought home to them that I am, after all, a human being and not just a machine. But it was an odd feeling, after tracking John and Cary home a long way back, to realise that just for once I didn't win the damn thing in front of my own crowd. It was a boiling hot day at Eden Park and I knew after the first 220 yards that the writing was on the wall for me. You can at times expect too much of yourself just as, at times, the public expects too much of you.

Peter later won the Auckland and New Zealand half-mile titles, but on the basis of these performances his prospects for the Olympic Games in Tokyo looked lean. He was generally regarded as having had it. John Davies was the man of the future, Peter's successor and the country's main hope for Tokyo.

> This attitude is not unusual. The public is very quick to forget or condemn a sportsman who lets it down in its expectations. As soon as you stop winning, you're forgotten or wiped off. In me, this reaction inspired a terrific determination to prove public opinion wrong and show that, while John might be a good Olympic prospect, I was still around and still dangerous.

CHAPTER SIXTEEN

Healing the wounds

In March 1964, Peter and Arthur, with their wives, were invited to tour South Africa — a chance to relax and recover rather than a major tour. The pair had reached an unspoken understanding that their quarrel would not be mentioned, and the tour actually helped to heal the wounds as each came to understand better the other's viewpoint. Arthur no longer advised Peter on his training, but Peter talked to him about his condition and was always given the same psychological encouragement Lydiard gave to his other athletes.

Peter, who was again affected by dysentery, ran a few races in surprisingly satisfactory times, including South Africa's first sub-four mile, a 3:59.6 on a rough cinder track in Durban, and the national half and mile titles in Port Elizabeth. They returned to New Zealand four days before he was to race John Davies at an Owairaka club meeting at Western Springs.

> There had been a definite change of feeling towards me since my reasonably successful running in South Africa. Now, instead of just writing me off, the opinion was that I'd have no excuse when John beat me again. Arthur had been building John up, too, as the man who could beat my mile record. John must have had pretty much the same feeling. He and Bill Baillie shared the running and John made a confident early move, which was a surprise change from his normal tactics. But I was determined to beat him, even if I killed myself in the process.
>
> I covered his early break and then took him on in a sprint with 220 yards to go. To my immense satisfaction, I beat him by two or three

> yards in 3:58.5, with John clocking 3:58. 6. Naturally, the public being as quick to forgive as it is to forget, I was immediately re-established in their eyes as, once more, a top prospect for a gold medal. I felt that I should improve another five or six seconds with five or six months of solid training.

Peter began running twice a day, aiming to reach 100 miles a week as soon as possible, with Barry Magee as an ideal companion because of his ability to maintain a uniform pace and his willingness to increase it when Peter wanted to push it. Over 10 weeks, Peter logged 1012 miles, much more than he had done in any similar period, with a 22-miler over the Waiatarua circuit every Sunday — a training element he could not afford to miss — and studiously avoided any speed work which might cause leg injuries.

He balanced his effort, alternating a hard session of six-minute miles with an easier one of seven-minute miles, spent a lot of money on shoes and good wet-weather gear, kept the cold at bay by rubbing olive oil on his legs, and took a multivitamin pill to avoid time-wasting colds and flu.

His daily runs were challenging. He would generally hit the road about 5.30 p.m. and was quickly in the dark, with only streetlights to guide his steps. As well as his Sunday runs through the Waitakeres, he also scattered the sheep on the undulating pastures of Cornwall Park. He then moved into six weeks of hill training, which ended nine weeks before Tokyo. This was over what Lydiard's runners called 'the Circuit', a square two-mile area in Blockhouse Bay which was selected for its imposing hills.

Peter climbed the hills in slow, exaggerated bounds and ran hard down them, perhaps four times in a single training session. He would add in some 700 yards of 30-yard dashes, alternated with 30-yard jogs. The conditions were often atrocious, with Peter battered by rain and sometimes hail while dodging cars.

> I was planning everything towards the 1500 metres. This had been my target since before Rome and, although I knew the Tokyo programme would suit an attempt on the 800/1500 double, this was more a dream

> than a consideration. I felt that some of my former sharpness, which was necessary for 800 metres running, had gone.

But Peter's hill training went exceptionally well, without a hitch. His downhill running was strong and his calves stood up to the punishment of the uphill springing, a key element in the Lydiard system. But for all athletes, midwinter track training in Auckland was a problem. Finally, they were offered the five-furlong trotting track at Alexandra Park Raceway, a crushed limestone surface which was too hard in summer but in excellent condition now after a great deal of rain.

> My track work began sensationally with 20 quarters in an average of 62.5 seconds. I had hoped for something like 65 seconds and it was a terrific boost to know that I'd gained so soon the rhythm of running at this pace.

The constant wind also made the running of satisfactory trials in Auckland impossible. In one trial, Peter, aiming for a 1:52 half-mile, battled the wind for nearly a full quarter on the trotting track and finished on wobbly legs in 2:02.

The Alexandra Park workouts tended to be quite informal. Halberg once warmed up by jogging a lap with his four-year-old daughter. Peter, Murray, marathoner Ray Puckett and hurdler Avid McIntosh ran several handicapped 100s. Peter ran some 220s with sprint star Doreen Porter, who had come under Lydiard's wing to improve her Tokyo prospects and was being hustled round Cornwall Park across the road by a sometimes jogger called Garth Gilmour to make sure she didn't renege on scheduled long runs, a part of training she didn't much like.

Meantime, John Davies was turning in training times which suggested he was going to be a real threat. He paced out twenty quarter-miles in an average almost exactly the same as Peter's series of twenty. And the 62.5s were the best Peter had ever done. On 17 August, Peter reeled off twenty 220s at a 27.83 average, which was a splendid performance; on 18 August he ran three miles in 14:35; on 19 August he turned in five poor 880s as a result of the previous great bursts; and on 21 August he pulled a thigh muscle.

In early September, with that minor injury behind him, he became dissatisfied with his training, especially a vile 2:02 half, the first quarter of which was run into the teeth of a cold, strong wind blowing down Alexandra Park's back straight. He stopped making entries in his training diary after that.

> I got to a pitch where I couldn't care less whether I missed the Olympics. There are times in your training when you wonder how on earth you could run a 4:30 mile, let alone a four-minute one. My training had been fantastic and then I hit a flat spot. I lost a few days because of my injury and because I was feeling sick of athletics.
>
> I had frenetically set my goal on the 1500 to the exclusion of everything else . . . suddenly you find you are no longer flogging yourself along, you no longer have the ability to push or punish yourself.

Then, on 8 September, Snell planned to run quarters in 55 seconds and peeled off four in 53.3, 53.6, 53.4 and 54.3 — the last as one thigh began to bother him.

> It was quite pleasing. When you've lost it, you have no idea how you feel. Those quarters made all the difference to me mentally. When I did those 220s in 27.8, I was supposed to be doing them in 29. Was I going too fast? I asked myself. There is a danger of overdoing it.
>
> Or could this mean my training times had to be considered in terms of a 3:50 mile? I felt everything had to be revised. Perhaps I should be running 53 seconds. It was all supposition. From now on, I decided, my training times have to be better. I've tended to underestimate myself, so when I do far better I get a mental lift.
>
> However, looking back, it seems to be necessary for me to have at least one trial in which I fare badly. Having got through it, plus some short work, it has been amazing how I've come up and somehow captured totally different form. So I was satisfied to continue training without worrying.
>
> I calculated that in the 1500 in Tokyo, no one would be capable of breaking away from the field before the last lap. If the pace was killing,

I'd wait until the stretch to make my sprint — the length of the straight at least. If not, I'd start it around the turn. There's an advantage to having the turn to yourself. That initial move, those couple of yards, are invaluable.

Peter had a realistic attitude toward his abilities. He knew he would be weaker than runners such as Burleson after two miles because he did not run distance particularly well. He attributed his cross-country success to the fact that he seemed to get momentary rests, when he was able to relax, and that ability to relax at a fairly fast pace was the secret of his success.

When the team gathered before the Games, I was given the responsibility of team captain and immediately decided I wouldn't be too conscientious. I feared that could affect my training and racing. Fortunately, the team management was particularly good and there wasn't much need of a great deal of liaison between the athletes and the officials.

On a two-day stopover in Sydney, Snell scampered over 660 yards in 1:19, which astonished one spectator — one of his Tokyo rivals, Tony Blue. John Davies finished less than a second behind.

In Tokyo, the spotlight was on the marathon boys, Barry Magee and Ivan Keats, and Bill Baillie, as he and Jeff Julian had both been winners at Tokyo's Little Olympics the year before. Which was possibly fortunate, because Peter spent his fourth day in Tokyo in bed with a temperature and a very sick feeling and, when he recovered, found himself struggling to keep up with Davies in training. John's confidence was buoyant; Peter's was low. And when John, with Arthur's approval, cheerfully offered to pace Peter for the first quarter of an 800-metre trial and make it a race from there, it was obvious whose star was in the ascendant.

What did concern both of us was a suggestion by Arthur that the American Tom O'Hara, who Arthur was advising, should run the trial with us. This, he said, would give us a line on the form he was in. True, we said, but it would also give him a line on the form we were in. However, Arthur had his way.

Somehow, news of the run leaked out and, as we warmed up, several of our future rivals became conspicuous spectators, plus Roger Moens, who was covering the Games for Belgian television, and British journalist and 1956 steeplechase champion Chris Brasher. We tried to keep the time quiet by beginning in the back straight at the 220 mark but we didn't fool anyone.

As John took off, I was amazed at the change I felt in myself. I was suddenly fresh and eager and, before we reached the 200, I urged John to go faster. We ran through in 26 seconds, and at 400 the time was exactly 53 seconds. I faded a little in the last 200 but produced the quite amazing final time of 1:47.1. Moens shared my elation. He told me confidently I could win both events. This was the idea I'd toyed with but, until this trial, I didn't think I'd regained enough speed to be able to try with any prospect of winning over 800 metres. Now I knew.

Peter also now recognised the psychological advantage of letting his time be known among his opponents. O'Hara and John seemed to have the stuffing knocked out of them — they, too, knew he was right for the double.

Before I even got to Tokyo, the press carried a statement from me that I wouldn't be seeing very much of Sally there. Subsequently, I received a somewhat sarcastic note from Sally saying that if I wouldn't be doing anything else, she'd be arriving in Tokyo at a certain time on a certain day. As luck would have it, that was the time I was required as flag-bearer in the dress rehearsal for the opening parade. So I wasn't able to meet her. I smoothed that over by getting her tickets for all three 800-metre races. She hadn't booked for those because we hadn't known I was going to run the 800. I had to work a bit of a swizzle to get her in at such short notice but it was a matter of conscience.

In Tokyo, the press was controlled to a great degree and had to have special passes and permission from the management before they could speak to New Zealand athletes. We were accused of being reluctant to co-operate, and my opinion is that it's better to talk to reporters than have them fabricate stories or get their information from other, perhaps unreliable, sources. However, it is a fact that most of the questions they ask are ones an athlete doesn't want to answer — the open request to predict performances, to express opinions on rivals' prospects, to reveal training times, discuss conditions and so on. So many unpredictable factors can influence the result of a contest, and it's not easy or fun to have to find excuses after the event. In the stress and emotion of the Games' atmosphere, it's very easy for an athlete to say things they wouldn't normally say. You can be caught with your pants down in a moment of elation — or depression.

Peter, for example, remarked to an English reporter that the British runner Simpson was 'in great form' judging from his trials. The reporter's story carried the line that Peter regarded Simpson as the man to beat.

The huge number of athletes in Tokyo emphasised for me that the time must come when the Olympic Games are reduced to the basic sports only, when team games will no longer have a place. It'll be back to plain old human endeavour, without the technical skills of team play and so on. I'm not going to stick my neck out and suggest which should go because, in some sports, like rowing, there's a hairline difference. A soccer team can get through if one man flops but a rowing eight can't. That creates a different kind of team spirit which perhaps should be retained.

My most nerve-wracking period of the Games was the night before my first race. I'd made the decision to try for the double, and promptly all sorts of doubts crowded into my mind in a sleep-wrecking procession. Quite seriously, I wondered whether the decision was the right one. I felt I could produce a really good performance over 1500 metres. But if I ran in the 800 metres first, there was a strong possibility that not only could I run out of a place in that event — or even fail to qualify at all — but I could find myself too tired for the 1500. I could, through tackling both, miss out on both. Was I being too greedy?

Now I'd made the plunge, I was hammered by doubts that I did have the best possible chance of taking the 800. And added to my last-minute worries was the addition to the 1500 of an extra round of heats. When it really came down to a choice, the 1500 was the one I wanted most.

> This was the target set even before Rome. But obviously, now that I was committed to the 800, I had to ignore the 1500 to avoid holding any reserves back that might be needed to get me home in the 800. I was in a rather confused state.

Only four would qualify from each of the 800 heats for the semi-finals, and only two would go forward from each of the semis, plus the two fastest losing semi-finalists, which meant the semis would be almost as cut-throat as the final itself. But Peter was happy with his heat because he was opposed by only one accepted world-class half-miler, Jerry Siebert of America. And he was even happier when he went to the warm-up track just before the start of his first heat.

> A quick search disclosed familiar faces of old rivals and gave a feeling of satisfaction to discover many of them had been warming up for some time. A full warm-up can be a tiring procedure, and to me it shows signs of jitters when men overdo it. Arthur was with me — to make sure I got there and to make my half-hour checks at the roll-call station.
>
> Once I began warming up, my feeling of apprehension left me. Any more thinking was purposeless, anyhow. What happened from now on was out of my hands. I think this was the stage where I really arrived at the 'business' of Olympic competition. And, partly because I was defending champion, I had a 'better-than-you' feeling as I moved around. I couldn't help feeling that I was having a disturbing effect on the others just by being there. I hoped so, anyway.

CHAPTER SEVENTEEN

'Oh, well'

Ten minutes before the gun, we were led through an underground tunnel under the track and onto the centre. We emerged in time to see the first heat and it was with some degree of shock that I saw an unknown from Kenya, Kiprugut, run a terrific solo time of 1:47.8. He won by nearly a full second and the slowest qualifier registered 1:48.9. The other three heats were more realistic, won in 1:50.3, 1:49.5 and 1:49.5. I breathed a little easier.

As in Rome, I'd drawn an outside lane. I used a crouch start, intending to get away fast and settle into a good position when we broke lanes. But as we swung out of the first curve, I found that the others had also got away very quickly. I was near the rear of the field. Oh, well. The rest were closely bunched and there was nothing to be lost by staying there and settling in to watch race tactics. The pace felt quite fast. I was running easily enough in the back straight second time round to improve my position to within striking distance of the two leaders.

I ran two out on the last bend to avoid being boxed and I moved up then and took the lead, keeping a close look both sides to make sure I wasn't caught by a sudden rush. I won by a narrow margin but, although I aimed to win as slowly as possible, I had an almost irresistible urge to surge away as soon as I hit the straight. My time of 1:49 was pleasing in relation to the effort it took.

The semi-final draw pitted Peter against six runners of good calibre, but it was the easiest heat and likely to be run fast because of the even ability of the field. Peter, delighted to see Kerr drawn against

Kiprugut and the vigorous front runner John Boulter of Great Britain, ran the semi much the same way as the heat, always aware he needed to win to be sure of qualifying.

> Running into the final bend, I found myself third behind Pennewaert (Belgium) and the Russian champion Bolyshev. Perhaps unfairly, but mainly to avoid being boxed, I moved out a lane and ran shoulder to shoulder alongside Bolyshev, making it impossible for him to manoeuvre behind Pennewaert without falling back at a stage of the race where falling back would be fatal. I reached the tape first and still had something in reserve.

Peter stayed at the track to see history repeat itself as Kerr again broke the Olympic record with a time of 1:46.1 after tremendous front running by Kiprugut. The German Bogatzki was the fastest loser with the same time as Peter — 1:46.9.

> I'd been absolutely sure that my Olympic record of 1:46.3 wouldn't be broken in Tokyo, and logic battled with inner fears as I tried to tell myself that this fantastic semi-final time would spell disaster for these two in the final. In the third semi-final, I felt sympathy for Tony Blue, who ran the last 600 metres with only one shoe. Someone had stepped on his heel and ripped the shoe off.
>
> My tactics at this stage appeared well defined. As long as Kiprugut had not tired himself too much, it was logical that he was going to make the pace in the final. And, since none of the others, with the possible exception of Crothers, was well performed over a mile, they would be suffering from the effects of the first two races because of their lack of stamina.
>
> In the final, I drew lane one — an awkward position in a way, because you are faced with this decision: either you go like a madman and hit the front so you can manoeuvre with the field behind you and allow only as many past as you want, or you can start slowly and try to work your race from the back of the field. Either way can be troublesome, and an in-between start can cause all sorts of jostling and tangling.
>
> I figured Kiprugut would fire in a fast first lap, with the others not

prepared to chase him closely. So my plan was to start fast, get in behind Kiprugut and then sit on his shoulder.

Some plan. Kiprugut didn't start as fast as I expected and the others kept right up with him. I got into second all right but, before I could get out to the position I wanted, Farrell was alongside, quite prepared to run a lane wide to keep me where I was. I thought, at this pace, he won't stay there much longer than 200 yards. So I chose not to drop back through the field to avoid the box. I stayed where I was. So did Farrell.

I began to realise the perilous position I was in when, approaching the bell, several runners moved wide past me and Farrell. One was George Kerr. I was powerless to chase them. My pre-race plan had called for a sustained sprint from about 250-to-go. Now the whole position was confused. I was running easily within myself and I felt I was capable of dropping back out of the box, going round the field and still being able to challenge.

This involved a surge from the rear to about fourth position with a clear run three or four wide which took me to the end of the back straight; then a second and final effort as I fought past Kiprugut and Kerr, who were locked together, and sprinted desperately into the curve. It was desperate because my plan had gone wrong and my run was coming late against fast finishers.

Just before the end of the curve, I had a look back and saw that Kiprugut and Kerr had followed but they weren't challenging. I felt I was giving it everything I had down the straight, although there was no sign of weakening but, on reflection, I think that, in spite of the desperation, I subconsciously held just a little bit back for the 1500. I know anyway that, with the lovely feeling of the tape against my chest, a terrific load seemed to leave me. I couldn't resist flinging my arms in the air. I hadn't messed it up after all. I could now enter the 1500 with virtually nothing to lose. So far, it was a gamble that had paid off.

Even more satisfaction came when the time was announced — 1:45.1. I'd got my record back — the first really good 800 metres time I'd run in two and a half years. And, with four under 1:46.0, that final rated as the greatest 800 of all time. Crothers clocked 1:45.6, Kerr and Kiprugut 1:45.9.

When Sir Arthur Porritt breezed in to the medallists' waiting room to tell Peter he was going to present the medals, as he had done in Rome, Peter didn't even have the energy to get to his feet. He just accepted his handshake in a semi-daze.

CHAPTER EIGHTEEN

No mug field

The next day, Peter faced the 1500 heats. Four would go forward from each of the four races, plus the two fastest fifths, which gave him a fair bit of leeway. He drew the third heat, and Tom O'Hara was the only runner he recognised.

> I realised the best chance for the others to eliminate me was to take advantage of my weakened condition and force the pace. As I trailed round the early part of the race, my hopes for an easy pace clashed with my expectations of an imminent increase in speed. But, incredibly or luckily, the pressure never came. This heat was the slowest of the four, and my qualifying time, in fourth place, of 3:46.8 was the lowest individual time of all those who went on to the semi-finals.

John Davies was also in a slowish heat, splitting Witold Baran and Dyrol Burleson with a time of 3:45.5. The fastest heat went to Britain's Alan Simpson in 3:42.8. The overall indications were that the line-up was no mug field. Next day, Peter had an easy hour's jog to recover from four days of racing. On the day of the semi-finals, he did an easy 30-minute pre-breakfast run and felt the strength had come back into his legs. His heat included Frenchman Michel Bernard, a compulsive pace-maker who had paved the way for Herb Elliott's world record in Rome.

> The rest of the field, aware that one world-class runner among us faced elimination and possibly pinning a last hope on at least the fastest fifth, chased him anxiously. I nursed myself along at the back of the field.

After a lap, 17-year-old American Jim Ryun had already dropped back — he eventually finished last. I was completely unaware of any times. I was conscious that the pace was fast but felt I was holding it comfortably.

It was so fast, in fact, that there was no sprint over the last 200 metres and, although I had intended not to win, I found myself passing the finish, looking sideways at and right alongside Baran, in the front of the field. My 3:38.8 exactly equalled Murray Halberg's best 1500 time in Oslo in 1958.

One heat was tense for the New Zealand camp. John Davies finished in a group of four fighting for third place and all were timed at 3:41.9. Two had to miss out and it appeared that one of them would be John — but after an agony of waiting, he was placed third. Bernard's fast early pace in Peter's heat had sounded the death knell for most of those who got through, and even Peter didn't appreciate how much the run had taken out of him until he was running in the final.

The warm-up of the other finalists seemed to be a little less vigorous than usual. There was more easy jogging round the track and fewer of the customary strenuous full-speed run-throughs. The semi-final had given me a great feeling of confidence as it had indicated my recovery was fairly complete. I had made up my mind that in no circumstances would I attempt to run a record. It was going to be a matter of waiting as long as possible and concentrating purely on winning. I knew John's plans were to ensure a truly-run race and not the sort of tactical jostling mêlée with the medals going to the fastest sprinters. By this time, too, I was beginning to enjoy racing over the 1500-metre distance, something I hadn't done until I reached Tokyo.

Bernard took us through the first lap in 58 seconds. Burleson was in second with the rest of us bunched behind him. I was drifting along at the tail of the field. In the back straight for the second time, Bernard appeared to slow down, look round and motion the runner behind him into the lead. This was a tricky situation because the front wasn't the position Burleson liked to be in at this stage of a race.

So there was a confused lull for about 200 metres. No one particularly wanted to set the pace until John, who had hoped to begin making it tough from about 600 metres to go, was stimulated by the prolonged indecision and time-wasting into taking the initiative. He had to make it a hard race for his own preservation. So, entering the home straight for the second time, he moved round the field into the lead, a lap sooner than he had intended.

The 800 metres time was outside two minutes and, rather than continue running in a group who were all moving well within themselves — but without the confidence to make any positive early move — I moved up to second behind John. I was so determined not to be boxed in I was quite often running a lane wide yet, before I realised it, we were back in the front straight with just over a lap to go, the field began jockeying for the all-important position for the run home — and I found myself trapped in a box.

I wasn't going to go again through my 800 metres performance of dropping back to the tail of the field and running right round the outside to regain the initiative, so set about extricating myself by the direct route. Fortunately, it wasn't necessary to use the discourteous elbow-jolt so common in races of this kind. I merely glanced back to see who was behind me as we rounded the bottom bend and then extended my arm, rather like a motorist's hand signal, to show my intentions. I breathed a sigh of relief when the athlete on my shoulder, John Whetton, with the manners of a true Englishman, obligingly moved aside. As simply as that, I was out.

Baran came up forcefully as we moved into the back straight. I was well positioned and unworried. I was feeling a little tired and decided to leave my move right to the end of the back straight. I just ran along, making sure I was dictating the position and, with 200 metres left, threw everything into the final bid. As I let go, I had the strange feeling that this was what the rest had been waiting for me to do, as if it was an inevitable part of the race over which they had no power of control.

Coming into the home straight, I felt I could renew my effort if I needed to but, when I looked to see what had been the effect of my break and saw a sizeable gap, I knew I wouldn't have to bother. If anything, my run down the straight was easier than it had been in the 800 metres — so easy that I was amazed to learn later that the time for the last 400 metres

> was 53.2 seconds, and for the last 300 38.6 seconds, which represented the pace of a full lap in 51.5 seconds.

Peter won in 3:38.1 — 2.5 seconds slower than Elliott's 1960 world record but good considering the fierceness of the heats and the slow early pace of the final itself. Davies was elated to win bronze, though he apologised to Peter for not gaining second. He had tried but Alan Simpson got in his way just long enough to let the Czech, Josef Odlozil, past. Then, from the New Zealand Broadcasting Corporation's box, he and Arthur watched Abebe Bikila win his second Olympic marathon. His performance, Peter recalled, made his own seem insignificant.

Peter returned home to find himself standing at the first of the crossroads at which his choice of direction were critical to the years which lay ahead. He had poured everything into winning his double on the promise to himself that he could then relax; but he would probably never be in such splendid form again and therefore should take advantage of it to run some record attempts. What was the sensible way to turn?

CHAPTER NINETEEN

Cinder heller

If I was to run well in the farewell trip I planned to make to Europe, it was important to resume a regular training routine as soon as possible. However, public interest was high following the Games, the New Zealand track season was just beginning, and it was obviously going to be difficult to ignore pressure to capitalise on my Games form or resist the many pleas for help from worthy causes and struggling clubs. The only reason I could give for refusal was my personal ambition to do something spectacular in Europe in seven months' time — and what right had I to be thinking or speaking in this vein?

I took the easy way out from this confusion. I decided I would allow myself to be used on a limited basis, comforting myself with the thought that I would never again be in demand as the brand-new winner of two Olympic events.

The New Zealand Athletic Association was organising a late December–January tour by Americans — which was fine for athletes just approaching their summer form but hopeless for those trying to hold the peak they had attained for Tokyo. The Auckland Athletic Centre, with a sharper eye for the main chance, promptly trumped that by arranging two major meetings in mid-November on Auckland's Western Springs cinder track.

Murray and I both felt that our first obligation was to our club, Owairaka, and to the helpful clubmates who had deliberately freed us of the worry which probably besets every sportsman in New Zealand — the endless tearing around with raffle tickets and other fundraising schemes to produce the money needed to keep their clubs functioning. Their help enabled us to concentrate wholly on training, so they were justly entitled to share the financial bonanza which Tokyo's successes promised to create.

I announced I would attempt the world records for 1000 metres and the mile, and Owairaka was accordingly allotted the less appealing 1000 metres while the Auckland Centre had the crowd-pulling mile at the second meeting. This arrangement satisfied virtually everybody, including those who bleated that all meetings should be run for the benefit of all athletes and not just those of a particular club. The Czech Josef Odlozil was in New Zealand and would run the races.

The 1000 metres record was 2:16.8, held by East Germany's Siegfried Valentin, seemingly a very easy record to break although we managed to make it quite difficult. Auckland sprinter Rex Dabb agreed to help me over the first 400 metres but unfortunately a special arrangement he made with a timekeeper at the end of the first 200 metres nearly cost me the record. About 12,000 were watching as Rex led off as planned and, according to my pace judgement, seemed to be going too fast, so I let him gain a lead of about five yards. I wasn't going to throw away my chances with a suicidal first 440.

Then, as I passed the 200 metres mark, someone yelled out 'twenty-six'. If anything, that made me relax a little more as my aim was to pass the 400 in just under 54 seconds. With 100 yards of the first lap to run, I closed up on Rex and waited to hear the time for 400. I was shocked to hear 'fifty-five'. I found out from Josef after the race that he had been fooled, too. The timekeeper hadn't been calling to me or Josef but belatedly announcing, for Dabb's benefit, the time he had taken.

Anyway, it shocked me. The record was slipping through my fingers and it shouldn't be. To regain my grip on it, I immediately had to put the pressure on. I ran 1:49.5 for the 800 and struggled frantically over the last 200 to make it by a bare tenth of a second.

Peter almost wept when, at the end of the track meeting, a demonstration of sidecar motorcycle racing took only seconds to rip the beautiful cinder running surface to shreds. He could not believe it could be restored to peak racing condition in time for the mile race five days later. Although Josef offered to be pace-maker for the race, Peter had already decided, to avoid any further blunders, to run 58-, 59- and 60-second laps to give himself a three-second advantage over his three-quarter times in the previous two races in which he had beaten 3:55. He reasoned that John and Josef could handle this and still be with him with 300 yards to go. Billy Sutcliffe, a youngster from Putaruru, John's old club, and Bill Baillie's protégé, Kim McDell, had volunteered to run the first and second laps for the 1:57 half Peter wanted.

A capacity 25,000 crowd jammed into the stadium on a still, overcast night, perfect for racing. Rex Maddaford proved that when he ran 4:08.2 for a New Zealand junior mile record. The great Australian Ron Clarke and Halberg clashed over six miles and Aucklanders for the first time saw Halberg mastered. Clarke's ruthless precision pulled him away, and with a mile left he seemed in total command. Halberg fought back but Clarke hung on — 28:29.6 to Halberg's 28:33.

Eight runners started the mile and Sutcliffe shot off like an 800-metre runner ahead of McDell.

> Again, my sense of pace told me we were too fast. A decision had to be made quickly: to run with this pace and take advantage of the pace-making or attempt to run my own race. I decided to risk the former with the intention of easing back later. So we flew round the first lap in 56 seconds. Yet the effort was barely noticeable at this stage. McDell shot to the front and ran strongly and evenly and the trail was perfect. I realised I was running hard but it was a very free sort of feeling and, as Kim slackened, I yielded to an urge to continue at the same rhythm. I passed Kim as we raced up to the half. I was now running entirely against the clock. The half-mile time was 1:54, three second faster than planned.
>
> My common sense and experience told me this couldn't last. Yet I chose to think I was committed to continuing it. I managed to convince myself I was feeling good and that this was the race in which I could run close to 3:50.

Peter reasoned that, since he'd run a 50-second quarter in Christchurch and held on for a world half-mile record, he could do it again. So he kept the pressure on.

> About halfway round the third lap, with 660 yards to go, the feared oxygen debt began to build up. Within the space of seconds, my legs, which had been feeling so strong, began to cry out for relief. I ignored the warning. I was running a terrific time; I had set myself for it and I ploughed on. Even at this stage, I'd lost my relaxation. It was a straining effort to keep rhythm and pace. I ran up towards the bell, driving my aching legs. It was going to take a supreme effort in the last lap. I eagerly awaited the time call, hoping it would give me the extra stimulus I was now desperately needing.
>
> The call came — 2:54. Despite an acute awareness that I'd need all I had for the final 250 yards, I made a conscious effort to raise my pace again. Then, as I swung into the back straight, the last shreds of my concentration seemed to ebb away. For the first time, I became suddenly aware of the people and surroundings and found myself listening for the crowd as if groping for something to make me work my tiring legs harder.
>
> Yet the harder I fought, the slower I seemed to be getting. This was a far cry from my feelings in many of my other races. I'd been tired before but I'd always managed to delve deeply into reserves to produce a fantastic finish. This time, the reserves had already been expended. There was nothing there. Somehow, hanging on to that crowd encouragement, I finished the last 200 yards. It was mechanical desperation running, completely without inspiration. I knew confusedly that I must have broken the record; I'd known that since I heard 2:54 called.
>
> Reflecting on it now, I believe that if the record I was attacking had been a little harder or the competition had been more intense — despite the almost ruinous mental and physical processes of that last lap — I could have pulled even more out of myself than I did. But I made it in 3:54.1 — 0.3 seconds inside my 1962 record — while John and Josef fought a bitter last lap, closing on me in the process, until Josef nosed in front. He ran 3:56.4 and John was 0.4 seconds behind. Personal best times for all three of us.

Some experts criticised Peter for a tactically wrong race. As the one who suffered, he knew that better than anyone. But he also learnt from it. He had, at last, run himself to the limit over a mile; he had put himself in a position to achieve 3:50 or better; but to have done it he would have had to be superbly fit and, that night, his condition was waning from its Tokyo peak. He proved that four nights later when he outsprinted John in a mile in Wanganui in a lethargic 4:03.9 to 4:05.2.

He did little more than light jogging until early December, when he, John and Murray raced in Melbourne and he ran an Australian record of 3:57.6. Murray ran a 13:31 three-mile looking at the back of the amazing Ron Clarke as he slashed the world record to 13:07.6.

So, with two post-Olympic world records and an Australian record to his name, Peter faced a struggle to get ready for his planned farewell tour. Mentally and physically, he was tuned to the idea of rest and relaxation after months of intensive training and racing. But, on New Year's Day 1965, he began again the chore of pursuing racing fitness, training alone while everyone else was track racing.

> I indicated quite clearly that I would not be entering any major races this New Zealand summer and I possibly made a tactical mistake by yielding to the temptation of a last fling on the boards in Los Angeles early in February, joining Bill and John, who were touring the board circuit. The trip was a notable first. I left New Zealand without a manager, reflecting that it seemed that at last the New Zealand officials considered me safe to go out of the country alone.
>
> New Zealand had a great night in LA. The [*Los Angeles Times*] meeting was, as usual, star-studded with athletes from Russia, Poland, Czechoslovakia, Romania, the United Kingdom, Formosa, Canada and Germany, and New Zealand pulled off all three middle-distance races. Bill won the two miles comfortably; John took the mile from Billy Mills and Witold Baran; and I was able to hold off Bill Crothers in the 1000 yards.
>
> However, I now found it rather difficult to stick to my original story that I wouldn't accept any more of the invitations constantly coming

forward. Most country clubs in New Zealand consider their meetings just an important as overseas international events and can't appreciate that theirs can be far more demanding on the guest runner, who draws the crowd and is obliged to satisfy them with his performance. If he flops, the meeting flops.

Despite being involved in various local appearances and commitments, Peter's training seemed to progress reasonably well enough, with a final pre-tour race in Hastings at Easter, where he ran a mile in just over four minutes. Convinced he would be all right, he continued stamina running, with no hill work and very little speed work, before leaving New Zealand at the end of May. He faced a long programme, a lot of races, and considered that stamina was his first requirement and he could race himself back into form.

It has been suggested that my mental approach to my tour training was wrong; but that had nothing to do with it. Perhaps I wasn't as diligent as I might have been, but I knew all along how I felt. A physical condition is apparent and no amount of thinking is going to change it at the crucial moment. Mental effort may help 200 yards from the tape but not with over a lap to go.

My only serious hitch in training came two weeks before the tour began when I was in the early stages of a reluctant 18-mile run. It was a wet night and I slipped on a grass verge. I made a three-point landing on my right elbow, hip and side of the knee. I was shaken but secretly pleased with this excuse to cancel that night's run.

The following night I limped out and managed to cover my regular 10 miles, which quickly proved that, in many injuries of this nature, the real trouble comes from the extra stress and strain placed on other muscles in the effort to favour the injured area. Through nursing my right leg, my overloaded left leg packed up and threatened to ruin what skimpy speed work I had planned to do. It was an interesting but untimely and painful demonstration of how finely balanced, tuned and specialised the muscles of the athlete are and how easily that balance can be upset by a change in rhythm.

Nightly massage and optimism convinced Peter that, if he couldn't get enough speed work in for the American leg of his tour, he'd have plenty of time to develop more speed for the more important European section, when he hoped to chase a few records. He did fit in twenty 220s on the limestone track at Alexandra Park, averaging 28 seconds but struggling with the last five. The nagging pain in his left leg reached maximum intensity but he drove it off, hoping he wouldn't be building up trouble for the future. With some more work, he decided top condition couldn't be too far away.

From January on, Peter had the additional mental preoccupation of house-hunting with Sally, finding the one they wanted in Mt Albert, selling their house in Pt Chevalier and moving, all of which kept him busy until the night before he and Arthur left on his farewell tour — an expedition which was destined to take an unexpected and unfortunate turn.

CHAPTER TWENTY

Apricots again!

Peter ran a half-mile during a stopover in Honolulu. Hoping for around 1:50, he lacked fire and barely managed a narrow win in 1:53.8 over the American star Bob Schul. So he approached his first US race, a mile in Los Angeles on 4 June, with some trepidation about his condition. Against him were Schul, rising young star Jim Ryun, Jim Grelle and Josef Odlozil.

Warming up, his concentration was disturbed by the remarkable Ron Clarke's three-miler, in which New Zealander Neville Scott set a furious pace to make it hard for the Australian for as long as he could hang on. Clarke eventually overpowered everyone in running 13:00.4 and Peter remarked to Schul that, as long as Clarke was running middle distance, he'd stick to miling.

> The mile? Well, my quarter times were 58 seconds, 1:59, 3:01 and 3:56.8. I felt tired in lap two, lap three felt faster than it was and, although I was determined to hold back on this run, I then found myself up near the leader, Cary Weisiger. At 300 yards, the point where I'm normally keyed for extra effort, I was beginning to weaken. Quickly, I calculated that since Ryun, Grelle and Odlozil had run around 3:58 two weeks earlier at Modesto, it would pay to make a bid now, so I sprinted.
>
> I realised at the end of the back straight that I wasn't going to make it. Reassessing rapidly, I decided to ease off round the bend, wait till the others came up and then go again, if the ability to go again was still there. That's exactly what happened. Coming out of the curve, a white-vested athlete challenged strongly. I caught a quick glimpse of him without

really seeing him and thought: it must be Ryun. I called for more effort, poured it on and saw immediately that I still wasn't gaining. I called for maximum effort.

We still appeared to be running neck and neck. The tape loomed up. I took a desperate swallow dive at it, hitting it without being sure who won.

Peter won by six inches, and the other runner, Grelle not Ryun, was given the same time. Even George Kerr had never made Peter run that hard up the straight.

Next stop was a hugely hyped half-mile in Toronto against local hero Bill Crothers, with whom Peter had formed a close friendship and who possessed what Peter described as 'the most fabulous display of trophies I have seen'.

The ornate nature of the display — mainly collected in the States — emphasised that the Americans haven't got the knack of designing trophies which are truly symbolic or which don't depend on size and ostentation to show how important they are. Everything they produce tends to be too big. I was somewhat surprised when Bill said that he treasured most his little Tokyo silver 800 metres medal.

Peter got a call from *American Track and Field News* writer Dick Banks. He said: 'Jazy has just run 3:53.6. Give me a quote.' Peter replied: 'Oh.'

A crowd of 18,000 turned up to see Crothers beat me by a fifth of a second in 1:48.4. My disconcerting experience against Grelle, where I ran out of steam, had made me reluctant to force the pace, and I knew after a slow first lap of 55 seconds that I had little show of winning against the fast-finishing Crothers. I let the pace-maker carry us round the penultimate curve before trying to make it difficult for Bill with 300 to go, but he merely cruised easily behind me, waiting his time to take me. I was well in front going into the straight but a deafening roar from the crowd told me exactly what was happening. Bill went past and once again there was that lack of fire when I tried to match him.

Bill Baillie finished fifth in the three miles behind another brilliant run by Clarke in around 13:04, and John Davies lost the mile to Grelle. Peter remarked that this defeat further emphasised John's need to change to a longer distance — a viewpoint he shared with Arthur Lydiard. The circus then split, with John and Bill leaving for Poland, to be followed by Arthur three days later, and Peter moving on to Vancouver, where he felt fine through an hour-long run and looked 'confidently, though guardedly' to his mile race, his first since the Frenchman Michel Jazy took his world record from him.

But, while the sports reporters conjectured on his chances of recovering his record, Peter had no intention of busting his boiler over a race that had been added to his original tour schedule. He was saving himself for a big effort in San Diego. However, Vancouver wanted a repeat of its famed 1954 Landy–Bannister classic and brought in the Americans Grelle and Weisiger to add to the competition. Peter pointed out that the track was in a loose and unsatisfactory state, but, still, 15,000 packed into the meeting.

> The night before the mile, I attended a dinner organised to promote New Zealand lamb sales in Canada. I made short work of three slightly fatty lamp chops and several generous slices of leg. Before the meal began, I was talking in a group and a waiter with a tray of drinks asked, without any 'excuse me', if I was going to break the world record. He shoved this question into the conversation three times and backed up his persistence by tappng me on the shoulder. The question was so damned stupid and so rudely posed that I ignored him. A Vancouver newspaper columnist, Jack Wasserman, noted this and wrote in his column later of my 'offhand treatment of the little men at the hotel' and expressed the view that because of it he was quite pleased when I was beaten.
>
> I awoke next morning to find that my bowels had turned to water. But I felt okay generally and reached for one of the last of the two pounds of apricots I'd bought the previous day. Immediately after eating it, I felt like throwing it up again. Still feeling otherwise all right, I had a light jog and then breakfast. Apart from continued and uncontrollable bowel activity, I felt fine and, since I wasn't planning to consume anything

more than a cup of tea for the day, didn't worry unduly.

My warm-up for the race felt reasonably good — I didn't find out until much later that what was affecting me was only aggravated by the cumulative effect of exercise. The first lap of the race was run fast, paced by Neville Scott. I sat back in 59 seconds, feeling quite normal.

In the second lap, I drifted a little. Disturbed, I tried to make contact with the leaders, but found it increasingly difficult. I passed the half in 2:02 and lost more ground in lap three. Lap four was terrible. Two juniors passed me with about 220 yards to run and I floundered on and was booed all the way up the straight. I finished dead last in 4:15.

I realized that the crowd, by its attitude, must be thinking I hadn't tried or had purposely run badly. I reacted in annoyance. I congratulated Grelle, who'd won in around 3:55, then I grabbed an official and said I wanted to say something over the public address system. I felt I had to straighten this out. I told the crowd:

'Ladies and gentlemen, first my congratulations to Jim Grelle, who ran a fine race. Secondly, I know a lot of you came to see a top-class mile — a miracle mile, possibly, being fought out by sub-four minute milers — in which, no doubt, myself as a former world record-holder would have played a large part.

'This is possibly the first time in competition overseas that I have run such a terrible mile. Because I have performed like this, it will no doubt take a long time to get over the shame of having run last. It is not my habit to make excuses but I can honestly say that, this morning, I possibly suffered a mild form of gastric enteritis, which of course means numerous visits to the toilet.

'This happened once before in my home town in 1964 and in front of a big crowd I ran 4:07 for third place. My own home town almost wrote me off. To run a first-class mile, everything has to be for you. I felt absolutely terrible round there and must have looked as though I wasn't trying. In fact, I was doing it harder than in some of my greater races.'

The response was a staggering ovation. More than the booing, it upset me emotionally. I turned from the microphone and walked away a few paces. I didn't know what to do. Neville came rushing over and his genuine efforts to be soothing upset me even more.

Unable to leave because he had to present the Peter Snell Trophy to a junior mile winner, Peter was forced to wander about the centre of the ground. The following morning, he lasted a mile and a half of a light jog with Neville Scott, made a frantic dive into the nearest bushes and had to walk back to his hotel. His next slow jog ended in 10 minutes. He rationalised that it would be great if he bounced back before San Diego but, if the peculiar effects of the illness persisted, he could go right down the drain.

He and Neville moved to Los Angeles' Laguna Beach and he continued light running, but it was five more days before he managed 12 miles in 75 minutes. It was panic training because he was determined to do something respectable and just churned away until he finished.

In San Diego, he submitted himself to physiological treadmill tests at the state college. His trouble was diagnosed as lower colon irritation caused by excessive consumption of the wrong kind of food. This tied in because, in Toronto and Vancouver, he had steadily hogged off the baskets of grapes, peaches, plums, bananas, pears, apples and cherries placed in his room every day by the hotel management. The physician in the testing team gave him drugs to combat the problem, and the panel of assessing doctors classed him as the best athlete they'd tested and ranked him not far behind their top endurance groups, a bunch of cross-country skiers.

Peter was further cheered by a number of apologetic letters from people who had booed him, including one who wrote: 'You taught thousands of us a lesson in fairness and understanding . . . we will remember you as more than a champion athlete . . . we will remember you standing at the microphone alone, yet bathed in a glow of greatness.'

The mile heats were run on 16 June on the hard track at Balboa Stadium. Peter wore shoes with a spongy heel to protect his legs and had to run his last lap in 55 seconds to qualify in 4:11, unaware that, even with the padded heels, he was building up yet more trouble for himself.

There was nothing outstanding about the mile. I made up my mind that I was going to sit on Grelle all the way and, if possible, leave my finish as late as the finishing straight. With 560 yards to go, Josef Odlozil made a break. I was tucked in behind Grelle and Ryun and decided to play safe and stay there rather than go after Josef.

With 300-to-go, we'd caught Josef, and Ryun moved past to hit the front. He ran away strongly but he was not yet sprinting, and Grelle and I covered him comfortably to the 220 where Grelle began challenging. He couldn't make it past Ryun and they ran together round the bend; this made it difficult for me to get past until we hit the straight. Then I found I could get past Grelle all right but not up to Ryun. It was as far as I could get. I could run strongly but without any extra, the explosive burst, that I had produced so often before and which I needed now to win. This was to be my trouble for the rest of the tour. Plenty of strength but none of the extra fire that makes it effective.

Peter's time was 3:55 and he still felt quite good, but thought Ryun looked washed out by his great effort.

The next day, Peter began a series of flights which took him to Helsinki on 19 June. It was 10 p.m. but still light so he ran five miles to shake off the effects of the long trip. On the first day of the Helsinki meet, he watched Clarke and Jazy clash over 5000 metres. The pre-publicity had built the race up on Jazy's superior speed against Clarke's ruthless, machine-like running — nobody gave a thought to a relatively unknown Kenyan called Kip Keino.

Clarke appeared to make a determined effort with a fast lap after about two miles. Jazy and Keino clung to him and it seemed Clarke decided he couldn't make it and, rather than help Jazy to beat his (Clarke's) world record, eased the pace off. When Jazy did spring in the middle of the back straight, he dragged Keino with him and the pair left Clarke. I felt oddly nervous during the race. It wasn't cold but I was actually shaking, even though I couldn't care less who won. Perhaps it was because I knew so clearly what the runners were trying to do to each other.

In the 1500, I finished fifth, hit now by the effect on my legs of the hard San Diego track. I'm heavily muscled and hard surfaces affect me considerably, particularly when I'm also tired. This upset me because it made me unsure of myself. Arthur, who hadn't seen me run in LA, Vancouver or San Diego, told me I was just unfit and needed to get stuck into some solid work. I accepted this but realised later that unfitness wasn't the reason I was running poorly. Arthur left the following day and John and I left for London.

Before they parted company, Peter decided to scratch from a scheduled race in Dublin. But as soon as he announced this, Dublin was on the line. Arthur took the call, saying, 'Leave it to me'. He began confidently enough to explain why Peter wasn't going to run, but then it turned out that the wife and daughter of the Dublin meeting promoter, Billy Morton, were attacking him because, they said, Billy was ill and likely to have a heart attack if Peter didn't run there. He wasn't winning races but he was still drawing the crowds and, in this situation, he and Arthur committed him to run.

Peter's main concern was running well in Czechoslovakia, so he trained harder than he usually did close to races, running six-and-a-half-minute miles round Hyde Park for 90 minutes the day before his London mile.

I was briefly in the lead after one and a half laps. I somehow knew I wasn't going to do well, but John [Davies] must have thought I was having a go because he whipped past and cracked on the pace. I promptly drifted away, unable to match him. Three English runners passed me in the back straight and I seemed to be going slower and slower. Odlozil, who didn't seem to be running any faster than he was when I was beating him, was the eventual winner, but I was a long way from being interested. However, I did feel my legs were getting stronger, which was what convinced me that my trouble was muscular and not unfitness.

In the Dublin mile, Simpson and Wiggs buzzed off and left me, although I again ran under four minutes. I reached the three-quarter mark in around my usual time but, instead of doing it easily, I was working hard and my form was already beginning to taper off. From that race onwards, I did very little training. Getting stuck into it wasn't the solution. But I was sure that I could run every second day and still do a four-minute mile. Winning was another matter.

Peter rejoined Arthur, John, Odlozil and Odlozil's coach in Prague and raced a mile against Odlozil and Jurgen May, of Germany. With 220 to go, he was sitting third behind them and feeling confident of being able to win. Then May sprinted, Josef sprinted and Peter sprinted. He got past Josef but could not find any more speed and Josef passed him again in the straight. In Czechoslovakia, John ran 3000 metres in 7:51, only two seconds outside Jazy's world record, which underlined his prospects at 5000 metres.

In Odlozil's home town, Otrokovice, Peter decided to help Josef in his attempt on the Czech 2000 metres record. A local runner took them to 800 metres, Peter led to 1200, Josef led to 1600, then Peter set the pace going for the last lap. Josef sprinted away with 200 to go, beating Peter by about four seconds and gaining the record he sought. Peter was off then to Oslo, where he and Bill Crothers were matched over 800 metres. The race was to follow a 10,000 metres race featuring Ron Clarke, who had just lost his six-mile record to Billy Mills.

This was crazy planning because Ron was running a lane wide to get a better footing long before he finished and we were presented with a cut-up track. Even more completely than in LA, I forgot my own warm-up to watch another race. But what a race! The crowd were quite carried away by Clarke's awesome performance. He threw his cards down for all to see with a cracking 63-second first lap and hammered out the first mile in 4:20. That's good time for a first-class three miles and Ron was running six and a quarter miles.

I missed the middle of the race — I thought I'd better do some warming up — but was back to see Clarke in colossal form as he finished, waving the photographers back to let the other two runners finish the laps they still had to run — and they were world-class runners. When Clarke lapped them, he went past like a Jaguar passing a pedal car.

His bearing afterwards was as amazing as his running. He seemed to treat his fantastic time as an everyday event . . . Machine-like is certainly an apt description of him. Somehow, he didn't seem quite real.

In my 800, I was beautifully placed after a brisk first lap. I decided to make a run with 300 metres to go — but when the time came, I couldn't even get past the leader and Bill [Crothers] had no difficulty in coming past to win in 1:47.1. I didn't bother to find out what my time was, which about sums up my state of mind at the time.

I wanted to go home. I was determined to tell that to Arthur straight, as he wanted me to go and join him in East Germany. But since he was in Yugoslavia with Bill Baillie and I was in Norway, I didn't really have a chance. I finally decided I would wind up with my race in Berlin, on the track where Lovelock won the 1936 Olympic 1500 metres for New Zealand. Because of the tradition he had established and because it would signal the end of my career, this, I decided, would be a full effort — I wanted it to end in victory.

I told myself I wasn't going to be talked out of this decision, but, once I rejoined Arthur, it became difficult. He had set his heart on Sweden and, of course, without me, there wasn't much point in going there. He knew I had made up my mind that my fitness wasn't there and went to great lengths to convince me that, with another couple of weeks of training under my belt, I could do something worthwhile before I quit. It was, he argued, a question of not being sharp.

But I knew from my running that it wasn't a lack of sharpness but lack of condition that was beating me. You don't fold under pressure in the straight just because of a lack of speed. However, having made my decision in Norway, I declined to run in the 1608 metres race (an English mile) promoted for the second day of the Oslo meeting. I jogged around the forest tracks for an hour and three-quarters, lunched on reindeer meat and red wine, played tennis, had supper of smoked leg of mutton and goat's milk cheese, went down to watch John win comfortably from Grelle in 4:00.6 and next morning saw him off on his way home. Then I headed for Berlin to rendezvous with Arthur.

But would he, as he intended, sign off his tour and his career with the kind of performance that would satisfy a perfectionist such as Peter Snell?

CHAPTER TWENTY-ONE

'No kick, no life'

I had every opportunity to win that last 1500 in Berlin but I was unable to. The last lap was quite fast and I ran about 3:44, but there was no kick, no life in me. I was totally without enthusiasm. Grelle and a local runner finished ahead of me and Schul was fourth behind me.

From Berlin, Arthur and Peter travelled to Leipzig, crossing through the eerie no-man's-land between East and West Germany — where all doors had to be opened with keys because there were no door handles — as guests of the Sports Medicine Academy. Arthur was to lecture the doctors and a few selected coaches at the academy — a strange contrast with New Zealand, where one or two doctors might decide to attend when Arthur spoke to coaches but never invited him to *their* sports medicine conferences.

Later we went to the magnificently reconstructed Leipzig Stadium, where the academy has its laboratories and clinics, and I was put through a physiological test, disconcertingly carried out entirely by women doctors. They checked my weight, height, bone structure, the fat on various parts of my body, gave me a barium test to determine my heart capacity by x-ray, and then got me on a bicycle, wired to an electrocardiograph and rigged up with a mask so that every breath I exhaled could be collected and analysed, with resistance controls to vary the effort I was required to make. I pedalled for seven minutes, had a rest, pedalled another two minutes against increased resistance, then two more minutes harder again, then more against added resistance.

Someone said, 'Stop when you've had enough', and I lasted another four minutes before I was almost sucking the mask into my lungs in the battle for air. I learnt that I'd achieved a standard which only the top cyclists have exceeded. Since cycling isn't an activity for which I've developed muscles, this was quite surprising and emphasised the value of developing the cardio-respiratory system, through running, to give stamina to the muscles.

Heading home, I was concerned because I wanted to get back without any fuss. In the past, I've had some pretty nice welcomes home, and I knew that on this occasion people would make sure I wouldn't feel let down by finding no one at the airport to greet me. This I didn't want. A public welcome would seem too much like a gesture of sympathy. I didn't want sympathy.

Peter indulged in various subterfuges and evasions about his immediate travel plans, which worked perfectly until he reached Sydney. Until then, he hadn't even told Sally what he was doing. But then the manager of the airline saw his name on the passenger list and informed the media.

However, they were the only ones who did meet me. I wasn't feeling exactly delighted with my exploits on the tour. I had failed in what I set out to achieve. But with what I knew about training, I was able to accept this quite readily. When I was honest with myself, I saw that, since Tokyo, there were many reasons why I was not running well. I was trusting in my ability to rise to the occasion. This had worked out for my first couple of races. I had hoped I would come completely right and I wasn't unduly concerned — not as much as I would have been had I been unsure that my opponents were not better runners.

It's rather difficult to explain exactly how I was feeling. I knew that if I trained hard and reached my peak, I could beat the best milers in the world at the moment. I knew what I was capable of and what they were capable of. Also, I was in the unusual position that, even though I was being consistently beaten, people were still coming along to watch me run. I mention it again because I found it significant.

At no stage was I disillusioned. To a lot of people, I must have appeared to be a winning athlete who found himself suddenly unable to win and unable to figure out why. In fact, I was discovering that it wasn't possible for me to train just for a world tour to preserve an unbeaten record. I needed something like an Olympic Games or as-yet-unattained goal to steel the resolution.

I had made only two world trips — the last one and the 1961 one in which I was still on my way up. On all the other occasions I had left New Zealand, I had been going for special events and had been able to set myself for them.

Perhaps, Peter concluded, he had been mentally geared to giving up. He recognised that he could succeed again if he went out to 5000 metres and a new series of goals. But that had never been necessary — he hadn't been forced to consider it and he didn't want to do it.

I retired fully satisfied, and I would even go through that last tour again exactly as it was — except perhaps for the Vancouver episode. It's the only one I wouldn't care to repeat.

And, having retired, Peter came to appreciate the extent to which athletics had dominated his life from the time he left school in 1958 and began seven years of the rigorous Lydiard training system. In that time, nothing was attempted before its possible effects on his training had been considered — if it did threaten to interfere with training, it wasn't done.

There's more to training than merely allocating two hours a day to be spent at it — your whole life revolves around it. The conscientious athlete has to moderate his approach to everything. I became a bit sheltered. I didn't know a great deal about living except as I knew it as an athlete, and that isn't the average, normal way. My circle of friends became smaller. If someone invited me out and it got past 9.30 p.m., I began to look at my watch. Not all athletes do this, but not all athletes get to the top.

Throughout his running career, Peter Snell was possessed of — or possessed by — a great driving force towards his chosen goals. It was something he saw as a gain for his future, that enabled him to close off anyone who started to mess around with his state of mind

— a single-mindedness 'developed to protect my concentration from people who bored me' — which made him to some extent come across as an introvert and a very intolerant person.

Retirement spun his life upside down. It threw him back into the real world. He relaxed into it and actually found himself enjoying it.

> Once my motivation went, the strain of living up to the expectations of myself and others became too much. Retirement meant the end of making sacrifices and the beginning of my enjoyment of golf — I joined the Grange club — tennis — I played interclub — and squash.

In fact, Peter never stopped running either — in his second life he became a successful age group orienteer right up until 2006. Finally, however, the effort became just too physically painful. Yet the will to achieve, temporarily suppressed after 1965, remained strong, and was soon to turn his life upside down once again in the pursuit of a new and daunting challenge.

Of course, one of the greatest influences on his decision to quit was the 1965 publication of our book, *No Bugles No Drums*. The day it came out, Peter disqualified himself under the rules of those days, which had also seen Arthur Lydiard threatened with loss of his amateur status if he continued to write columns for the newspaper I worked for, the *Auckland Star*, even though those columns were of potentially immense benefit to New Zealand athletics.

Peter Snell's record-breaking races:

17 July 1961, Dublin, 4 x 1 mile relay — 16:23.8

27 January 1962, Wanganui, 1 mile — 3:54.4

3 February 1962, Christchurch, 800 metres — 1:44.3; and 880 yards — 1:45.1

10 February 1962, Los Angeles, 1000 yards (indoors) — 2:06.0

18 March 1962, Tokyo, 880 yards (indoors) — 1:49.9

19 November 1964, Auckland, 1000 metres — 2:16.6

24 November 1964, Auckland, 1 mile — 3:54.1.

Olympic records:

31 September 1960, Rome, 800 metres — 1:46.3

16 October 1964, Tokyo, 800 metres — 1:45.1.

PART TWO

CHAPTER ONE

Global circuit

My new, laid-back life wasn't without its interesting experiences. For example, early in 1967, I was invited to run around the world. The invitation came from the American Ambassador to New Zealand, Jack Henning, a Lyndon Johnson appointment with a keen interest in track and field. It was the US Navy's custom then to provide an annual tour to the Antarctic, to show US politicians and business leaders the American operations down there. Normally, a Member of Parliament from each of the main New Zealand political parties — National and Labour in those days — was added to the group.

Jack called me and asked if the trip would interest me. He added: 'I want you to go to the South Pole and run around the world.' This was one of those invitations I didn't even have to think about, so in mid-February I was off to Christchurch and the Operation Deep Freeze headquarters to join the party, which included the head of IBM, James Watson III. We were outfitted with thermal clothing and climbed into a piston-engined Super Constellation for the trip south. Oddly, for some reason which was not explained to us, the seats all faced towards the tail.

The flight was several hours long, and as we approached the point of no return the pilot had to make the decision whether the conditions were suitable for continuing on to McMurdo Sound. What he decided had us arriving on the McMurdo sea ice, near the edge of the Ross Ice Shelf, on a beautiful day. At this time of the year, the sun stays up day and night so we were treated to some fabulous sights, highlighted by a three-hour flight to the South Pole on a skiequipped Hercules transport jet.

We landed and lunched and then I fulfilled Jack Henning's wish, plodding through six-inch-deep snow for something less than 100 yards on a 15-metre radius circle round the striped barber's pole which denotes the geographic pole. The altitude at the pole is 10,500 feet (3200 m), 7200 feet (2200 m) higher than the Ross Ice Shelf, and although some of the older members of the party became breathless on the walk from the Herc to the underground station, I was in pretty good condition and felt all right after the 'run'. I had a crowd of about a dozen witnesses — and I have the photograph as further proof that I did, in fact, run *right round* the world (wearing a Rothmans tracksuit).

On the flight back, I was invited on to the flight deck as we approached the Beardmore Glacier, which was the route taken by Robert Falcon Scott on his ill-fated expedition in 1910–12. The pilot flew the full length of this 200-kilometre-long, 40 kilometre-wide glacier at 500 feet, leaving me in awe of the challenge it must have presented to the early explorers. It validated the description of Scott in his epic book, *South with Scott*.

Other side trips included a flight to the ice-drilling project at Byrd Station and, before landing, a low-level run over the crater of the active volcano, Mt Erebus, where, less than 13 years later, an Air New Zealand DC10 was to crash, killing all 20 crew and 237 passengers. Helicopters also took us to historic places such as the hut used by Scott and his party. I made one trip by myself: the New Zealand operation, Scott Base, close to Erebus, was just a mile away so I jogged over one evening to join the Kiwis for dinner and learn about their research in the unique snow- and ice-free dry valleys, including Lake Vanda, which lies in an arid Antarctic valley ringed by 5000-metre-high glaciers.

Another interesting experience involved the medical field. Led by an ear, nose and throat surgeon, Noel Roydhouse, Auckland had a group of medical doctors, physiotherapists and athletics coaches interested in sports medicine who periodically met to discuss topics such as sports injuries and treatment, exercise physiology and training. Invited to one of these meetings in 1969, I found some of my core beliefs challenged and I yearned for more information to defend my ideas instead of having to rely heavily on the bald statement, 'This is what I did and it was successful.'

These challenges arose when I discussed how the resting heart rate became lower in response to endurance training — mine was 36 beats a minute compared with the normal 72 — and the value of warming up. Both these concepts were rebuffed by educated 'experts'. The physiologist at Greenlane Hospital disagreed with the lower heart rate idea and supported his view with a report on studies done with top US miler Jim Ryun, whose resting heart rate was about 70 when measured in the laboratory. My support of warm-up was countered by a physical educator, who cited a research study showing that warming up had no effect on 100-metre sprint times and then patronisingly said that, if you believed it, there would be a *psychological* benefit. Oh, I thought, for the tools and the knowledge to be able to respond! After all, if you read something in a book, or particularly the report of a study, it must be right. Right? Wrong — as we shall see later.

As for Ryun's normal pulse rate, that was something that bothered me. I have wondered whether, when he showed up at the lab for testing, he was a little bit nervous and not properly relaxed. The only really reliable way to check your pulse rate is to take it yourself when you wake up in the morning. I have people showing up at my laboratory and they're just sitting there and their pulse rate is 100. They're nervous. It's the same with blood pressure. Many people have high blood pressure when a doctor takes it as part of a consultation.

The other issue is that it is not all about heart size. There are complicated mechanisms that regulate the heart. The vagus nerve slows the heart down and the sympathetic nerve accelerates it, and it's the balance between those two that is complex. We have someone at the University of Texas Southwestern Medical Center who is very interested in this subject but he hasn't been able to give me an explanation for this yet.

The scientist doing the Ryun research was Jack Daniels, who was the cross-country coach at the University of Texas, and he was well known and respected for his work *Running with Jim Ryun*, which reported on five years of testing with Jim. That included the pulse rate result; and people who read it concluded that it meant that the heart rate didn't necessarily come down with runners like him. But he is the only one I have heard of and I still don't believe it.

In fact, I did finally talk to Ryun about it and said, 'Jim, it has always bothered me that Jack Daniels said that your resting heart rate was a normal 70 when everyone else who ran like you did came down into the thirties.' But he maintained that was correct — it was 70. Whether he took it himself and in what circumstances, I don't know. I should have quizzed him more closely about it, I suppose.

The same sort of problem arose when I became interested in overtraining and tried to understand some of the ways of predicting overtraining. When people ask me what I've learnt that would cause me to do anything different from what I did as a runner, my answer is always 'Not much'. Lydiard had it right all along, without knowing exactly why, and he then created the physiology to justify it. He did do a lot of reading, but some of it was off-the-wall. What I have gained is a much better way of explaining *why* what he did worked.

Then, in the early 1970s, Rothmans decided the Sports Foundation would benefit from administrative expertise and hired a retired army officer, Colonel Frank Rennie, who was given the title of Chairman since we were all directors. He brought useful skills with him in defining our objective and setting goals — and he also loaded the gun and pulled the trigger that was to get me out of the Foundation and into academia.

Frank Rennie managed to convince the purse holders at Rothmans that it would be beneficial for me to have sabbatical leave to study coaching schemes in Britain, while based at Loughborough College, which was famed for its physical education programme and expertise in athletics. This reputation was no doubt earned by the legendary Geoffrey Dyson, who taught the top New Zealand coaches Jim Bellwood and Frank Sharpley at the college. Bellwood coached the world-beating New Zealand long jumper Yvette Williams. Frank reasoned that I would benefit from taking classes in the sciences relating to sports performance, such as anatomy and physiology, biomechanics — the study of movement — motor learning and psychology. This was to provide a backbone to my practical experience and allow me to interact knowledgably with 'educated' people in the coaching field, especially the knockers and doubters in Roydhouse's group.

The trip, in 1971, happily coincided with an invitation to speak at the International Olympic Academy. The Academy is Greece's contribution to the Olympic movement and is sited close to where the ancient Olympic Games were held in Olympia, some distance from Athens, on the Peloponnesian Peninsula. Conveniently, this fitted in on my way to England and it proved an interesting detour. Arthur and I had been to Greece before, stopping over in 1964 on our way to South Africa, but we were there only long enough to rush round the Acropolis.

Now, on the way to Olympia from Athens, historians told us all about the places we were passing. One stop was at Corinth, on the neck of the peninsula, which had been the site of the Corinth or Isthmian Games, which were organised about 581 BC, and are now held at Corinth in the spring of the first and third years of each Olympiad. The contests were generally like the Olympic Games,but were conducted on a smaller scale. We were taken to see the marks on the stones which indicated the starting lines for the long-ago sprint events. But, of all these various games the Greeks held, the Olympics were the most famous and we arrived at Olympia to find that the old stadium had been excavated and provided an ideal backdrop for the buildings of the Olympic Academy, where the conference was held.

My talk was about my training and my Olympic experiences. At this stage, my training was still fairly novel to many people. However, I do remember that, as I sat listening to the various coaches, I thought, 'I could make similar presentations'. And probably it had been in the back of my mind for some time that, with formal education in physiology, I could effectively discuss the science underpinning

Lydiard training. I had never been interested in coaching athletes but I did like talking about why things worked. Arthur said that was what he was now doing by working with coaches rather than with athletes. In training, he had never wanted to be a coach of athletes, but he also underestimated one of his great talents — his ability to motivate people to do the demanding work he outlined for them. He was helped in that area by early converts to his training system, such as Murray Halberg and Barry Magee, who made it easier for those of us who came along later to respond to his methods.

After Greece, I flew to Mexico to join Sally and the girls, who had gone there to spend some time with a diplomat friend in Guadalajara, Gordon Dugan and his wife Gloria. We had met them when he was vice-consul in New Zealand and we had kept in touch. In England, I was formally enrolled in the human biology group within the Department of Ergonomics and Cybernetics — two words I had to look up — at the Loughborough University of Technology, which shared the same campus as the Loughborough College of Education. Under this arrangement, I could pick courses of interest in both the college and the university. We spent a week in a guesthouse and then found a house to rent in the nearby village of Shepshed.

Attending university proved a very positive experience, especially at the phys ed college where the course material was directly related to my growing interest in training and physical activities. One of my mentors was Clive Bond, a soccer coach with a strong interest in sports psychology and skill learning. Our University of Technology group was headed by Dr Ernest Hamley, an interesting character who insisted on being addressed as Ernest and was a refreshing change from the rest of the status-conscious academics and upper-crust Brits.

It wasn't all work, though. I visited the national coaching centres, Bisham Abbey National Sports Centre in Marlow, Buckinghamshire, owned and Lottery-funded by Sport England, and Lilleshall Hall in Shropshire, close to North Wales and now better known as the Lilleshall National Centre of Excellence, a flagship training ground for many of the UK's top sportsmen and women. And we visited an old rival, John Whetton, who was teaching physiology at a college of education in Nottingham; met up with a former schoolmate, Graham Day, in North Wales; visited Scotland; took a train to London to visit the laboratory of Vaughan Thomas at St Mary's College; and took part in a coaching weekend organised by the British Milers Club, where I met Roger Bannister.

However, as the year rolled on and the knowledge poured in — I was determined to soak up as much information as possible — I found myself wishing I was enrolled for credits so that what I learnt could help me academically in the future.

CHAPTER TWO

Muscling in

The Science of Sport, a book by Vaughan Thomas, was produced in the 1970s after he earned his Master's degree in Loughborough. It contained much of the stuff that I was interested in and it was also a subject we covered during the course. The technique, called electromyography, produced records from which you could establish what muscles were most used in a specific exercise.

One subject was a weightlifter who was studied during a 'clean and swatch' with electrodes attached to the main muscles he was using — the thighs, triceps and biceps. As the muscles were used, they produced electrical activity in proportion to the number of muscle fibres that were activated. This could be shown as a series of spikes on a graph, varying in size according to the effort involved during the lift. So, on a time line, you could see the progression of the fibres in the quads coming in, then the triceps and biceps as the lift advanced. I found it fascinating.

Another who was tested both for the book and in the lab was Tom Simpson, an Olympic and Tour de France rider and one of the greatest British cyclists, who died five years later, aged 30, after collapsing on the Mont Ventoux climb in the 13th stage of the Tour de France. The post-mortem determined that he died from a diuretic cocktail of amphetamines and alcohol combined with the heat of the climb and a pre-existing stomach complaint.

Loughborough is also the place where I was turned on to sports psychology. A lot of British people were working in this field. Barbara Knapp, a researcher at the University of Birmingham, had written a book which dealt with that oft-repeated theory that practice makes perfect. The sports psychologists, of whom she was one, would say that practice makes perfect *when* it is accompanied by knowledge of the results of practice which are known and cared about. What they were trying to say was that, if you don't know or don't care about what is happening during practice, you are not going to get any better. In other words, just going through the motions is no good. You've got to have feedback as to how you're doing, and you've got to care about that feedback. It makes a lot of sense.

Clive Bond, with whom I became friends, gave me some insights into skills learning, and a psychologist helped me to understand a bit about personality testing, which I got very enthusiastic about. One particular measuring instrument, which are called pencil and paper tests, was the Edwards Personal Preference Schedule, which purported to measure 15 of an individual's manifest needs. Among these needs were achievement, heterosexuality, affiliation (which is the need for interacting with people), abasement, succour and nurturing, and aggression (which some people apparently have a need for). I thought this made a lot of sense, because at that time it seemed that physiologists weren't coming up with anything that helped coaches very much. Instead of presenting new methods, they would come in behind and say, 'Well, we've done some tests here and we know you are a good athlete because you have a high VO_2max.' That kind of thing really wasn't very helpful.

Later on, before I got to university in the States, I did some further reading, including a book by two clinical psychologists from California, Bruce Ogilvie and Thomas Tutko, called *Problem Athletes and How to Handle Them*. I really enjoyed the book but I was to learn that such anecdotal accounts were not appreciated as much by research psychologists.

Loughborough, as I have said, was where I discovered I had the capacity to learn to become a scientist. The material was interesting, and I felt I was capable of doing the courses I sat in on. I didn't have much hard-type science stuff to get my head around, and I divided my time somewhat between the human biology group at the university and the physical education people down at the college. I worked fairly hard and involved myself in some of the activities outside: I was a member of the Loughborough hockey team and I made trips to different coaching courses to pick up all the information I could about coaching schemes in Britain and how they educated their coaches.

With our Loughborough year almost over, Sally and I planned a camping tour of western Europe with the girls. We took our little British car across on the hovercraft from Dover to Calais and drove south through western France, eventually pitching our tent at the seaside resort of Biarritz, not far from the Spanish border. From there, we drove into the Basque country and the Pyrenees, visiting the high-altitude training camp at Font Remur. With the Munich Olympics so close, I expressed surprise at the absence of athletes and was told that the camp had been built for preparation for the Mexico City Olympics.

We made a brief crossing into Spain and then headed over to the Mediterranean coast and meandered through southern France, living off cheese and salami, local boulangerie bread and cheap wine, and marvelling at the spectacular tunnels and viaducts which took us through Nice, Monaco, into Italy and on to Genoa. We then turned back north through the breathtaking Dolomite mountain region, into Austria for a quick look at Innsbruck and then into Germany and on to Luxemburg.

Before the Munich Games, I took part in a series of Rothmans United Kingdom promotions. My fee for this was to join their party of executives who were attending the Games. Although it was now eight years since I had competed, sitting in the stands did not compare with being part of the action. Just before the awful, horrible Israeli hostage crisis, I joined a group of the Rothmans executives on a day trip to Garmisch-Partenkirchen, a ski resort in southern Germany, not far from Munich, so I missed that tragedy.

After the Games, I returned to Loughborough, the family was reunited and we carried on back to New Zealand. I was eager to pass on my new expertise in sports science and especially sports psychology. At this stage, I guess the seed of what I wanted to do may have been planted in my mind, but I was obligated to go back to Rothmans and I had no plan beyond that. So I settled down to family life, playing tennis and golf, and making Rothmans trips, one of which was to Dunedin where I was invited to give a talk on training to the School of Physical Education at Otago University. During the question session after my presentation, the head of the school, Phillip Smithells, suggested that I was perpetrating the 'cult of the champion', whereas the goal of physical education was to encourage widespread participation and not a nation of sports spectators obtaining some vicarious thrill from the sports equivalent of gladiators.

While I agreed with the general idea of broad participation, I could not resist suggesting that Smithells might be fostering the 'cult of mediocrity'. He and the other influential physical educator of the time, the superintendent of phys ed in schools, Dudley Wills, overlooked the fact that New Zealand sports successes actually *increased* participation. Wills, talking to his student teachers (some of whom were runners coached by Arthur) and during interviews, was particularly derogatory about the contributions of Arthur Lydiard, referring to him as a 'monomaniac'. This insulting label was in reference to Arthur's jogging movement, which Wills insisted was not rounded enough. He was enamoured with Swedish gymnastics and apparently did not have the foresight, as Arthur did, to see that cardiovascular disease was New Zealand's big problem.

In terms of some of the philosophy that exists today on how children should be encouraged, I'm all for fostering participation. I believe competitiveness is good, but it should not be developed to the stage where all the emphasis is on trying to produce the top teams, as it is in the United States — where, for example, there is only one baseball team in each high school; if you don't make the team, you don't play baseball. I like the situation we certainly used to have in New Zealand where there is competitive opportunity all the way down through the age groups and so on.

Nevertheless, it is my strong belief that the competitive situation is one that challenges people to do better. If everyone is a winner by simply showing up and going through the motions, that's not going to produce any great improvement in overall performance. Young people like to be competitive. Recently, in New Zealand, I watched Massey University experts testing young talent, identified by the Peter Snell Institute of Sport, in a variety of exercises, which quickly became competitive as the youngsters tried to outdo each other. The testing became a challenge.

It had been my firm intention never to become a coach, but I enjoyed talking about training and trying to understand the physiology involved in the adaptation to endurance training. I never thought then that it would become my lifelong pursuit and passion. However, I had a visit from Rex Maddaford and his father, who asked me if I would guide Rex in his preparation for the Mexico Olympics. Rex, who lived nearby and belonged, like me, to the Owairaka club, was New Zealand's outstanding young distance runner. He had already won New Zealand titles at three miles and cross-country, and in 1968, while he was still only a few days over 21, ran the second-fastest mile and the fastest three mile of the New Zealand season, was the world's fifth fastest of all time over 10,000 metres, and ran a 2:23.16 marathon.

I did some interval work and other workouts with Rex at Mt Smart Stadium. It was quite a lot of fun for me and kept me in good condition. But Rex knew what to do and what worked for him, as most athletes do after a while, so the coaching was easy. In Mexico, the 5000 and 10,000 metres races were dominated by runners from the highlands of Kenya, Ethiopia and the Soviet Union, but Rex, although he had done no altitude training, finished in the top 12 in both. The German Harald Norpoth, who was a 5000 metres silver medallist four years earlier, collapsed in pain from oxygen starvation. Rex then went to a minor league college, Eastern Mexico University, in New Mexico, and fell victim to the American system, which requires athletes to run their hearts out to pay for their scholarships and for the futures of their coaches.

Many years later, when I was in Dallas, Rex and I made contact again through his sports-writer brother Terry, back in Auckland. We got in touch and decided to do a ski trip together with our wives. Rex had done very well in the teaching profession since we had last met. He now lives in Tucumcari in New Mexico, about 500 miles from Dallas, with a population under 6000. It is fairly close to where he went to college and he has settled down there, married an American girl, and had a start as acting principal of Tucumcari High School. We arranged to meet in Santa Fe, which is a ski resort, and the plan was that my second wife Miki and I would head off from Dallas after work on Friday night, stay the night in Santa Fe with the Maddafords and be on its ski field early on Saturday morning. Unfortunately, Miki and I tend to swoop in at the last minute to catch flights and this time we were just a little too late and didn't make it. Embarrassingly, we had to wait and catch a flight in the morning. Rex and his wife stayed the night in Santa Fe and we got there around ten in the morning and finally got to start skiing in the afternoon.

Santa Fe is the capital of New Mexico and a beautiful city. All its buildings, by city decree, are built in the traditional adobe style (sun-dried clay bricks) developed by the southwestern Indians — even our hotel, which was part of a major chain. We had a lot of fun together. Rex is a good skier, and I had learnt to ski in California, when I was at Davis, and had done a little bit of cross-country skiing at Pullman — where I even skied from home to university on one occasion. It was a great opportunity to meet Rex, who, as Miki remarked, was pretty energetic.

Miki recalls: 'It was my first ski experience and I enjoyed it and meeting Rex and his wife, but I found Rex to be one of the most energetic persons I have ever been around. He jogged everywhere — he just never walked and was over-abounding in energy. I remembered him from when I was a runner. I ran in New Mexico several times and Rex was a big star at the meets.'

Early in 1974, I was becoming increasingly restless about my future with Rothmans. With my overseas educational experience, I sought to interact with graduates of the national physical education system, but my tobacco connection reared its head as a perennial problem. It wasn't a question of rejection or insults and so on, but in terms of invitations to participate in activities that had anything to do with the Department of Physical Education there was a reluctance to involve me, because of that Rothmans link. The Department, in the era of Smithells and Wills, did not want to have anything to do with us, even though the individuals they had control over did. We were offering coaching services, so ended up working with sports clubs and schools which made their own decisions.

In addition, I was becoming increasingly aware now that when I got involved through Rothmans in sports discussions involving medical people, I could say nothing — or at most very little — because I would be dismissed as an individual who did not understand the processes about which I might talk. There were no long-term prospects in what I was doing. I wanted — maybe *needed* is a better word — to work in an area that gave me pleasure and fulfilment and which maybe could help other people.

I was still conscious of what I learnt when I underwent the maximal treadmill test at San Diego University in 1965 about the possibility that talent could be measured by tests that determined the quantity of oxygen the body could consume, the range of the rate of the heartbeat, the critical amount of body fat and so on, to add to knowledge about hard training, good coaching, mental toughness and other abstractions. And I also met people there who would soon have a great influence on my future. And, of course, the more recent experience of Loughborough had whetted my appetite for what I might be able to achieve.

So, in 1974, I made the decision to toss my financial security away and go looking for my own answers.

CHAPTER THREE

Not one of the 'old boys'

I didn't devote a great deal of thought to what I might do once I had attained a university degree, but, at the time, I was concerned that a third of the deaths in New Zealand were due to heart disease — and mainly coronary artery disease, degenerative types. My reading indicated that maybe a lot of those deaths could be prevented through exercise. I was also interested in looking at sports from a social science viewpoint. How did sport affect social behaviour? Could it reduce crime and juvenile delinquency?

However, the beginning of the year of my change of life was pleasant. I was honoured to run the last leg of the Queen's Baton Relay into the brand-new QEII Stadium in Christchurch for the 24 January opening ceremony of the Commonwealth Games, and then had an arrangement with Auckland journalist Phil Gifford to give him regular reports to send up to the *New Zealand Herald*.

I was also appointed athletics training officer, responsible to Harry Blazey — the brother of the renowned rugby and athletics administrator and New Zealand Hall of Famer Ces Blazey — and was the liaison person advising arriving teams about the venues available for training. In this role, I sat in on meetings between team managers, at one of which the business was to appoint three people to form the International Jury of Appeal, the group which would rule on any protests lodged during the Games. Although this was officially a democratic election process, the jury members were normally selected in advance by members of the 'old boys' network' led by British administrator Sandy Duncan.

Apparently, some 'insignificant countries' were not in on this arrangement, and when the chair of the managers' meeting called for nominations, my friend from Western Samoa, Pita Ali'ilima, stunned me and probably some others by nominating me. Before Harry Blazey could say anything, the Australian manager seconded the motion and my appointment was carried. Sandy Duncan, according to insiders, was not pleased, and the following day I was asked to resign. The impression given was: how could a mere competitor occupy this lofty position, which was the preserve of the administrators? To their credit, Games chief Ron Scott and fellow jury member Ces Blazey supported my election and Ron advised me to hang tough.

Personally, I had no doubts that I could be a good jury member, because I felt the official rules did not always have to be applied rigidly and there had been, in my opinion, instances of bonehead rulings in the past. A classic example was Dorando Pietri's disqualification in the 1908 Olympic marathon because, following his dramatic collapse close to the finishing line, he was helped across by officials. More recently, Jim Ryun, then the world mile record-holder, was fouled in the first round of the 1972 Olympic 1500 metres and took a bad fall. His protest to the jury was rejected and probably the best runner in the field was out. If it had been my decision, I would have ruled that Jim was denied a place in the semi-finals through no fault of his own and should be advanced as an extra runner so that no one would be displaced. Unfortunately, this is only common sense.

Meanwhile, my frustration with my life with Rothmans grew. We had assembled quite a good group of coaches in a variety of sports and periodically would travel to communities for a week to provide coaching sessions and stimulate enthusiasm across a wide cross-section of sports. Arthur had left us by then, but we had Don Clarke in rugby football, Bert Sutcliffe in cricket working full time for special occasions, and we would bring in coaches from other sports for the week, such as rowing's Rusty Robertson. Some of the sports also had Rothmans money to import other coaches — among them the squash coach Dardir el Bakary and Leith Sand, who was a badminton expert. (Incidentally, I didn't learn until 2006 that my co-author Garth had written a squash coaching book with Dardir, which was published in 1971.)

These excursions were enjoyable to a degree. We saw that we were generating a lot of interest in the communities we visited. They ranged from mid-sized cities, such as Wanganui, to quite small towns, particularly in the South Island. It was also a PR campaign to an extent, and my job was to co-ordinate the visits, lead the team, and participate as well. Ultimately, however, it was not making me feel satisfied job-wise. I felt that I was not achieving much and realised that I could be doing this for the rest of my life unless I did something about changing it. I know now that, if I'd had my life over again, I'd have lived it differently. I would have taken an athletic scholarship when I was 21 or 22. But that's hindsight. Under the circumstances, I'm glad that I didn't go down this route. There would not have been double gold at Tokyo and I may not have found the satisfying career I have today.

Finally, not long after the Commonwealth Games in Christchurch in 1974, I contacted acquaintances I had made at San Diego State University in 1965, when I did the maximal treadmill test there, and discussed with them how I could further my interest in adult fitness. The physiological jargon with which they bombarded me was more than I could comprehend at the time, but I was intrigued by the thought that it should be possible to translate the data into useable information. And, once I had overcome the mental barrier of not believing I could do the academic work I needed to reach that stage, I was ready to change my life totally.

The leader of the exercise laboratory at San Diego State University, Dr Fred Kasch, strongly recommended that I study for a Bachelor's degree and gain experience I could put to use on my return to New Zealand. He said I should contact Dr Jack Wilmore, at the University of California, Davis, about the programme he was running. In June, I visited Davis to explore options with Dr Wilmore and the head of the physical education department, Dr Dean Ryan. While I was there, I gave a talk to the faculty and students and generally laid the groundwork for accommodating Sally and the children. Jack was extremely positive and said that I had a grasp of exercise physiology equivalent to his Master's degree students. The informality of all my talks with faculty members indicated I was going to enjoy the experience of studying there.

However, UC Davis is a top-echelon university—Jack claimed they selected students from the top 10 per cent of high school graduates — so I had to establish my credentials for admission. The nearest New Zealand equivalent to graduating from high school in the States was the School Certificate exam but, whereas most US students graduate from high school, the New Zealand system was structured by scaling to fail 45 per cent of those taking the exam. I was still hung up about failing the New Zealand University Entrance exam twice and did not have my School Certificate to prove my graduation.

Which is where my running reputation came to the rescue. The registrar, Dr Maynard Skinner, was an avid jogger and finally resolved the predicament. 'Okay, jog four miles with me and you're in,' he said. So, my running career, the Loughborough experience, my San Diego episode, and my subsequent enthusiastic reading were paying off. I became one of the 17,000 students at the Davis campus, roughly half the population of this small agricultural town 80 miles northwest of San Francisco.

Financially, it was not going to be easy. I was entitled to $900 a year relief from the government — a kind of break on the fees for needy students — because I wasn't working and had no means of support for my family; but I needed $2500 a year for instruction fees and about $150 for books. So I was living off our capital, which we received from the sale of our Auckland home. I calculated the capital would last us through three years, but then we would be scraping. The Bachelor's degrees at American universities are all considered four-year programmes but I was told that, by carrying a high course load and taking summer school, the degree could be completed in three. Thus, I decided that, rather than try to work in a fast-food joint to earn some money for the fourth year, it would be better to take on a heavy load and try to get through my degree quickly. With our limited finances, this was clearly the path I needed to follow — there was no other choice we could afford.

For that first year, we lived in an apartment, which had no access to a garden. However, UC Davis provided little plots of ground for students and, after my first year, I had one so that we could grow our own vegetables, mainly tomatoes. It measured maybe 15 feet by six feet and was in a row of plots. It was an agricultural school after all. I also kept reasonably fit, cycling all over the place, taking regular runs and playing a bit of tennis as a break.

The UC Davis year, excluding the summer, is divided into three 12-week sessions, known as quarters, which differs from the traditional two-semester per year system used by many universities. And, unlike most students, whose majors are standard areas of study offered by the various departments, I was permitted to create an individual major that fitted my particular needs and interests. Using this option, and with Jack's help, I was able to figure out the coursework I would need for my academic objectives. He encouraged me to structure my own degree plan but to include a rigorous dose of basic science — chemistry, physics and calculus — which had been my nemesis subjects at Mt Albert Grammar in 1957. So I constructed a degree programme that comprised a third each of physiology, psychology and the science courses within physical education — exercise physiology, biomechanics, tests and measurements and motor learning. For breadth, I included courses in child development, rhetoric and pharmacology. I titled this combination 'Sports Science' but the Dean's office told me to pick another, 'more academic-sounding' name. My second choice, 'Human Performance', was accepted.

And so I was very well treated. Considering I was a foreigner, I got an excellent deal that enabled me to get my feet firmly on the first rung of the academic ladder I wanted to climb.

CHAPTER FOUR

Going for it

After looking at the offerings for the year's summer school before I began at Davis, I decided I had time to enrol for the second summer session. Thus, I signed up for two four-hour graduate-level classes that ran for six weeks through mid-July to the end of August and provided eight units towards the total of 180 I would need to graduate. Because I had developed an interest in psychology, I chose physiological psychology, a general course about neurology and brain function, and sensory processes, which was the detailed anatomy and physiology of how sight, sound, taste and smell are sensed and processed by the eyes, ears, tongue and olfactory bulb of the nose. If I survived this lot, I reckoned, it would be a great start to my degree.

Again with Jack's help, I was able to line up low-cost family housing, and Sally and our daughters, Mandy, now 8, and Jacqui, 6, arrived in August and moved into the apartment about a mile away from the campus.

In that first year at Davis, I acquired 67 units of the 180 needed for my Bachelor's degree. I got another 21 by attending summer school in July and August instead of taking time off. I was nearly halfway there.

I took extra stuff. For instance, I studied child development. I don't remember if there were any other males in the class but I was certainly the only student with children, and I was motivated purely to try to learn more about being a better dad. I'm telling you this because I got my worst grade ever out of it — a D! I'm not entirely sure why, but we had to go out to migrant camps, observe kids interacting and playing and then write about it. My instructor for the course, a crusty middle-aged woman without a doctorate, met my ex-wife Sally recently and told her I was the worst student she had ever had. However, I could just as easily respond that she was probably the worst instructor I ever had, and that the 'worst student' she had known won good enough grades in everything else, despite the crummy grade she gave me, to go to graduate school, finish with a PhD and end up in the International Scholar-Athlete Hall of Fame. But enough said.

I ended up in a rather weird sort of situation because I was 34 when I enrolled at Davis, and found myself making friends with other students, many of them 18-year-olds, who now became my peers. Yet I was as old as most of the faculty. At the time, it didn't feel peculiar because it was something that I had to do. My lab partners didn't make me feel I was a lot older and that may have been because I was still pretty athletic and energetic. But even though the instructor you're learning from may be the same age as you, he's still the one who's going to be evaluating you and you're there to learn. And consider that, internationally, grey-heads like Garth are now being taught and evaluated by people who may be young enough to be their grandchildren, so maybe my situation wasn't quite as odd as it might seem.

My first chemistry course looked vaguely familiar so I looked through some of my sixth-form chemistry notebooks, which I had kept, and discovered that the material was similar. My New Zealand teacher had just read from a book and we'd copied everything down. What I now had to do was much more meaningful. But my first chemistry exam was a real disaster. I scored around 40 per cent and I was in trouble. But they have this rule that after four weeks you can actually drop the class and take it up again later, and because so many were taking freshman chemistry it was offered every quarter. So that's what I did — I picked it up again in the next quarter and this time I scored 90 per cent. There was so much that was totally new to me that I just needed a second look at it. The kids I was with had come straight from chemistry at high school whereas I hadn't touched the subject for 16 years. There were about 400 students in the class, using multiple labs with about 20 in each group. And the faculty member running the lab I was in told the class, 'Well, we've someone here who got 90 per cent in the exams,' and that made me feel pretty good. I wasn't able to keep it up, though; I wound up with an overall B.

But another important development at Davis was that I learned computer programming. I took a course and learned two programming languages, BASIC and FORTRAN, a high-level language used especially for scientific calculations. In those days, data was entered into the computer using a punch-card system which needed a card for every line of code; so a 100-line program gave you a pile of 100 cards. You'd see students like me wandering round with stacks of these cards, which you would take into the basement of the computer conference, run them through a card reader and, click-click whirr-whirr, you had a program result. Or it might not run and then you'd have to go back to your computer and check it through and maybe find a card which had some small error you'd made. When you think that you can now do all that stuff on your own PC or laptop, you realise how antiquated it was. But I gravitated to computers like a duck to water and in fact even owned a cheap early computer that had no storage capacity but a very primitive game on it called Pong, which was an electronic version of table tennis.

However, having learnt all this at Davis, I found there wasn't much opportunity to use computers when I went to Washington State. Word processing was available but not on my computer, and I had to type out my doctoral dissertation and have it sent off to be typed up properly by a professional. When I finally got to Dallas I purchased a Commodore 64, which wouldn't store anything but I could do some programming and make it run. My ability to master it stemmed from my quantity surveying days, when I had to do calculations all day with a paper and pencil. The only machine in the office was an adding machine, which could do simple addition and nothing more. Calculating areas and volumes using the old units of yards, feet and inches wasn't something you could do easily in your head. So I really appreciated the value of a little machine on which you could quickly handle such calculations, quite apart from the word processor, which came in quite handy when I wanted to write papers or reports. Later on, I bought an Apple 2-Plus and then an IBM-compatible computer with hard disk storage. Eventually, I bought the computer components and assembled them myself. This made upgrades easy to do and, if anything went wrong, I could fix it.

After I completed a year in Davis, Jack Wilmore decided to accept a position in a private clinic that specialised in executive physicals. This was unfortunate, because I was so buried in classwork that we had had only limited interaction and I had valued that highly. As the summer rolled round, I found myself in classes which, because of the shorter summer session, involved more class hours each week. But the first quarter of my second year was marked by making the Dean's list of the College of Letters and Sciences. The list recognises students with a grade-point average (GPA) of 3.5 and higher. An A in a class is assigned four points, a B earns three and the grade of C is worth two. The GPA is then calculated by adding the product of the class hours and the grade assigned for each class and then dividing this total by the total class hours.

I should add that I was on the Dean's list for only one quarter but it was a good indication that I was handling my workload and I was doing well in exams. I was pleased that I didn't screw up in any of the courses and, as I have said, I was taking a heavy load and aiming for gaining 15 credits a quarter to get myself through in three years instead of the normal four. How well you do depends on what sort of load you take on. Hindsight suggests that, if I had chosen a lighter load, I might have done even better.

In my second year at Davis, I was enrolled in a nutrition course. A requirement of this was that I had to do a piece of research. An Aussie postdoctoral student in biochemistry, Gil Stokes, who lived next door, suggested that I should grow some yeast at different temperatures and look at the variation in fatty acid composition produced by the yeast. Gil laid on the laboratory facilities for me and instruction on how to do the fatty acid assay. The experiment showed that the higher temperatures resulted in greater synthesis of unsaturated fatty acids.

Another useful laboratory experience was provided by Dr Don Curry, a physiologist in the veterinary school, who gave me my first lesson in animal surgery. Don was a diabetes expert, who isolated the pancreases of rats and perfused them with different substances to explore the effects they had on the secretion of insulin from the pancreas. The main stimulation of insulin was glucose, but the other substances added in varying degrees contributed to the glucose effect.

Don taught me how to do the surgery, which proved a minute and complicated task. Unlike humans, where the pancreas has a specific location, it is all over the place in the intestinal area of rats, so I had to extract it with extreme care. Then I sat it on a five-inch-wide plastic platform, kept it moist and viable, and perfused it on the arterial side via the celiac artery. Perfusion is simply a matter of pumping liquid through. It was vital, of course, to keep the blood vessel supplying the pancreas intact while perfusion was achieved. This involved slitting the aorta a little bit to either side and then at the back side so that I had a sliver of aortic tissue with the celiac artery in the middle of it. The sliver was about a millimetre square. I was then able to grab the flaps of the aorta and pull the celiac artery through to the underside of the tissue. On the outflow side was the portal vein where, once I had perfused the pancreas and introduced the glucose, I collected the perfusate at varying logged intervals into different test tubes and could then measure the different amounts of insulin showing up.

That was my first experience of rat surgery. My next meeting with them was concerned with their fitness.

CHAPTER FIVE

Inevitable end

Even before we left New Zealand for UC Davis, Sally and I had decided that we were going to separate — we already had an agreement drawn up by our lawyer. We had become aware of an incompatability in our relationship and recognised that nothing was going to change that.

Sally mixed socially with the wives of other students, mainly doctoral students. Among them were two vets, an Englishman and a South African, both of whom had their wives with them. We had been in our apartment for about a year when the English vet, Mike Burridge, suggested we should share a house, complete with swimming pool, with them. We did that but, after about a year, the Burridges left and we took in a boarder so that we could afford to stay in the house.

But when it became obvious that our marital situation was never going to improve, we separated. I found an apartment and moved out.

So I moved on and Sally remained in Davis until recently when she moved to nearby Sacramento to be closer to our younger daughter Jacqueline and the two grandchildren. We remain good friends and we occasionally see each other and can talk with complete amicability on the phone. Miki and I have enjoyed Christmas dinner in Sacramento with Sally and Mandy and Jacqui. In addition, Miki talks regularly with both daughters, realising the importance to them of having a good relationship with their father. I appreciate this communication for its contribution to happy and caring family interactions.

Jacqui graduated as a teacher in 1992 and decided to teach English in Taiwan; she spent four years in a city where little English was spoken and learnt to speak Mandarin fluently. When she later visited China on a trip, the Chinese were fascinated by this tall, blue-eyed blonde who could talk with them in Mandarin. She wanted to explore her roots in New Zealand and in 1998 decided to study for a Master's degree in Asian studies at Auckland University, from which she graduated in 2000.

Jacqui has produced two granddaughters, Samantha and Jodie, maintaining an all-daughters streak started by my mother's family (six daughters), and continued by me (two daughters). But she has separated from their father and is not on good terms with him. Meanwhile, Mandy, who graduated from Cal Poly at San Luis Obispo with a degree in Agricultural Economics in 1992, married a Canadian, Dave Lipsit, in 1997. They live in Dixon, a small fruit- and vegetable-growing community near Davis.

But I've leapt ahead of myself. I'd arrived at Davis with a whole lot of learning to do, I'd had an early introduction to academia's personality problems, and a streak of luck was about to change the whole tenor of my life.

The book that had impressed me when I read it in Loughborough, Ogilvie and Tutko's *Problem Athletes and How to Handle Them*, had received a cold reception when I mentioned it to the physical education department head, Dr Dean Ryan, at UC Davis. He said bluntly: 'I don't want you to mention those two guys around here again. If you're interested in the psychology of sport, I'll put you in touch with scientists doing peer-reviewed research in this area.'

Bruce Ogilvie and Thomas Tutko were clinical psychologists who worked with athletes in the San Jose area, and their book, I thought, was an interesting anecdotal account of their experiences in helping athletes. At Davis, however, they were plainly anathema. I was fast learning about scientific rigour and the potential jealousies and disagreements among the scientific fraternity.

Until he left Davis, Jack Wilmore and I ran together every morning. It was a good time to go over the problems of the day before, but the first couple of quarters at Davis were traumatic. Jack said he saw the struggle I was having but also that I was determined to succeed. There was also, around this time, the annoyance of reading reports from New Zealand that I had left the Rothmans Sports Foundation after 12 years because I was conscience-stricken about working for a cigarette company. Nonsense. I enjoyed working for Rothmans, and I was grateful for the overseas trip they had given me because they enabled me to discover that I could handle the demands of an academic career.

But once I realised this was the life I wanted, it dictated that I had to leave New Zealand to follow that path. It was as simple as that. I knew I wasn't cut out for a public relations career. It was all right in small doses and I didn't dislike it, but I had a need for something more solid — a stronger base for opportunity instead of being locked into a role which might have left me stranded with nowhere to go. In a short time, of course, the anti-smoking campaign would have made certain of that.

So, work at UC Davis became all-consuming. My working day ran from 8 a.m. to midnight as well as weekends. I wasn't much of a family man. I didn't run much either — I was too tired. I rode my bike between home and the campus, and every day when I cycled past the playing fields and saw teams training or individuals running, I wondered just how they could do it. I knew I was carrying a unit load heavier than average but I couldn't see how you could effectively combine sports and studies. I confronted this quandary squarely when I was invited to compete in the Superstars competition.

Incidentally, Davis is totally flat and well known for having more bicycles per head of population than any other US city, with designated bike lanes on the main streets making two-wheeled transportation both safe and efficient — an example well worth emulating in these days of 'carbon footprint' consciousness.

Thus, the first 20 months at Davis were not all rosy but, thankfully, some courses were waived. I got out of one English course by telling my counsellor I had co-authored a book, *No Bugles No Drums*, with Auckland journalist Garth Gilmour. But I still had physiological chemistry, physiological neurology, the biomedical applications of computers, exercise physiology and the psychological social factors in human performance to grapple with. I really wanted to know what made athletes tick. We knew how a runner functioned at the beginning and the end of, say, a 220 or 440, but what happened physiologically in between the start and finish?

Initally, my American sojourn wasn't going to be long term — my original thought being that I had to finish my studies in three years and then return to New Zealand and set up as a fitness consultant. And when, in the first year, I got turned on to research, I thought there was no way I could afford to continue with it, but that all suddenly changed with an unexpected opportunity to use my background in tennis and other sports to give me the vital financial break I needed.

CHAPTER SIX

Out of the blue — and the red

How I came by the extra money was completely out of the blue. Late in 1976, I received a surprise last-minute invitation to compete in a televised competition called 'Superstars', organised by ABC television's 'Wide World of Sports' programme. Apparently, John Walker had been approached but, for various reasons, the newly minted Olympic 1500 metres champion was unable to accept. And John suggested I might be a good substitute. What a windfall he handed me — and at exactly the right time to give me a chance at earning enough to get me the rest of the way through university. It was a fortuitous way to finance myself. All I had to do was compete — and do well, preferably win.

The contest brought together professional athletes from a wide range of sports at different times of the year to coincide with the off seasons, when the athletes were available. The most famous — eventually to be infamous — participant was gridiron running back OJ Simpson. The idea was that each athlete competed in seven of 10 events, excluding their specialty. For example, I was allowed to run the 100 metres but not the 800. The grouping I was in comprised retired athletes ranging in age from mid-20s to mid-40s. I was in between at 36, and up against a tough bunch: Jim Taylor, Leroy Kelley, Floyd Little and Bernie Casey from pro football; KC Jones and Bob Cousey (basketball); Al Kaline, Bill Mazeroski and Bobby Richardson (baseball); and surfers Fred Hemmings and Felipe Pomar. The top three from each of four groups would compete in a couple of months in the final event to find the overall winner.

My seven events were tennis, rowing, swimming, tenpin bowling, a one-mile bike race, the 100-yard dash and the obstacle course. I left out the 800, weightlifting and baseball hitting; but I later switched from swimming, at which I was fairly hopeless, to baseball hitting, which was more suited to my hand-eye co-ordination.

One problem was that I had just two and a half weeks to get ready. Part of the solution to that problem was that I knew more now about how the body worked and reacted to impetus, which helped to determine what I needed to do; another was that I was still in reasonably good condition; the rest was a regime of training in which a typical day might be: 7 a.m., 90 minutes cycling; 8.30, in laboratory; noon, bowl four games; 1.30–2.30 p.m., baseball workout; 6.00, two sets of tennis followed by rowing; 8.15, chin-ups and similar exercises. One immediate result of this programme was exhaustion!

Fortunately, at Davis, I was surrounded by people not only capable of helping but only too willing to help. A friend of Sally had a home on a small lake complete with a dinghy much like the ones we would be using in Superstars; UC Davis had a bowling alley on campus where Tom Compton provided coaching lessons; and the baseball team, who were having pre-season practices, allowed me to join them for batting experience. I bought a good second-hand Gitane 10-speed racing bike and went training with a rider who had ridden in US road champs. Cathy Carr initially gave me some coaching in swimming and Will Lotter helped in tennis — one sport I felt I could do very well in because of my background in the game in New Zealand. I reasoned that most of my opponents could not have become so good in their specialty events and still have had time for tennis. And, finally, it had to be of some benefit that I played regularly with the UC Davis tennis coach, Rex Davis.

The money involved in Superstars was great: the top three place-getters in the qualifying rounds got $10,000, $5000 and $2500, plus $100 for each point earned on a 10-7-4-2-1 basis, which seemed a rather pleasant way for an ageing undergraduate to make a living. In the final, the stakes were raised to $300 a point, with the winner taking home $25,000, second $15,000, and third $10,000.

The ABC televised event was held at a development resort, The Rotunda, near the Florida city of Sarasota, and I like to think it justified my sports-dominated 'misspent' youth because it was now potentially paying off. The first event was tennis — the first to win a set won — in which I beat Jim Taylor in the final. The next was rowing, which I was able to win through some teenage experience in dinghies and the understanding that rowing power is developed through the legs as much as the arms. I scored a few points in bowling and baseball hitting, but my 10-pointers for winning tennis, rowing and cycling were sufficient to give me overall victory and a $13,000 prize. Thank you, thank you, John Walker. This was a much-needed boost to my flagging finances.

It didn't take me long to realise that I had a good chance to do well in the final because of my teenage background in other sports. The other participants were, of necessity, successful players in specific top US sports and generally did not have much of a grounding in other activities — this was to change in the later international competition. So, with the possibility of even greater financial gain in the final, I put together a training plan which enabled me to concentrate full time on developing skills in sports such as tenpin bowling and baseball hitting, at which I proved particularly good, while continuing to work at my cycling, rowing and tennis.

In order to do this, I needed to get creative at UC Davis so that I could skip a quarter without compromising my overseas student status. After various consultations, I found the perfect solution: the 'planned educational leave programme', which was designed to allow students time off from classes to pursue an interest related to their field of study. As my major was Human Performance, I was able to make a successful case to investigate the training methods used in a variety of sports. I shared the fact that I was in the Superstars final with all these helpers, who were enthusiastic about making sure I would be well prepared.

The final was held in late February at the same Florida venue, The Rotunda, and it proved an exciting contest. Sally joined me there, along with friends from New Zealand, Doreen and Nick Caulton.

The first event was tennis and I played Kyle Rote Jr, who was the defending Superstars champion from the previous year. He played with the Dallas Tornados soccer team and was one of the better American-bred players. Tennis was one of his strengths, so he was somewhat stunned to be beaten by an ageing former Olympic runner.

The next event, rowing, was held on a canal which formed part of the venue development and had room for only two boats at a time. This meant a series of heats was needed, which suited my stamina background, and my opposition in the final was Steve Grogan, the quarterback for the New England Patriots. I was able to beat him, using a better technique which enabled me to get more leg power into the stroke. So, after two events, I had the maximum 20 points.

My effort in the 100 metres was somewhat puerile — zero points and a strained hamstring. The strain, however, wasn't likely to affect my other events. I gained fifth place and a couple of points in the tenpin bowling and another couple in baseball batting, so the training paid off. And, as we moved to the second-last event, the mile cycle race, the position was that Kyle had six more points than I did.

We knew neither of us would get any points in the last event, the obstacle race, which was the domain of football players and, in particular, former Pittsburgh Steeler and eventual Pro Football Hall of Famer Lynn Swan (who was a Republican candidate for the Pennsylvania governorship in 2006 but lost 40 per cent to 60 per cent to the incumbent, Ed Rendell). I calculated that, to get the big prize, I would have to win the cycling and Kyle would have to finish no better than fourth. But how, I thought, could I achieve this? Kyle knew that, if I did not win, it didn't matter where he finished.

After the cycling heats, it was apparent that the best of the other riders in the final were a 40-year-old football player, Jim Taylor, and a gold medal high hurdler from France, Guy Drut. That defined my strategy: cycling was my strength and I knew I could give Jim and Guy as much as 50 yards' lead with a lap to go and still reel them in. Hopefully, this plan would lull Kyle into thinking I was out of it and he'd be content just to finish.

With a lap to go, Jim and Guy had their 50-yard lead and Kyle was drafting me. I accelerated with all the power I could muster and the plan worked beautifully. Kyle could not stay in contact and was wallowing in fourth place as I caught the other two on the crown of the last bend. I was leaning into the slightly banked curve as my momentum took me past them, then my left pedal hit the ground and, before I could regain control, I hit the perimeter fence. This dropped me back to fourth from what, with only 100 yards to go, had seemed an overall winning position.

More importantly, the winner received $25,000 and my fourth place was worth only $8000 and also meant I would not be invited back the next year to defend the title. I still think about that last curve when I ride on the streets of Dallas and lean into corners . . .

CHAPTER SEVEN

It gets bigger

When Sally and I separated towards the end of my time in Davis, she retained possession of the family car, an old Buick LeSabre, so I went looking for affordable transport and acquired, for $800, a set of wheels in the form of a VW van. The van, a bit like one Arthur Lydiard once had, was 1964 vintage. It wasn't fast but it gave me long and good service until it expired, finally, in Dallas. It was ideal for me because it was something I could afford and, armed with an illustrated manual, I found I could fix just about anything that went wrong mechanically. It also had the room I would need to take all my possessions — not that I owned many — when I moved to other places in my new career endeavours. And I was later able to sleep in it with my cat for company when I moved on to Texas.

The Superstars circus wasn't entirely over. I had enjoyed the fruits of some success as an undergraduate at Davis, and now they were talking about having a World Superstars competition, to which the various Superstars champions from countries around the world would be invited. That meant I had to go back to New Zealand in an attempt to qualify as New Zealand's representative. The event was held in Christchurch in February 1978 and fortunately I was able to prevail, managing a win against John Walker in tennis along the way.

The first world event was held at a beautiful resort in Georgia called Callaway Gardens, not too far from Atlanta. I didn't win it but I did well overall finishing third. The winner was the American pole vaulter Bob Seagren, who was there because he won the US event in

1973. The man I should have beaten in the US event in 1976, Kyle Rote Jr, who was a soccer player, had been US winner in 1974, 1976 and 1977 but declined to attend the world contest. (Incidentally, the athlete who squeezed between Seagren and Rote to win in 1975 was OJ Simpson.) The second world event was won by another pole vaulter, Kjel Isaaksson, of Sweden, who held the world pole vault record before Seagren took it.

The World Superstars wasn't exactly the same as the American one. They had some European-type events in there, such as parallel bar dips, which were made to order for pole vaulters, who have a lot of upper body strength, but not for people like me. I won three events so I scored 30 points — but it wasn't quite good enough. I didn't get any points anywhere else, such as in gymnastics and the 100 metres. But I won the rowing, the tennis and, this time, I made no mistakes in the cycling and won that. For those wins, plus a bonus for finishing in third place, I took home $18,000, so it was well worthwhile — it helped a lot to have that money.

The following year, I competed again in the second New Zealand Superstars contest in Auckland. The final event, a one-mile cycle race, was another disaster, reminiscent of the American final two years earlier in Florida. I was leading into the last lap round the Tartan track at Mt Smart and looking around trying to judge where the opposition was so I could plan my finish. I ended up weaving over the trackside kerb, falling off and separating my right shoulder, which required a visit for repair at Middlemore Hospital. The small but aggressive New Zealand All Blacks winger Grant Batty ended up winning the event, and, even after falling off the bike, I finished in second place. Among the other contestants were Munich Olympians Rod Dixon and Barry Maister, who I met in the tennis final at Stanley Street court, and the swimmer Gary Hurring, son of Jean and Lincoln, all of them former New Zealand representatives. One of the events Gary and I clashed in was wood chopping, which I liked and did quite well at, although I can't remember whether I beat him.

Grant Batty, having won the contest, then decided for some reason I still don't understand, that he didn't want to go to the world event.

So, as second place-getter, I was promoted to go as New Zealand champion. Good fortune sometimes seems to ride on my shoulder — even a dislocated one and even when I fall off.

The second world event wasn't so good, as it turned out, although the contest was held in the Bahamas, which was a pretty nice place to be in. I won the tennis again and was a narrow second in the cycling but I made enough money to again make it all worthwhile. The only income I had in the US was from winning money at Superstars but, being a foreigner, I was unable to average out that income over the years when I earned nothing so I got a fairly big tax hit. Still, I had some money and I was feeling good about the United States.

Looking back, I can say that the Americans made a lot possible for me: the invitation to Superstars, the opportunity to study in their universities, and a wholly enthusiastic welcome and encouragement. Their outlook was in stark contrast to the New Zealand situation, where the system was steeped in the past. The breadth of programmes was not available back home, and the nearest I could get to my interest was to study physical education down in Dunedin. That might have been okay, but the wide range of activities in which I was able to get involved in the US was what mattered. And the number of people doing good research is quite considerable in America because of the much greater funding available than anywhere else in the world.

When it became a financial and academic reality that I would study for an advanced degree, I first considered the University of Illinois, in Chicago. I was interested not so much in the universities but the individuals who were at them. One I had met at Davis when he came to give a guest lecture was Larry Oscai, and I enjoyed what he had to say about his work. He was an exercise physiologist, doing research mainly on rats, but was interested in seeing how exercise helped the body to do better at using fat as a fuel and making the connection between that and human health. Larry was from the Chicago Circle campus at the University of Illinois and was an expert in fat metabolism, trained in the laboratory of renowned exercise scientist John Holloszy MD, of St Louis. Larry had talked about the possibility of doing a Master's degree with him and I decided to visit him on the way back to Davis from Florida after Superstars.

However, I realised almost as soon as I got there that, no matter how good the programme was, I didn't think I could live in Chicago. It was February, snow was piled high in the Chicago streets and the city-type campus was bounded by the downtown area on one side, the slums on another, and the Italian quarter on another. I just felt displaced there. It was a totally unfamiliar environment for me.

Then a New Zealander, Jeff Wood, who was a good runner at Mt Roskill Grammar and now at Washington State University in Pullman, called me and asked if I had thought about the Masters and PhD programme at Washington State. It was a nice school, he said, and Phil Gollnick had a great reputation as an exercise scientist.

I took Jacqui with me on an exploratory trip to Pullman and it looked and sounded good for me. Pullman had a totally different feeling from Chicago. Located on the eastern border of Washington State, it was a small town of 25,000 to 30,000 people with a country atmosphere among rolling wheat fields. Named after George Pullman, the railway sleeping car magnate, the town is situated only about 12 miles west of the border with Idaho and only eight miles from a place called Moscow, which is the site of the University of Idaho. Pullman is the location of Washington State University, which is well known for its agricultural and veterinary medicine schools. My move to work there with Phil Gollnick panned out perfectly.

So, finally, I graduated from Davis in June 1977 with a BS — they don't call it a BSc in the States — majoring in human performance. My mother came over to visit for the graduation and seemed to enjoy the two-hour ride in my VW van from San Francisco airport to Davis. I'm sure when I was doing so poorly at Mt Albert Grammar she would never have thought I would be a university graduate.

Later, my mother accompanied me on the long but scenic drive up through northern California and central Oregon to Eastern Washington and Pullman, where we inspected Washington State and I took a look at a house that was for sale. Later, back at Davis, I was able to complete a purchase deal over the phone. This was where the Superstars money came in so handy; I could make an acceptable down payment on the house and carry a loan for the rest. The house was a duplex (having two separate living spaces) with a very nice upper floor, which I would be able to rent out while I lived in the basement part. The rent would take care of my mortgage payments.

The day before finally leaving Davis for Washington State, I took Mandy and Jacqui out for a horse-riding experience. I think they had fun, but the horse I had was one of those smart old boys. He decided he would get me off his back and achieved that by galloping under a tree with low branches. I was knocked off and then he kicked me in the back as I was going down. The trip next day was going to be a little bit uncomfortable for a while.

Nevertheless, I loaded all my stuff, books and things I would need in Washington and headed up to take possession of my new home. The route north involved a beautiful drive up the Sacramento Valley and then past Mt Shasta and some very nice scenery in Oregon. I stopped to have a look at the Crater Lake area in southern Oregon and went on through the middle of the state via Bend, which is now a ski resort place and the area's largest city but was relatively small in 1977. I journeyed on to the spectacular Columbia River at a place called The Dalles, and farther up crossed the Columbia into a place they call the Tri Cities of Pasco, Kenniwick and Richland in Washington State and then angled northeast across some fairly dry country with a lot of wheat fields and eventually arrived at Pullman.

It was late summer and I had a couple of weeks to get myself organised before I had to show up at the lab and start involving myself in the coursework towards my PhD. I used the time to rotary-hoe and till the back yard of my duplex, re-lay the lawn and create a garden to make myself at home. I also arranged to let the upper part of the duplex.

But I couldn't afford the time away from my studies and I also had the feeling my professor would far rather see me in the laboratory doing research than out coaching. Recreationally, I didn't do a lot at Washington. My time was well occupied with the work I needed to do. I kept up with my running — I had a four-mile course worked out which I did fairly regularly in the mornings. If something came up, I might get into it, a 5 k race for instance, but I didn't compete much at all. I also maintained tennis as a sport, and during a summer tournament paired up with the 60-year-old chairman of the Art Department to win the doubles tournament at the university.

It was a life much like that at UC Davis, except a bit more rigorous and more focused because, unlike Davis, where I was able to pick out my own courses and choose research in different areas, the PhD programme was tightly structured and Gollnick insisted on high academic standards. For example, I had to do biochemistry and physical chemistry; and students who hadn't done organic chemistry had to do that. I had already taken the latter subject as an undergraduate, so not having that on my plate as well was an advantage and let me focus better on biochemistry and physiology. Then it was just a matter of working in the lab as well, where one of my main jobs was taking care of the animals, all the rats and hamsters.

Another graduate student, Ben Timson, and I took turns at exercising them on the treadmill for an hour each day. We could run 20 at a time. This was new stuff because at Davis I was in the Department of Physical Education, where there was none of this kind of research involving animals. Davis was a well-appointed human performance lab, with treadmill testing for humans, and it was set up for the science part of physical education. Pullman had a similar department, but Gollnick ended up in the Veterinary Medicine School working on exercise and muscle metabolism in horses at Washington State.

Using National Institute of Health (NIH) funding, he was able to develop an animal-based exercise biochemistry laboratory. A world-class physiologist, he was the only Physical Education faculty member to be granted support from this major government funding agency.

Also, because the phys ed. department was awarding our degrees, I had to take an obligatory course in physical education.

CHAPTER EIGHT

Oh, rats

The PhD programme is a minimum of four years after a Bachelor's degree or three years after a Master's. I didn't have a Master's but everything once again seemed to fall into place for me. It is fairly unusual to go straight into a PhD after a Bachelor's but I was allowed to do that. I think the fact that I was a mature student, plus the fact that I had already done the pancreas research as an undergraduate, helped.

A fair bit of coursework has to be accomplished but the main thing is the participation in research projects and learning lab techniques. To keep themselves afloat financially — and this is really part of the deal in being accepted into the programme — students are offered graduate assistantships, which involve teaching or research or a combination of both.

The research assistantship gave me work in the lab, where — as I've mentioned — my job, along with Ben Timson, another PhD candidate, involved looking after and training the animals. This involved checking their chow and water, mopping the animal room and running the rats on the treadmill five days a week. The treadmill was about 14 feet wide and three feet long and we had 20 caged lanes side by side, and at the back of the cages, a little four-bar grid with electricity going through it. The rats just had to keep running to avoid a shock. We lifted them from their cages by their tails, popped them in their lanes on the treadmill, started it up and put them through an hour's training at a pace they could manage. The hamsters were trained for 30 minutes per session at a slower pace.

Depending on the funding that was available, I also had to do a bit of teaching of activity classes, so I taught things like the beginners' tennis and racquetball classes and I also actually taught weight training in the gym. I hadn't done any weight training myself but I had a degree, I was in the phys ed department, and I'd read the book. So, and I can't help laughing about it, I was fully qualified to have them do all the work and then evaluate them and give them a grade. It was pretty logical stuff, anyway, and most of the students who took those sorts of courses just wanted a bit of a break from the academic grind. They also liked to do weight training because they got one credit for it out of the 180 they needed to accumulate.

I spent three of my four Pullman years working on studies in the lab that had nothing to with my PhD dissertation. These studies, using rats and hamsters as the subjects, were funded by a grant from the NIH and the Muscular Dystrophy Association. The rats were used for studies on exercise on calcium uptake by the sarcoplasmic reticulum, and the hamsters, specially bred with Duchenne's muscular dystrophy, were used for exercise studies on that disease. I did one of my own projects with rats which I presented to a meeting of the American College of Sports Medicine. It was a fairly sophisticated experiment with which I was quite pleased.

The technique that Gollnick's lab used for a variety of studies was to measure the uptake of calcium as part of the sequence of muscle contraction. Muscles contract as the result of calcium being released and then relax when the calcium is taken back into vesicles known as the sarcoplasmic reticulum (SR). We had a technique for isolating these SR membranes from, say, a heart or skeletal muscle. We removed the tissue, ground it up and subjected it to ultracentrifugation, which separated the membrane from other material in the tissue, which was precipitated down. We then incubated the membrane with radioactive calcium for different time periods, and the amount of radioactivity in those samples was an indication of how much calcium had been taken up. We theorized that, when muscles got fatigued, there was an impairment of the SR's ability to take up calcium.

The experiment I did was to make the heart fatigue and cause it to fail. The way I did this was to anaesthetise the rat and place it on a ventilator after opening the chest, cutting the trachea and inserting a small tube into it. This was to keep the rat breathing and alive while I did the surgery. This involved cutting through the ribs with scissors to expose the heart, beating away merrily, and placing a little plastic tube, or cuff, around the top of the aorta. I then pumped some liquid into this tube to make it compress against the aorta and squeeze the aorta down. It was surgery on a minute scale, but the result was that the pressure in the left ventricle of the heart would rise because it was pumping against the resistance of the tube. To measure the pressure, I inserted a needle into the apex of the heart so that it entered the ventricle and installed a ligature. The needle was connected to a pressure transducer and I could then read on a chart the pressure variations as the heart contracted and relaxed. By gradually increasing the systolic pressure until I got it up from around 90 to about 150 mm Hg, I could then determine, by trial and error, that under these conditions the heart would fail in about 60 minutes.

So that was my heart failure model. When the heart failed, I quickly removed it, put it on ice, ground it up and isolated the sarcoplasmic reticulum, incubated samples with radioactive calcium, and then used further processes and different time periods to construct a curve showing the uptake at those varying times. I then collected the various samples and put them into a gamma counter to measure them. Because all this had to be done without a break, it could sometimes take most of a night. We tested normal hearts as well, but the failed heart had a depressed ability to take up calcium.

I've made many presentations to sports meetings but this may have been my first scientific one because it was during my rats' period. However, Phil Gollnick knew I didn't want to work in 'rat land', that I wanted to work with people, so when he developed a health problem himself, he got me involved. He had a condition known as supraventricular atrial tachycardia, all of which means his heart was beating too quickly, which is similar to atrial fibrillation. His heart at rest was beating at about 140 and he wasn't feeling too good. It was actually associated with a diminished productivity period in his career and it was before drugs were available to control the condition.

So he decided that he would undergo a procedure whereby the conducting tissue between the atrium and the ventricle would be destroyed by freezing. Once that happens, the ventricle doesn't have any signal to go by to contract so you have to be fitted with a pacemaker. He had a normal fixed-rate one fitted under his skin but he could place a magnetic device over it to change its rate from 72 to 90 to 120. He then said that he would like me to study him because it could be an interesting project — and it certainly was.

We had the unique situation that he could be three different persons physically, based on what his heart rate was controlled at. We played racquetball at lunchtimes fairly frequently, along with six graduate students. We played doubles, which was pretty dangerous, or cut-throat, which was two against one. If he forgot to dial his heart rate up to 120, he was pretty poor on the court because he couldn't get the blood flow up and get more energy. We figured out how I would study him as a person and then I had a control group for comparisons. So, in my last year, I was able to do a thesis project involving human subjects. He was my patient and I successfully defended my thesis at the presentation.

Around this time, I'd had the occasional visit to New Zealand and I still didn't have any vision as to what I was going to be doing when I finished. There was a possibility in Australia. Max Howell, who I had met at the Olympic Academy in Greece in 1971, was then at the University of Alberta, Canada. Now he was head of the Exercise Science department at the University of Queensland in Brisbane and he asked if I would consider joining his faculty. But Gollnick said I wasn't ready for a faculty job and needed the benefit of some postdoctoral research. He suggested the University of Texas Southwestern Medical Center in Dallas, where Dr Jere Mitchell, a cardiologist, was a prominent exercise scientist. There was a three-way connection between Jere Mitchell in Dallas, Philip Gollnick in Pullman, and Dr Bengt Saltin, head of the Muscle Research Centre in Copenhagen. Bengt was to win the Olympic Prize for sports medicine in 2002, awarded at the Salt Lake City Winter Olympics. Phil had worked with Bengt in Sweden for a year during a sabbatical in 1972 and they had become close friends.

Meantime, I made occasional trips back to Davis to see my daughters, staying on these occasions with Sally, with whom I united as far as doing the best for our girls. In the summer, they would alternate spending time with me, so I was able to teach them tennis, take them on rafting trips and share their growing up. Jacqui is still an enthusiastic tennis player. They have fond memories of the times we spent together and so do I.

Pullman was a lot of hard work and, as I've said, some late nights were spent on experiments. But it was also where I learnt to cook. Sally had packed me off from Davis with a handwritten recipe book she had put together for me so I hardly ever ate out at Pullman. Eating out would have meant no more than going down the road and getting a pizza — when I had my own recipe for pizza. I bought wheat, which was grown locally, just over the border with Montana, and I made bread and also developed a very good vegetable garden. Tomatoes grew very well there and they've always been a favourite of mine.

I had also learnt to ski in California, where the Sierra Nevada ski fields were only a 90-minute drive away. The exercise phys lab group at Davis made a field trip to the mountains, where the instructor knew someone who had a cabin we could use. So we did some experiments to justify the trip and then went skiing. For the experiments, we took stationary exercycles and observed how the altitude affected exercise capacity.

I really enjoyed skiing, which subsequently I have experienced only once in New Zealand. That was when the flame was on its way to the Sydney Olympic Games and we took it with us on a helicopter trip from Queenstown to Coronet Peak. I was able to walk about 15 yards and hand it on to Annelise Coberger, who skied back down the mountain with it. I followed her down, on the ski lift, rented skis, boots and poles, was assigned a Swiss instructor and spent the afternoon skiing — it was a lot of fun. Unlike the United States, where the ski fields are created in forested areas, New Zealand skiing is above the tree-line, and in that respect less dangerous for me, as I had a tendency to have brief periods of skiing out of control. Fortunately, there weren't any ski-related injuries.

In Pullman there wasn't much downhill stuff to speak of, but we would occasionally have a decent fall of snow. So I had bought myself a pair of cross-country skis and, one day, after a gorgeous heavy snowfall, I skied the mile or so from my house to the university across pristine early-morning snow. It was about six in the morning and I was the only one out there making tracks. Unfortunately, by the time it came to ski home, the snowploughs had been out. I was able to ski along the footpaths, which hadn't been cleared, but at every cross street the snow had been piled up and it was mixed with sand and probably salt as well, so it was neither as much fun nor as easy as the morning run.

One of the several things happening for me at this time was that Emmy award-winning Bud Greenspan, the outstanding sports film producer, writer and director, was making a documentary called *Numero Uno*, so I got to go back to New Zealand for that. That has proved to be a wonderful thing for me because he brought together a lot of the highlights of my running career.

Sadly, Bud now has Parkinson's but it is interesting that, for some reason, he has always been impressed by my running. I don't know if it's just the running, but he always rates me very highly among history's 800 metres runners. There have been a lot who have run faster — for example, Alberto Juantorena, from Cuba, Joaquim Cruz from Brazil, Sebastian Coe and Steve Ovett from Britain. Murray Halberg was involved in the film, and in those days Murray sported long hair and bell-bottom pants. Bill Baillie was there too, being Bill as only he can be. There were one or two exaggerations in the script but Bud did a good job on the whole. He used quite a lot of material that Lynton Diggle, the internationally known New Zealand documentary film director, and I had put together when I was in the middle of my running career.

During my second year in Davis, I was invited by the popular magazine *Runner's World* to Los Altos, California, for the launch of a national running week. One of the speakers was Ken Cooper, founder of the Dallas Aerobics Center and the so-called father of aerobics, following publication of his popular book *Aerobics* in 1968. Initially, I thought there was nothing I would like more than to work at a facility like his Aerobics Center, and I was a little disappointed because I didn't have the opportunity to talk to him much because he was more interested in talking to people with shared business interests.

But when it came time to give his talk, I realised there was no way that I could ever work with him. Ken was another Arthur — but more so. He was a nondescript sort of man who, once he got behind a microphone, was transformed into this crusading dynamo. It wasn't quite religion, but he was just so positive that *his* was the only way. You got the impression that you could not argue with him. There was no other viewpoint as far as he was concerned. It was straight-out preaching. I know he is religious anyway, and one of the slides he showed was of him and Billy Graham in the soccer stadium in Rio de Janeiro. He was proud of the fact that Billy had invited him. Turns out Cooper is quite famous in Brazil. The Brazilians apparently had no word for jogging and so came up with the term 'coopering'. Apparently, Ken loved that.

I find it difficult to express my own views in the presence of such forceful personalities. Arthur was forceful, and when you were working with him to achieve a goal, it was okay — but there will come a time when sparks are going to fly and problems are going to occur — as they did between Arthur and me. Nevertheless, in recent years, I have come to think of Arthur as someone to whom I owe a great debt. I would not have had the career or the accomplishments that went with it had he not steered me into them.

Anyway, the religion in Cooper's case was fitness. He was preaching fitness. He didn't get it right necessarily, because he has had to back off some of the initial pronouncements he made about exercise and now realises that you can do some damage. For instance, he gave an address at the pasta-loading dinner just before the White Rock Marathon and actually told the runners they were all damaging their health by doing marathons, but then said the good news was that they could do something about it — and proceeded to do what was basically a commercial on his line of vitamins. That didn't go down very well. It wasn't totally crass, but you don't tell a bunch of marathoners they're doing themselves damage. He was more interested in putting across his views on antioxidants and so on. But the religious fervour with which he talked about exercise did remind me a bit of Arthur.

Before heading off from Pullman for Dallas, I had invited my mother over for my graduation. But I couldn't get my thesis completed in time, unfortunately, and, instead of graduating in 1981, I officially graduated in 1982. I was working frantically on the thesis but I just wasn't able to manage it. The process of acquiring a PhD in the American system is that there is a certain amount of coursework that you have to complete in the area of the degree programme, and then you have some research and also the somewhat intimidating oral exams where you are grilled in front of your PhD committee to see if you are competent enough to justify going forward for the degree. When you pass those, you become a 'candidate' for a PhD and finally earn the degree by completing your research and writing up a dissertation. It was a long and arduous process and I just could not complete it within the time available for graduation in June or July of 1981 — I had to stay through to October to finish. But my mother had arrived in anticipation of my graduation so I had the opportunity to take her around a little bit in the VW van. Mum was then in her 80s.

Anyway, I finally got my thesis all typed and bound and delivered to the committee members and then had to defend it in front of the committee and anyone else who wanted to sit in. This was a very good situation to be in because I felt that none of my examiners knew any more about the subject of my thesis than I did. Although it doesn't always work out that way. A New Zealander at Pullman was working on a project in water and soil research which overlapped several departments, had a heck of a time fielding specific interest questions from *his* examiners.

As I was preparing to leave Pullman for Davis, an incoming faculty member of the Department of Physical Education wanted to rent my duplex, which was very convenient, so I was going to get some regular income. I held a garage sale and got rid of what furniture I had and then packed the few bits and pieces which were my total belongings into the VW van. I took a heap of books that I had accumulated, a lot of papers, my clothing and, of course, my cat — Pekoe — and headed off to California, planning to call in on my daughters and Sally on the way through.

That trip was a fairly long one. I stayed overnight in a rest area, sleeping in the van with the cat, and then continued on down through the centre of Oregon, which was an area becoming quite familiar to me because I'd gone back and forth through there several times in the four years that I was in Portland. It was always a beautiful trip. I spent a night in Davis and saw the family, and then the cat and I headed off towards Texas. I knew what I was doing in heading there. Others in my programme under Phil Gollnick also had postdoctoral scholarships from Dallas, so it was obviously the place to go.

My plan was to meet up with one of them, Russ Moore, who is now Chairman of the Kinesiology Department at the University of Colorado. Russ was staying in a house owned by Dr Gary Klug, who graduated from Gollnick's lab at Washington State two years before Russ and myself and was completing a postdoctoral fellowship in pharmacology at UT Southwestern. Russ and I planned to find an apartment to share, so the arrangement was to stay at Gary's while apartment hunting.

They were expecting my arrival at the end of a long trek. It was pretty well a straight shot east through the Mojave Desert, Arizona and New Mexico to hit the Texas Panhandle but still a very long way from Dallas. The old VW behaved flawlessly as I drove 10 hours each day, munching on fast food as dictated by hunger before pulling into a rest area and settling down for the night with Pekoe. After a delay in Davis when Pekoe had disappeared, I kept him on a leash for visits outside. The van had the back seats removed and a two-foot-high carpet-covered platform across its width that served as a back seat but also extended all the way to the rear door so it could double as a bed. Underneath was storage space full of gear. Boxes of books were tied onto a roof rack. It was pretty obvious that I was moving house. Pekoe existed on dry cat food, which was his normal diet, and a sand box located on the floor behind the front seat provided for his other needs. Perhaps surprisingly, there were no problems or incidents until we were almost at our destination.

I'd overnighted and slept in the van all the way. The conditions generally were ideal, dry and sunny but, after passing through Fort Worth, with only 30 miles to Dallas, it was getting late and the rain started coming down in buckets. I was bowling along on the freeway when, all of a sudden, my lights went out. Pulling to the side of the motorway, I decided I couldn't risk carrying on and resigned myself to spending the night there. I guessed something electrical had got wet and ceased to function, because it was a pretty reliable vehicle even though there were more than 100,000 miles on the clock.

When I woke up in the morning, non-stop rush-hour traffic was hurtling past and it was still raining. I couldn't see well enough and this low-powered VW van of mine was so slow to get moving I couldn't get into the streams of traffic without risking getting creamed. So I had to wait there until after the rush hour then slowly find my way into Dallas and, somehow, to the medical school. I'd already spoken to people in the division I was going to be working with, so I called them and they directed me to the lab. Eventually, I arrived, still in one piece, with Pekoe and some water-damaged books. I'd found my place of work. Now I had to set about finding somewhere to live.

CHAPTER NINE

Good luck holds

Russ Moore and I stayed a couple of days with Gary and Marilyn Klug from Pullman while we went looking at apartments. We didn't really know what we were doing and nearly settled on a place which we thought was a reasonable price but — unbeknown to us — was right in the middle of a dangerous neighbourhood. But once again, my good luck held.

Gary had been in Dallas for a year or so doing postdoctorate fellowship work and he now had an opportunity to go to work for an expert in his field in Germany. I should mention here that before graduation from Pullman one of the requirements was competency in a foreign language and I did German through an eight-week, all-day immersion programme through one summer — and I should also say that I now know very little German, apart from 'ein', 'swein', 'drei' and so on. Anyway, Russ and I jumped at the chance to share the house, and later on we were joined by Jim Stray-Gundersen, who was to play a large role in my Dallas activities.

UT Southwestern was a medical school with 800 med students, grad students in biomedical science, and a School of Allied Health with undergrads in professional programmes to become nutritionists, physician assistants, med technologists, and physiotherapists. My postdoctoral goal in Dallas with Dr Gunnar Blomqvist was to continue my interest in human research, hopefully get some publications under my belt and experience to improve my chances of a teaching and research faculty appointment elsewhere.

Gunnar, a cardiologist with expertise in electrocardiogram

analysis and non-invasive measures of heart function, had arrived in Dallas from Sweden in 1966 to join a team that included Jere Mitchell to put together the classic Dallas bed rest study. Five students took part in a summer-long study of the effects of bed rest and training on cardiovascular and pulmonary function during exercise. The study was in three stages: a complete evaluation of cardiovascular and pulmonary function, plus electrolytes and blood work; a three-week period of bed rest (when the students wanted to use the toilet they had to use a wheelchair); followed by an eight-week training period of mostly running, after which stage one was repeated. After completion of the study, Gunnar accepted an invitation to join the faculty permanently.

Blomqvist's real interest was space flight, so when the shuttles started flying he was well positioned to have some experiments done in space.

Meantime, I was learning research techniques in the lab. We were working on a couple of projects, one of which I had to myself and which led to my first publication. It was about the relationship between calf muscles and blood flow, determining the maximum capacity of the muscles. Gunnar had given me a new way of thinking about how the blood vascular system works. We knew that, when you measure oxygen uptake, it's really all about the ability of the heart to circulate oxygen to the working muscle.

When you do these tests, you arrange a sufficiently high level of exercise to be placed on the muscle to create a demand for oxygen until you eventually tax the limits of the heart to pump enough blood to satisfy that demand. Well-trained people are better at reaching that level and they have much more muscle capacity. It's easier to test on a treadmill than on a bicycle because you get much better muscle recruitment and activity when you're supporting your own weight on a treadmill rather than carrying it on a bike.

But our lab had a bicycle — a clumsy-looking machine that was designed by NASA and was used in the old Skylab experiments in space. After a few years, Skylab was abandoned. It spiralled out of orbit and eventually crashed somewhere — maybe in the middle of Australia or some remote place like that. So the bicycle became jobless. It was a huge and heavy contraption that was electronically braked, which meant you could dial in a resistance level and the total power was maintained no matter how fast you pedalled. It was very convenient, because when you're using exercise bikes that have a fixed resistance you have to have a metronome going to maintain the pedalling frequency. This machine was independent of that kind of requirement. When you measure up consumption on these bikes, individuals have to have reasonably strong legs to give a true max.

My thesis work had been in this area, so I thought I already understood it pretty well. But what Gunnar educated me on was that the muscle blood flow was important and that what we call the peripheral resistance, which means the condition of the blood vessels in the exercise muscles and their ability to dilate, was a significant performance factor. The more they were able to dilate and the higher the blood flow through the exercising muscles became, the more blood was able to return to the heart, and that actually had an impact on heart performance because, after all, the heart can only pump as much blood as is being returned to it. The heart cannot be thought of as just operating by itself and its efficiency does depend in large part on the filling pressure created by returning blood, which is a determinant of the organ's performance.

As we train and do a lot of endurance exercise, the heart is constantly being subjected to higher filling pressures, or volume overload. The ventricle gradually remodels and gets bigger and the chambers have a greater volume and capacity to fill. This makes sense when you think of the very large cardiac outputs, which is the measure of blood through the heart. Those high cardiac outputs are possible only by having, as Arthur Lydiard knew, a very large stroke volume of blood being pushed out with every beat.

This is the characteristic which is important for athletes and is the effect of endurance training. It's the main way in which to increase the amount of blood the heart can pump, other than increasing the heart rate. But the maximal heart rate of athletes and non-athletes is essentially the same — roughly 220 minus one's age is the normal way of figuring that out. Athletes may, if anything, be a little bit lower at the top end, because their resting heart rate tends to be very much lower at the bottom end of the scale. However, the difference between athletes and non-athletes lies in the amount of blood pumped with each beat, and that depends on what we call the 'compliance characteristics' of the heart, or its elasticity — i.e. the ventricle's ability to stretch to accommodate a larger amount of blood.

Shortly after arrival in Dallas, I had a call from a local coach, Robert Vaughan, who turned out to be a Lydiard disciple and had even made a 'pilgrimage' to New Zealand. It turned out that Arthur Lydiard had been visiting Dallas on a fairly regular basis to carry out running clinics. He would run week-long training camps, which attracted people from far and wide, even beyond Texas. Apparently, he often used me as an example of his training system, so the running community in Dallas felt that, through Arthur, they already knew me. After a *Runner's World* article on my university work and plans for a postdoctoral fellowship in Dallas appeared, Robert contacted me and invited me to join his runners for a 10-mile run and dinner. The plan was that we would all show up after work, about six o'clock, at Southern Methodist University, a renowned private institution with a running track, where Robert's club did their training, do the 10-miler on the streets and then adjourn to a local Mexican restaurant.

I had no idea what a significant change of circumstances would follow on from this simple invitation.

CHAPTER TEN

The tender trap

It turned out that a woman called Miki Hervey, Robert and another coach, Terry Jessup, had founded the running club, called the Metroplex Striders. Miki was a qualified physical education teacher, specialising in dance, but for many years she had been a flight attendant with the big international airline Braniff. In 1968 she read Dr Ken Cooper's book *Aerobics* and, coupled with the inspiration of the Mexico Olympics, started to run at the age of 26; by the time she was 29 she had a respectable 2:12 for 800 metres and twice won the Dallas 8 mile Turkey Trot race held on Thanksgiving Day.

Terry Jessup was from South Africa, where I competed against him in an 880-yard race in Blomfontein in 1964. After completing a Bachelor's degree at a small Texas university on a track scholarship, he moved to Waco to complete a Master's at Baylor University and started coaching. Among his runners was Doreen Barker, well known to Kiwis as 1964 Olympic sprinter Doreen Porter. She is now married again, to an engineer, Rick Shann, lives in the hill country in west Texas and has established herself as a successful painter, mainly in pastels. Terry later moved to Dallas where he discovered Robert and Miki and teamed up to create a thriving club.

But back to Robert's invitation to the run/dinner. Miki wanted to come but unfortunately had a flight for Braniff that day that would prevent her. She tried to trade the trip with other flight attendants, which they were allowed to do, but couldn't manage it this time. So, eventually, in desperation, she called in sick, knowing that her supervisor knew she had tried to trade her trip. And then, rather than come along in a tracksuit like everyone else and do her 10-mile run, she did her run in the afternoon and showed up to go to the dinner looking fresh and very attractive. She was not, as she would call it, 'slimed with sweat' when I met her. She was three and a half years older than me, blonde, and stood out in the company of runners. And, somehow, she engineered the seating arrangements to get to sit next to me among the 15 runners at dinner. I was impressed. Not only was she very attractive but she was also an engaging conversationalist. Prior to meeting Miki, I was job focused and not looking to meet women, but now I found myself anxious to find out more about her.

The opportunity to do just that came up a couple of weeks later. The Internal Medicine Department at the university were having their Christmas bash — a dinner and dance at a local hotel, which promised to be fairly fancy because Internal Medicine was a big department with a lot of money. The cardiology division, where I was doing my fellowship, was part of Internal Medicine, so I was invited. The invitation included a partner so I called Robert and asked him if he thought Miki would be interested. I didn't at that time know what her status was. And that's where it all started. Miki didn't say no, because she was hoping to escalate things herself, and was in the very process of trying to figure out how to do that when I called her.

During the interim before the dinner/dance, Miki called me and suggested that we should get to know each other better by going to brunch — for which she paid. She felt that, since it was her invitation, she should treat (shout). This was a first for me. During this initial date with Miki I was immediately attracted by her slim, athletic figure and beauty, which was combined with an engaging personality. There was an immediate chemistry between us.

For the impending second date, I decided to get my only suit dry-cleaned. But when I went to pick it up, the place was closed. This made me realise that I couldn't actually remember which one it was that I had taken the suit to. I desperately needed to look right, so I rushed out and, extravagantly, bought a new one. That dinner/dance was the beginning of committed dating during which I learned a lot about Miki's background.

I respected the way in which Miki had managed her life thus far and had returned to college to attain interior design qualifications to add to her degree in physical education. I admired her wide-ranging artistic ability, her athletic accomplishments and healthy lifestyle. It became apparent that her values, aspirations, religious and political views and goals were similar to mine, and I felt incredibly lucky that such a wonderful person with such complementary interests and attitudes was still available. In addition, she was confident, independent and well organised. We enjoyed doing activities together — competing in triathlons and other athletic events, gardening and travel, among other things. When Miki was asked what attracted her to me, she replied that I had many admirable qualities. I'll let her tell you in her own words:

> I saw Peter as a strong male figure, but in turn, he had a gentle personality. I highly appreciated his accomplishments, especially his running successes and his pursuit and achievement of high academic status. I was thrilled he was a scientist, as my father was a microbiologist, and I have much respect for scientists. Peter's physical appearance was most appealing to me. I like blond-headed and blue-eyed men. His physique was stunning. I appreciated Peter's willingness to be helpful in any circumstances, his enthusiasm to try new things, and his sense of adventure. He was fun and adorable.

Miki had majored in dance at Texas Woman's University and then graduated with a degree in health, recreation and physical education from North Texas State University. During her university years, she had interim jobs as a dancer in shows, including the Six Flags Over Texas theme park and the Texas Pavilion at the World's Fair in New York in 1964. Returning to Texas from New York, she completed her degree with a period of student teaching. But, after a stressful experience during her student teaching phase, where she was involved in managing 150 girls each period in a big gym, she questioned whether that was what she really wanted to do. While

Above: Noted New Zealand TV and radio commentator, the late Peter Sinclair, talks to Snell and Barry Maister (member of the 1978 gold-medal-winning New Zealand hockey team, now Secretary-General of the New Zealand Olympic Committee) after Peter won the tennis final at the New Zealand Superstars contest in Christchurch.

Below: Snell, far right, was one of the many who paid tribute to Australian mile-star Herb Elliott on TV programme This is Your Life, one of the many occasions his life was celebrated.

Left: Tennis was Snell's first love and he continues to play the game.

Left: On the last curve of his 800m semi-final in Tokyo, Snell positions himself for the run home. ART RICKERBY// TIME LIFE PICTURES/GETTY IMAGES

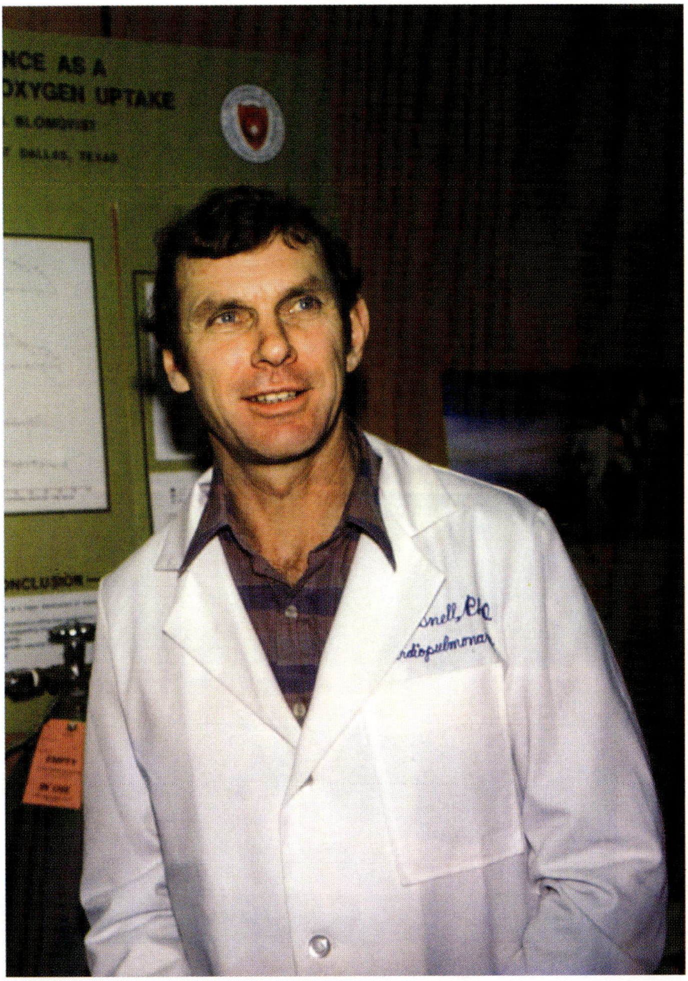

Right: Snell in his lab, 1987.

Below: In Miami for a 'legends' mile race in 1994, the 40th anniversary of Bannister's first sub-four-minute mile. Top row: Filbert Bayi, Snell, Steve Cram, Jim Ryun, Roger Bannister, Kip Keino; bottom row: Marty Liquori, Frank Shorter, Rod Dixon.

Above: Snell with mentor Arthur Lydiard, at Arthur's training camp in Dallas, Texas, 1989.

Below: Snell, Jim Grelle, Jim Ryun, and Wes Santee in Bermuda for a 'legends' mile race, 1996.

Above left: Peter with a model yacht, named in his honour, displayed at an Atlanta Country Club reception for the New Zealand Olympic Team, 1996.

Above right: Miki on her way to winning her age division at the US Orienteering Championships at Quantico Marine Base, Virginia, 1997.

Below: Peter heads towards the finish at an orienteering event at Lake George, Colorado, 1997.

Above: Miki and Peter following an orienteering event in Chicago, 1994.

Below: Snell, Lydiard and Halberg at the Sportsman of the Century and Halberg Awards, 2000.
PHIL WALTER/GETTY IMAGES

Above: Peter and Roger Moens meet in December, 2005, at the university in Leuven, near Brussels, where Snell delivered the annual lecture in sports medicine. Moens was the world record-holding Belgian beaten by Snell over 800 metres in Rome, 1960. They became firm friends and met many times through the years.

Right: Peter conducting a treadmill exercise test in his laboratory at UT Southwestern Medical Center.

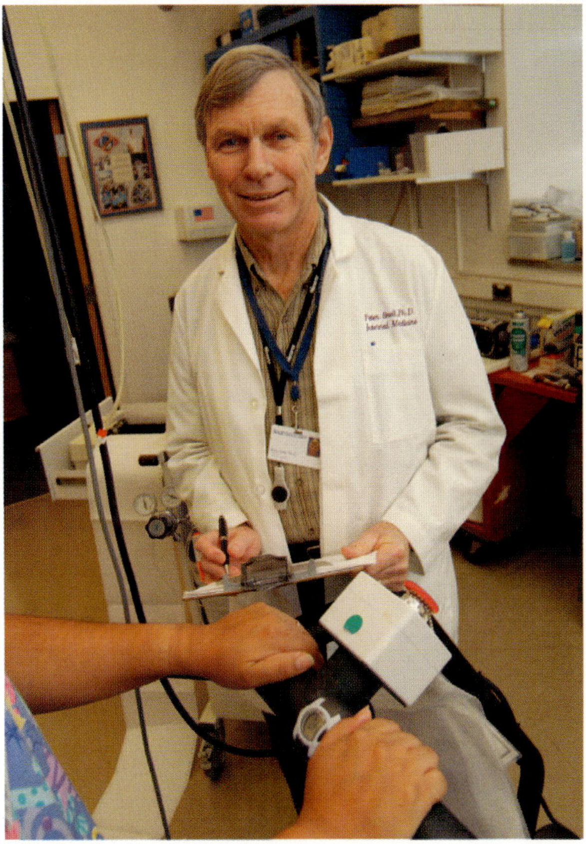

Above: Opunake's tribute to their famous son: a bronze statue erected in 2007.

Below: Peter wearing his UT Southwestern 2007 Intermural Racketball winner's T-shirt, with his defeated opponents who good-naturedly posed for this photo by Dave Gresham. Victims from right to left: Assistant Professor, Matthew Lewis (34), Graduate Research Assistant, Andre Durudas (33), and medical student, Philip Lieu (25).

the teacher who was supposed to be in charge went outside to have a smoke, Miki was left in control of these screaming girls who didn't want to exercise at all.

Wondering if there was anything else she could do rather than teach, as a temporary job, Miki decided she would be a flight attendant for a year or so. She was employed by Braniff International Airlines, a large Dallas-based airline that flew all over South America, to Europe, Asia, Hawaii and within the United States. This was a convenient job for her because she soon afterwards embarked on a career as a runner and so was able to travel inexpensively and race all over the world cheaply. She worked for Braniff until the airline unfortunately went bankrupt in 1982, most probably from a combination of mismanagement and overexpenditure. As Miki recalls: 'For instance, Braniff flew the Concorde — which Britain and France brought to the States — from Washington DC to Dallas. They flew these SSTs subsonically at a loss just for the prestige.'

During the next two years following our initial encounter, Miki and I did a lot of fun activities together. We took several camping trips, and I was pleasantly surprised to discover that she was prepared to 'rough it', sleeping in the back of my newly acquired, used Toyota station wagon and enjoying the outdoors. Miki was an established Veterans competitor, who had run in the World Veterans Champs held in Christchurch in 1980 and had spent a month travelling around New Zealand. It was natural for us to compete in local track and road races. Since Miki held American age group records at 400 and 800 metres, she was interviewed for a women's sports television programme at the US Masters Champs in Houston, where a number of Kiwis were participating. I was filmed timing Miki in her race and referred to as Miki's 'boyfriend'.

Miki, being a good swimmer, wanted to try her hand at medium-length triathlons and asked me to help her with bike preparation at an upcoming event. After being on the sidelines for this first event, I decided to get in some swimming training myself and join her in subsequent races. Miki and I routinely finished in the top three places in the over-40 age group and Miki was often the top female overall.

Meanwhile, I was regularly invited to give talks at clinics associated with big running events. Among these was the Deseret Marathon in Salt Lake City. Though we were not yet married, I convinced the organisers to pay Miki's way, assuring them our wedding was imminent. This provided the opportunity for me to see Miki's childhood home at Bear River Bird Refuge on the Great Salt Lake near Brigham City. Miki's dad, Ralph Hervey, was, at the time, a microbiologist employed by the US Department of the Interior. Other important trips involved visits to Temple, the Texas city where Miki spent most of her childhood, to meet Miki's parents and grandparents. Miki's elder sister, Madeleine, lives in Dallas with her two teenage sons, Paul and Bruce.

During this period, the delicate task of introducing my teenage daughters Mandy and Jacqui to Miki was accomplished. During Jacqui's visit, we took in the theme park Six Flags Over Texas, 'Southfork' of the TV series *Dallas* fame, and splashed around in a huge water park, which featured a mechanical wave-making machine. Mandy visited at a separate time and interacted pleasantly with Miki while I was working. Unlike Jacqui, who didn't say much, it was my feeling that Mandy was more reluctant to accept another woman in my life. Fortunately, and much to my appreciation, Miki ultimately gained their acceptance.

While we were enjoying ourselves during this period of dating, one contentious issue arose, that could be described as having a cultural basis. Americans tend to express their appreciation of others with compliments, whereas Kiwi males in particular are more understated and reluctant to overtly compliment women, which may be seen as manipulative. Also, when we like something we'll say it's 'not bad' — which, translated, means 'very good'. As an example, our friend, New Zealand runner Glenys Quick, who lived many years in Dallas, returned to New Zealand for a visit. Having been used to expressions of approval in America, the lack of this behaviour in New Zealand caused her to wonder if there was something wrong with her.

Miki, therefore, was not feeling particularly valued. This was a problem that was not readily resolved. In addition, there were stresses surrounding the uncertainty of my future employment possibilities.

Immediately after meeting Miki, I realised that I had to address the status of my marriage to Sally. In spite of being officially separated for over four years, we were not in fact divorced. This was primarily to protect her immigration status and that of the children on my student visa. As I was no longer a student, I decided to go ahead and initiate divorce proceedings, which were accomplished without contest.

CHAPTER ELEVEN

No time to waste

The course of my relationship with Miki changed in 1983, when I was offered a faculty appointment with UT Southwestern. This provided the security that allowed me to offer a tangible future to Miki and so I asked her to share her life with me. Fortunately, Miki said yes and we immediately went shopping for an engagement ring. Because we were both in our 40s and didn't have time to waste, we set the wedding date for two months later and began looking for a house. The recent sale of my property in Pullman allowed us to combine our financial resources for a downpayment. We eventually found an ideal, affordable house on a creek lot, close to our favourite running area at White Rock Lake. It was always Miki's dream to have a creek flowing through the back yard.

Instead of a traditional wedding, Miki came up with the brilliant idea of having it in the garden of our new home. We took possession a few weeks before the wedding date, 29 October 1983. The property, previously owned by two elderly women, required a lot of work to get it into shape for the occasion. Consequently, friends were pressed into service to help us. My mother arrived from New Zealand, and for the two weeks prior to the wedding she and I lived in the new house, which was so sparsely furnished that she occupied the only bed.

The wedding was held on a beautiful fall (autumn) day with some cloud cover. Chairs were set up on our patio and a string quartet played from an adjacent grassy area. Handel's 'Water Music' served as the wedding march music. The garden had fall colour but the landscape was still mostly green. My best man was my current roommate Russ

Moore, and Madeleine, Miki's sister, was the matron of honour. The ushers were Bruce Hervey, Miki's nephew, and Jim Stray-Gunderson, another roommate of mine. Miki's parents attended, as well as her grandparents, Mr and Mrs William Maurer, and of course, my mother. Two of Miki's friends helped serve the refreshments at the reception, which was held in the far back lawn area. A judge, wearing his black court robe, presided over the ceremony. There were over fifty friends and relatives in attendance, including Miki's aunt, Helen Clayton, and her uncles, Quentin Clayton and Bob Hervey. The patio was decorated with pink azaleas in pots and many ferns. Miki wore a long white Victorian-style dress, with a veiled, lacy hat. I wore a black suit. When the judge pronounced us husband and wife, the sun, in celebration, broke through the clouds with a large splash of golden light.

Over the ensuing 25 years, we have enjoyed our life together. The house has been remodelled several times, starting with the kitchen and conversion of one bedroom into a closet and master bathroom. Later, we added a second storey and a large garden room. Finally, there was a major kitchen redo. Both of us have always been keen gardeners, with Miki's interest being more on flowers and shrubs and mine on vegetables and fruit trees. We worked together on landscaping improvements, laying a new brick patio surface and creating waterfalls within the creek bed. While our property has extensive grounds, there is not much sun because of the many large and lovely trees.

There is, however, one sunny patch. I've always wanted to have citrus trees, but in Dallas, for eleven and a half months a year, citrus are fine, and then, for maybe a couple of weeks, the temperature drops sharply and kills them. I bought a Quonset hut, with a PVC frame I could put up myself at the beginning of each winter, and installed an electric heater in it to protect the little citrus grove — a mandarin, lemon and grapefruit — out there in my sunny patch. They were pretty successful for quite a few years but one year I was very busy and decided it was too much hassle to put up the frame. With the first big freeze, the citrus grove croaked.

Our life has always involved many pets, particularly cats. I arrived in Dallas with Pekoe, while Miki had Tibby, Bunny and Pumpky as well as a cockatiel. Later, we acquired more cats, miniature rabbits, mourning doves, chinchillas and a southern flying squirrel. In the wild, there were raccoons, mallard ducks and exotic-looking wood ducks. Occasionally, a blue heron or screech owl would appear. Some of the raccoons, though, weren't wild — they were very young ones which somehow became trapped behind the brand-new wall in our house. I had to take to the wall with a drill to get them free and we raised them as pets.

When Braniff reorganised from bankruptcy, after two years, as a very small airline which operated only around the US, Miki flew with them again from 1983 to 1987 until she decided she was tired of it — by now she was in her 40s and ready to retire. So she did.

From 1988 to 1991, I was a wellness consultant to Merck, Sharpe and Dohme (MSD) at major medical meetings in Stockholm, Brussels, Rome, Sydney, Vienna, Rio de Janeiro, Nice, Bruges, Montreal and Amsterdam. Miki accompanied me on these trips and was able to see the scenic highlights while I worked all day testing people who came through the MSD booths in these cities and generally giving them healthy guidance (my own sightseeing was second-hand, as in the evenings Miki described where she'd been and what she'd seen).

Merck's aim was to interest physicians in wellness-type tests they could use for their patients. Since a wellness programme was part of what I was doing in Dallas, this was no problem. I helped to design the booth and my job was to test those who visited it — a body fat measurement with skinfold calipers, a session on an exercycle, a finger prick cholesterol test and a blood pressure reading — from which I produced a coronary risk profile. These trips provided money for the lab in Dallas and some for me as well.

On many of these occasions we were able to take side trips — for example, after the Rome meeting, we visited Capri and stayed next door to the hotel I had stayed in after the 1960 Rome Olympics. It was fun to see that again. However, another trip to Sydney was less fun. We were to open our booth on a Sunday, but, on the day, we found that none of our equipment had arrived. My associate Bob Yamin and I phoned frantically around and then used taxis to race around the city collecting computers, printers and anything else we needed to put together a makeshift booth. Somehow we did it, and I rate it as a pretty heroic effort.

Then there was the trip to Rio de Janeiro, which was interesting — but scary. The head of Merck's international division, Mike Noar, walked onto the beachfront from the convention site one afternoon. While he was taking in the view, a car drew up, some men sprang out and Mike was knocked down and lost all his money and his watch. The muggers jumped back in their car and raced off. The booth girls never wore jewellery when they left to go home, and hotel guests were warned never to leave the hotel grounds.

Miki and I hired a taxi to take us up to the famous Rio statue of Jesus and were driven around for two hours with the driver insisting he was trying to find the road up the hill. We finally told him to take us back to our hotel and that took another hour and ended in an argument, even involving the hotel staff, because we refused to pay the additional fare for the runaround.

We both found Rio very sad. The famous and beautiful Ipanema Beach was polluted by open sewers and we were told that if you went into the water you were committing suicide because the sea was so foul. Rio's problem is that it has a small, very wealthy upper-crust class, no middle class, and a huge and desperate lower class — some of them incredibly impoverished. There were beggars everywhere on the streets and people crowded into shanty towns on the hillsides.

It was around this time that Miki got interested in orienteering and went to her first event while I was in Colorado Springs for an Olympic meeting. It was such fun, she got me involved in the next one, and since then we have both competed in the sport for 20 years.

In 1989 I was recruited by the local arm of a national bread company that was sponsoring Iron Kids Triathlons. My job was to visit various centres where events were to be held and talk up the concept. It was later introduced to New Zealand as the Weet-Bix Tryathlon and I was involved in a launch function in Auckland.

Meantime, in Gunnar's lab, I worked with Steve Lewis, a physiologist; Willie Moore, the lab technician; Drew Gaffney, a cardiologist; and Linda Lane, a research nurse, who took care of subjects enrolled in studies. Drew was taking flying lessons in the hope of enhancing his bid to become an astronaut (payload specialist) for the life sciences mission in 1991. Later, two other Southwestern faculty members, Jay Buckey MD and Jim Pawelzek PhD, would also conduct experiments in space.

Other postdoctoral fellows arrived — Chip Martin, Jay Buckey and Jim Stray-Gundersen, who were all MDs. Postdoctoral fellows within the Mitchell-Blomqvist group included Tim Musch, a collegiate swimmer, and Tony Waldrop, who in 1974 as a senior at the University of North Carolina ran 3:55 for a world indoor mile record. In 1976, many expected Tony to concentrate on the Olympic Games but, after the indoor season, he decided to retire and pursue a PhD in Physiology. Tony didn't seem to regret his decision in the least, as he directed his competitive determination into his research career. Today, he is Vice Chancellor for Research and Graduate Studies at UNC, where he oversees the $577 million in research conducted annually at his alma mater.

Jim's background as a surgeon fitted in nicely with a lot of work being done in the dog lab run by a physiologist, George Ordway, who was a regular runner. In our weekly research meetings, discussions were held on potential research questions that might be of interest. One such topic, on the filling capacity of the heart, arose from my own doctoral dissertation.

When my PhD mentor, Phil Gollnick, required a heart operation to destroy the electrical conducting pathways from the upper to the lower right chamber, the surgeon had to cut the pericardium, a tough inelastic fibrous sac surrounding the heart. I had reasoned that this procedure would release the constraint on the capacity of the heart to expand during filling. This was supported by the fact that when Phil's pacemaker was fitted and he exercised at a fixed HR of 70 beats per minute, the amount of blood pumped per beat was exceptionally large.

With this background, Jere thought that the hypothesis could be tested in dogs, and Jim was given the task of performing a partial pericardiectomy in 10 untrained dogs and a sham operation in seven others (the control group). After recovery from the surgery, there was an impressive 20 per cent increase in cardiac output in the pericardiectomised dogs during treadmill exercise and no change in the sham-operated dogs. This translated into an 18 per cent difference in maximal oxygen consumption between the two groups. The study was published in *Circulation Research* in 1986. Jim speculated, tongue in cheek, that the East Germans might be interested in the technique, given their widespread use of doping in athletes. As an explanation for the effect of endurance training on heart size (athletic heart), the constant 'volume overload and expansion stimulus during exercise causes the pericardium to "remodel" and get larger over months or years'.

Blomqvist's lab was set up for non-invasive (no needles or catheters) measurements of cardiovascular function — echocardiography, VO_2max arterial blood pressure and cardiac output by the technique of acetylene rebreathing. In this procedure, the subject breathes through a scuba-type mouthpiece from a five-litre bag containing 90 per cent oxygen, 9 per cent helium and 0.6 per cent acetylene. The small concentration of acetylene is enough to measure its disappearance into the circulation through the lungs as the subject rebreathes the bag mixture for several seconds. The rate of the acetylene uptake is proportional to the blood flow through the lungs. My early training involved learning the techniques. Gunnar was working on a NASA grant which would ultimately result in experiments in space to understand how zero gravity affected the cardiovascular system. Such experiments would require measurement of CO (carbon monoxide) and it would not be possible to risk the use of C_2H_2 (acetylene) in space. So, because of my experience with CO_2 (carbon dioxide) rebreathing, he sent me to Buffalo to spend time with another NASA-funded investigator, Leon

Fahri, who had proposed a new method involving CO_2 to measure CO in space.

Early on, I was assigned to work with Steve Lewis, who had completed a fellowship with Gunnar and was now working on a variety of his own studies. As I've said, Gunnar taught me to think about cardiovascular performance in different ways. For example, the heart's capacity to pump blood was dependent upon the amount of filling during diastole and then the extent to which this volume could be ejected during systole (SV). The filling depended on the size of the heart and its elastic properties and the SV on contractile properties of the heart and in particular the resistance of the systemic circulation. This meant that the heart's performance was dependent on how well the arterial system could reduce resistance by vasodilation. Was this a structural or regulatory property of arteries and arterioles or both?

To answer this question, we designed a study that would relate maximal oxygen uptake to maximal blood flow, or, more accurately, conductance of arterial blood in the lower leg.

CHAPTER TWELVE

Ouch! That hurts

In order to measure the maximal capacity for blood flow in the muscles of the lower leg we had to devise a method that would maximally dilate the blood vessels. The measurement of flow itself was no problem, as there was a well-established technique known as venous occlusion plethysmography.

Briefly, arterial blood flows into the leg at high pressure and leaves at low pressure in the veins. Thus, when a blood pressure cuff above the knee is inflated above venous pressure at about 60 mm Hg, blood flows into the leg unimpeded but cannot get out and the leg muscles expand. A calibrated strain gauge is used to measure this rate of expansion, from which a volume is derived. The method was in common use to detect peripheral vascular disease, known as intermittent claudication, which is often seen in patients with heart disease. Patients with this condition experience periodic leg pain, particularly during walking, because their blood vessels are too narrowed by arteriosclerosis to allow adequate blood flow and therefore oxygen for muscular contraction.

There were published reports indicating that if the leg was occluded for 10 minutes and then flow measurements were made, the blood flow was 10-fold higher than at rest in normal subjects. We decided that the combination of exercise and occlusion (ischaemic exercise) would provide a greater arterial dilating stimulus than occlusion alone. We tried this by occluding the circulation with a pressure cuff above the knee and then doing heel and toe lifts in a rocking motion so all the muscles of the lower leg were activated.

Our reward was a massive 25- to 30-fold increase in blood flow above resting. Our only problem was that we had to use four-inch-wide cuffs, which imposed a heavy high-pressure crush on the lower thigh just above the knee because the blood vessels are fairly deep inside the muscle. For some of our subjects, it proved very uncomfortable. I should know — I was one of them! This work was eventually published in the *Journal of Applied Physiology* in 1987.

When Steve Lewis left for an appointment in Boston, I had the opportunity of working with his colleague Ron Haller, a neurologist interested in muscle metabolic abnormalities. Ron had built a worldwide reputation for his work on rare muscle diseases, the best known being McArdle's syndrome, in which patients lack the muscle enzyme phophorylase, which is necessary for releasing glucose stored as glycogen. As glucose is the most important fuel for exercise, these patients have low exercise capacity. The body interprets this lack of fuel as a lack of oxygen and responds with increased heart rate and cardiac output to deliver more oxygen. When Ron infused glucose into an arm vein, the exercise capacity in these patients increased dramatically.

One of his more interesting patients was Bill Byrd, whose syndrome was not diagnosed until he was in his 20s. As a teenager, he was a running back on the high school football team. The coach accused him of being lazy, he told me, because he could not run a lap of the track (400 metres) without slowing down over the last 200 metres. The sad truth was that no amount of training would help. Once, in a game, he received the ball close to his end-zone, broke clear and was on his way for a score. About 20 metres from the goal line, his muscles cramped severely and he couldn't make it. Unfortunately, his disease is so rare doctors couldn't figure out his problem. Another of Bill's stories was that he learnt that, if he got into a fight, he had to finish it off quickly!

These patients provided us with important insights into the mechanisms of fatigue and the regulation of the cardiovascular system. For example, the prevailing dogma in exercise physiology was that with increasing levels of exercise, a threshold is reached where anaerobic metabolism and lactic acid production in the blood rises. This acidity stimulates the respiratory centres, causing breathlessness, and inhibits muscular contraction, resulting in fatigue. Because the McArdle's syndrome patients cannot get glucose from glycogen, lactic acid is not produced, yet they still get fatigued and breathless.

One of the research goals for such patients is to understand how the cardiovascular system is regulated and to design some dietary interventions that will allow fuel to more readily enter into the muscle. For example, blood-borne fuels, such as fatty acids and glucose, are beneficial, and one possibility is that short-chain fatty acids will be more effective than the normal long-chain fatty acids because their small size enables them to get into the muscle faster.

In 1983 I was invited, along with Phil Gollnick, to give a presentation at an orthopaedic conference in Denver primarily concerned with knee problems and treatment. Phil gave his usual talk on metabolic properties of muscle fibres, and I gave a presentation on how the physical requirements of any sport or athletic event can be isolated (i.e. speed, strength, aerobic endurance, anaerobic capacity, technique etc) and training devised to strengthen these individual physical characteristics rather than just playing the sport. This was an interest I had been developing for several years. The proceedings were published in *Clinics in Sports Medicine* in 1985.

This was also the year in which I and colleagues began presenting our laboratory work annually, usually at the American College of Sports Medicine. The first meeting we attended was in Montreal, where I presented work on maximal muscle blood flow conductance in trained and untrained men. Later that year, I did a similar presentation at the American Heart Association meeting in Dallas, where the thrust or the emphasis was on how calf muscle blood flow is a determinant of maximal oxygen uptake. My colleague, cardiology fellow Chip Martin, who had been conducting a study on the cardiovascular responses to exercise of large and small muscle groups in patients with ischaemic heart disease, also presented his results at the Dallas meeting.

The following year, at San Diego, Chip delivered the results of intensive swim training on maximal oxygen uptake and calf muscle conductance. This study was undertaken because the chief of cardiology, Dr Jim Willerson, under whose supervision Chip was doing his fellowship, was a friend of Jim Montgomery, a gold medallist swimmer at the 1976 Olympics now coaching in Dallas. Jim Montgomery wanted to demonstrate the benefits of swimming scientifically and supervised all the training, making it a good arrangement for Chip, who performed the measurements in the lab.

At that same meeting, I presented work done on conductance and muscle fibre type in sprinters. This study was initially designed to try to understand more about the relationship between muscle fibre type and hypertension. A Swedish researcher, who was a friend of Drew Gaffney, the budding astronaut, felt that individuals with a lot of fast-twitch muscle fibres, which are poorly supplied by capillaries, would have less resistance to blood flow and therefore be at greater risk of high blood pressure.

When we first talked about this study, I suggested recruiting black track sprinters from a local university team because I was sure that they would have a high percentage of fast-twitch fibres. Surprisingly, this turned out not to be the case. Yet another example of the sort of dogma that becomes established and is not necessarily correct.

The 1984 year was also the year in which my research interests changed direction somewhat and led me into the kind of work I have been doing increasingly since then. Again, it was Jere Mitchell who set me on the path.

Another highlight, this time of late 1990, was the Commonwealth Games, held in New Zealand for the third time. In 1950, when they were still known as the Empire Games, track and field was staged at Eden Park in Auckland. I was then an 11-year-old at primary school in Te Aroha and as yet knew nothing about either my running ability or the Games, but the regular *School Journal* put out by the Education Department carried stories about athletes who were to compete there. I was particularly taken with a story about Duncan White, a hurdler from Sri Lanka (then Ceylon), who developed his running ability by running through the olive groves in his native country. Little did I realise that the next time the Games were to be held in New Zealand — in Christchurch in 1974 — I would be involved with them myself.

In 1990 they were in Auckland again, this time at Mt Smart Stadium. This festival was a great sporting success and the first to use the spectacular opening ceremony to tell a story through dance. The theme was New Zealand: how it was uplifted from the sea and populated first by Maori and then by Europeans following the voyages of explorers Abel Tasman and James Cook.

I know how good these particular Games were because Miki and I were there as special guests, and I played a part in them as the last athlete to be the bearer of the baton which carried the Queen's message round the world. The baton was brought into the stadium by Olympic equestrian champion Mark Todd astride his gold medal-winning horse Charisma — a master-stroke of showmanship suggested by that doyen of athletics administration and promotion Joe McManemin. Mark completed a circuit and passed the baton to me. I carried it for another half-lap, climbed the stairs to a landing and passed it off to Games Federation chairman, Peter Heatly, to pass to the Queen. The Queen then opened the baton and read her message to the crowd.

My connection to coaching and sports science was maintained by appointments to the US Olympic Committee Sports Medicine Council and as a scientific advisor to US Track and Field. These responsibilities involved meetings with other scientists at the Olympic Training Center at Colorado Springs. The chairman of the middle and distance coaching committee, John McKenzie (a friend of Arthur and representative for Brooks running shoes), invited me to an annual week-long camp for 'emerging elite' middle-distance runners.

The idea was to invite the best college runners who were about to graduate and provide them with tools for survival as a runner beyond university. They were good runners (around 1:47 for 800 metres), but not good enough to secure a running shoe contract. The trouble with the US scholarship system is that everything for the athletes is handled by the coach — training, travel, entry to meets and so on. However, once the athletes graduate, they are no longer eligible for these services and are cast out to fend for themselves, with little training to do so. Consequently, many retire with unfulfilled potential. The purpose of the camps, held in Camden, Maine, was to address this issue.

I was brought in to talk about how it was possible to work an eight-hour job and still do the training necessary for world-class results. Many of these 22-year-olds were of the opinion that they could not be successful unless they were full-time athletes. The argument they wanted to make to me was: 'Things are different than in your day.' That may very well be so, but as my personal best was about three seconds faster than theirs, their case was weak. Another prevailing attitude was the belief that the best thing that could happen was to be given an air ticket to Europe so they could try their hand in money races. My advice to them was to train hard and improve times in the US until the European promoters extended invitations.

CHAPTER THIRTEEN

Faculty appointment

The university President, Charles Sprague, was persuaded by Jere to offer me a faculty position as an assistant instructor in the Department of Internal Medicine. My role was to do research and to design and carry out initiatives for faculty-staff wellness. This was the beginning of my interest in preventive medicine — the science of understanding and measuring risk factors for disease and screening for its early development. In this capacity, I organised an annual health fair, offering free screening on various health topics — vision (glaucoma), skin cancer, fitness, cholesterol, blood pressure, safety, nutrition and health. I developed a fitness profile involving measurements of blood pressure, skinfold caliper estimate of body fat, cardiovascular fitness (estimating VO_2max) and muscle strength (sit-ups, leg press, handgrip and bench press). Later, this expertise was put to good use when I set up the Wellness screenings for Merck, Sharpe and Dohme at medical meetings all over the world.

In my spare time, I wrote a computer program in basic language to handle data input, storage, calculations and report functions. I converted these programs into a database language which I still use today.

The importance of cholesterol measurements in the prediction of coronary heart disease risk encouraged me to learn phlebotomy at Parkland Hospital so I could draw blood in my office without sending subjects to a clinic. I also initiated a research project with med students on the hypothesis that the health and fitness of students in their first year would be better than in their fourth year. About 50 per cent of the class of 200 volunteered for the testing, which included a skinfold estimate of body fat percentage, a short bicycle test for the prediction of VO_2max, and a blood draw for a coronary risk profile (total cholesterol, triglycerides and HDL cholesterol; using a calculation from these values, I was able to derive the atherogenic LDL cholesterol).

Medical students spend their first two years in classrooms and laboratories learning anatomy, physiology, microbiology and other medical sciences. The third year is the busiest as they get hands-on experience in the hospital with very little spare time. In other words, no weekends off or time for working out. Consequently, I expected fitness and health levels to decline and persist into the more relaxed fourth year. This turned out not to be the case, and I was left to ponder whether the 50 per cent of the class that participated were more fitness conscious than the other half and were able to maintain an exercise programme even under adverse conditions.

I also assumed that fourth-year students would be competent at phlebotomy, so I had everyone pair off, provided collection tubes, needles and other equipment and stood back and watched. The sight was not very pretty and, even though they were about to graduate with an MD, there was still a lot of practice needed before most of them would be competent doctors.

Late in 1984, I was invited to speak at the Sports Medicine of the Year awards dinner in Dunedin. On the way, I called into Wanganui to meet with chiropractor Clive Moon, who, along with local community leaders Ted Fox and Gordon Swan among others, had set up the Life Foundation for Health and Science in Sport, which would encompass three key components — a health clinic with a strong chiropractic influence, a fitness centre, and a sports science research laboratory.

Sports and exercise science normally exists within universities, where its presence can be justified by the teaching of students studying physical education. In the community, despite its importance in evaluating and understanding human physical performance, it cannot survive without funding support.

Clive's ideas were far-sighted and appealing. He foresaw how the interrelationship of the treatment, the rehabilitation and the science underpinning these disciplines would be mutually beneficial. Importantly, he saw the health centre as providing revenue to support the research laboratory. Clive, who had done his chiropractic training in the US, saw me as fitting into the scheme by developing protocols for the sports science part of the Life Foundation. I left with the promise that I would give serious consideration to their invitation to come back for an extended visit.

Consequently, in October 1986, Miki and I were back in Wanganui for a month to advise the Life Foundation on their sports science research programme. Miki's sister Madeleine joined us for a couple of weeks and stayed with us in a small apartment on the banks of the Wanganui River. On weekends, we were able to do some adventurous activities, such as rafting on the Tongariro River and visiting historic Pipiriki up the Wanganui.

My days in the city were spent developing a software program for fitness assessments, and planning with Clive and Life Foundation personnel how the research laboratory could best be set up to support the goals of the Foundation. I was able to run 40 miles a week on firm grassy verges along the river bank and also ran a 10 k in just under 39 minutes. These were the days when Miki and I competed in medium-course triathlons back in Texas.

Unfortunately, Clive's and the Foundation's objectives were tragically cut short when, at the age of 40, he developed multiple sclerosis and lost his eyesight. He was a good friend of John Davies (later president of the New Zealand Olympic Committee) and teamed up with him to promote 'Olympism' — the ideals of the International Olympic Academy, in which participation, fulfilling your potential and fair play are emphasised. Today, Clive is director of the New Zealand Olympic Academy and an inspirational example of one's refusal to allow adversity to limit life. At 62, he runs 10 km regularly, has jumped out of an aeroplane at 12,000 feet, has flown in a fighter jet, and challenges himself in many other similar ways — out of his comfort zone — every year.

In 1985 I wrote my first grant application to the National Institutes of Health (NIH), in which I proposed to study the effect of endurance training on the development of muscle blood flow. Like many first-time grant applications, it was not ranked highly enough to be funded. Fortunately, a portion of my salary was paid from private funds administered by Jere Mitchell, which eased some of the grant pressure. The terms 'hard' and 'soft' money are the parlance of research scientists. Money that is from an enduring source such as the State of Texas or from a donor's endowment fund is *hard*, whereas grants from funding agencies is short-term *soft* money.

The American Heart Association (AHA), which has its national headquarters in Dallas, is an organisation that makes a huge contribution to fighting heart disease and stroke through its educational programmes, by funding applied and basic research, and by providing a forum for research presentation. UT Southwestern's scientists have benefited from the grants awarded by the AHA and it is expected that we volunteer our time with the local Dallas division for talks, committee assignments or other duties as requested.

Jere Mitchell was president of the American Heart Association in Texas in 1983 and, about this time, Texas adopted an initiative to promote fitness to the business community. He must have mentioned my interest in this area, because I found myself in charge of setting up a committee to handle the project in Dallas. I recruited runners who were businessmen, such as Ed Jackson from the Overhead Door Company and Mike Metheny, an executive for the restaurant chain Steak and Ale.

A module on how to set up fitness programmes in the corporate setting, utilising free material and literature from the AHA, was developed by a team of experts. Our task was to target some big companies and talk them into adopting the programme. Although I abhor selling, I figured that this was different in that I was giving something away which was worthwhile and would help the companies' bottom line in terms of reduced healthcare costs, fewer employee sick days and improved employee productivity, as had been shown by research.

We have had reasonable success but it wasn't all that easy. I had called Core Laboratories, a large company that provides services for the oil drilling business, to set up an appointment to discuss the programme. As soon as I introduced myself as a Heart Association volunteer, it was as though I had ignited a fire.

'I'm having nothing to do with the AHA,' the executive bluntly told me, without any explanation, adding, 'and don't call us again.'

As chair of the Fitness Task Force, I was also on the board of directors of the Dallas division, attending monthly 7.30 a.m. meetings, and eventually finding myself on a ladder of leadership culminating in presidency of the division from 1990 to 1991. One of the ventures I initiated was a tour of the annual meeting exhibits with a cardiologist guide for lay board members — this enabled them to see directly the advances in technology of treating heart disease.

Jere arranged a fellowship for middle and distance running coach Robert Vaughan, who was working on his PhD at North Texas State University and for whom I was research supervisor. Robert and I set about recruiting female distance runners for regular physiological testing. For some reason, Jere saw Dallas as a centre of excellence in sports physiology. He was impressed with the enthusiasm of Jim Stray-Gundersen, who convinced him that a physiological approach to sports performance could lift US cross-country skiing from the doldrums into Olympic contention. Jere also could not understand why Jim, a board-certified general surgeon, would give up a lucrative career in surgery for a lowly-paid fellowship to work with athletes. But he encouraged Jim and I to form a sports research team.

St Paul Medical Center across the street from Southwestern, run by the Catholic Sisters of Mercy, had recently built a new clinical facility, complete with a nicely appointed health club to emphasise the hospital's focus on preventive medicine. The planners included an underwater weighing tank for body composition measurement and exam rooms, in anticipation that physicians would use these to undertake health screenings on their patients. Unfortunately, the physicians, who were not consulted about this idea, were not interested in seeing patients outside of their own offices. This proved to be a windfall for us. Hospitals in Dallas and, no doubt, everywhere in the US are in the business of attracting paying patients — this, to me, is at odds with promoting wellness, which is bad for hospital business. But the administrators decided that their hospital would derive good PR if they could claim that their facility was undertaking exercise research. Jere Mitchell was consulted and St Paul offered us the space that was originally to be used for wellness screening. In addition, they provided a generous budget for equipment, a technician and a receptionist.

Jim and I now had our own lab in spanking-new carpeted rooms and we were soon planning for new equipment and discussing ideas for studies. Jim, who grew up in areas where ice skating and cross-country skiing were popular winter activities, was a competent athlete in his own right, and I felt somewhat regretful that he had been unable to explore his own athletic potential, choosing instead four years of college, followed by four years of medical school and then six years of surgical residency. But his passion was to use physiology to transform US cross-country skiing from its lowly world status to an international force.

But how do you study cross-country skiers in Dallas, where it almost never snows?

CHAPTER FOURTEEN

Rolling on

The answer to Jim Stray-Gundersen's dilemma was the use of cross-country roller skis, which work well on smooth pavement and on treadmills that are wide enough. To accommodate Jim's ambition, Jere Mitchell funded the construction of a large treadmill with a six-foot-wide belt. The nation's best young skiers in their late teens were invited to come to Dallas for a week of intensive testing in which all the tests we could think of that might give us some clue on future potential were undertaken.

Being a surgeon by trade, Jim naturally included a muscle biopsy on the protocol. The small sample of tissue, taken with a 'needle' the size of a pencil, is quickly frozen in liquid nitrogen and stored at –160°C until analysis by a pathologist. Typically, measurements are muscle fibre type, capillary density, and enzyme activity in the energy-releasing pathways where glucose and fat are completely oxidised. Jim's belief was that, as the skiers matured, the physiological testing would provide objective information on strengths and weaknesses, allowing their coaches to more accurately target their training.

Whereas my appointment was in the Cardiology division of Internal Medicine, Jim's was in the Department of Orthopedic Surgery. One of his department's specialties was fixing back problems. As a result, our first research presented at the American College of Sports Medicine (ACSM) in 1985 involved assessing the safety of an isokinetic trunk testing device during one-minute bouts of repeated extension and flexion (forwards and backwards bending) of the trunk for patients who may have co-existent heart disease.

We measured oxygen consumption, blood pressure and heart rate during the exercise to calculate demands on the trunk and heart. Jim discussed our assessment of the energy cost of performing exercises on the device at that year's meeting of the ACSM, held in Nashville, Tennessee, which is the home of the Grand Old Opry of country singing.

The following year, 1986, was particularly busy with research meetings. Our group had expanded to include an outstanding marathon runner, Geoff Moore, who had completed his physician residency in Dallas; Andrea Katz, a national-class racquetball player with a Master's degree in exercise physiology; and Claire Kispert, a physical therapist.

Ken Pitetti, a Vietnam War veteran, who had lost a lower leg in combat, arrived in Dallas to study for a PhD in physiology. While visiting the Dallas Veterans' Administration Hospital for a new prosthesis, he met up with other amputees, many of whom were sedentary, overweight and at risk for heart disease. Ken felt he could motivate them to exercise and improve their health, so we decided to do this in the context of a research study. We found that they were able to exercise and improve their fitness on an air-braked stationary cycle, which had arm levers linked to the drive chain. The amputees were able to use their arms and 'good' leg to exercise while resting their amputated limb. The unanticipated finding was that the amputees improved their ability to walk following the cycle training.

Among our group at the ACSM meeting in Indianapolis, I presented the study of oxygen on recovery from exhausting exercise in soccer players. Ken Pitetti presented his study on amputees and training on the fan-braked bicycle; Robert Vaughan did a presentation comparing physiological characteristics of elite women runners who had a good competitive season, with those who were less successful; and Jim discussed results of our 10 k training study comparing interval training with sustained hard running of equal distance.

The following year, when the meeting was at Las Vegas, I deferred to Ken Pitetti for the presentation of our work on the prediction of maximal oxygen uptake from cycling.

But why would you hold a sports meeting in Las Vegas? Well, it's an interesting city and during our week there all the drinking, gambling and cigarette-smoking people who were normally in residence had quit the hotel we were occupying, so it was a pretty nice place to be. Truth be told, we probably did a bit of gambling ourselves, and there were shows to go to for those who had enough of attending talks.

The physician for Dallas' professional soccer team, Dr David Winter, approached me to ask if I thought that the use of 100 per cent oxygen on the sideline in football games was effective in facilitating recovery. My impression was that it was probably not. We consulted Jim, who suggested that the oxygen might result in reduced levels of lactic acid, which, in the mid-1980s, was heavily implicated in fatigue.

It was decided that we would design a study to test the oxygen hypothesis. Briefly, we settled on a double-blind crossover protocol. In the morning, we tested the entire soccer squad, starting with a treadmill running test that resulted in exhaustion in eight to 10 minutes. Lactic acid was measured and we then allowed the subjects to recover for three minutes, breathing from a tank containing either oxygen or compressed air, and then repeated the earlier procedure. Colleagues prepared the tanks, labelling them 'A' or 'B' so that neither the players nor the investigators knew whether it was oxygen or room air that was being delivered. In the afternoon, the two treadmill tests were repeated with a different treatment (gas A or B) — the crossover part of the design. After each player completed a series, we asked them to state the treatment (oxygen or air) they thought they were getting.

I presented the results to the ACSM and the full paper was published in the *Journal of the American Medical Association* in 1989, with Dr Winter as first author, which fulfilled part of his requirement for admission into the American College of Physicians. Our findings were that supplemental oxygen did not enhance recovery from exhausting exercise and that the only benefit that American football players who took oxygen received was purely imaginary — the placebo effect, which should not necessarily be discounted. Dr Winter did not recommend the procedure for the Dallas soccer team. Of all the research I have done, this study aroused more attention and media coverage than all the others put together.

During this time, Tapio Videman, an orthopaedic sports medicine surgeon from Finland, was visiting Dallas and had some discussions with Jim. He was very knowledgeable about the doping situation in Europe and interested in the way anabolic and catabolic hormones were affected by hard training, suggesting that overtraining was a result of imbalance of these hormones — testosterone and cortisol respectively. The thinking was that testosterone protected the body from the negative effects of too much cortisol, stimulated by demanding training, which is why endurance athletes benefit from controlled doses of testosterone.

This made a lot of sense to me and fitted in with what I knew about the dangers from overuse of cortisol injections to reduce inflammation in joints. While cortisol is anti-inflammatory, its action is catabolic, meaning that it facilitates tissue breakdown. In starvation states, cortisol rises markedly to provide the body with life-sustaining glucose from muscle proteolysis (breakdown). Thus another study was born. The hypothesis was that overtraining, defined by reduced performance after weeks of hard training, resulted from a decrease in plasma-free testosterone (the active form) and an increase in plasma cortisol. In particular, the ratio of these hormones (cortisol/free testosterone) would be significantly elevated.

At the 1986 American College of Sports Medicine meeting in Indianapolis, along with eight presentations from our lab by co-investigators, Jim presented our study on hormonal markers of overtraining and I discussed our findings in the Dallas soccer team study on the use of 100 per cent oxygen on recovery after heavy exercise. Robert Vaughan presented our work on elite women distance runners, who we were testing on a yearly basis for US Track and Field.

Other studies that year included histology on Jim's biopsies from dogs, a couple of cycling studies, and an MRI evaluation of heart size in long-distance runners, cross-country skiers and cyclists. Jim fully expected that the cross-country skiers would have the biggest hearts and therefore demonstrate their superiority among endurance athletes. However, it turned out that, while all the endurance athletes had big hearts, there were no differences among the sports when heart size was related to body size.

I collaborated with Jim on his cross-country skier project in the lab we established at St Paul hospital, where we did testing on trained and elite athletes. The 'name' athletes included Francie Larrieu-Smith, who set 36 American track records during her career, the world-class marathoner Alberto Salazar, and the Hall of Fame triathlete Scott Tinley.

Salazar made an unusual slice of history when he collapsed after a furious sprint finish with Dick Beardsley at the end of the 1982 Boston Marathon and subsequently received six litres of water intravenously — he had not drunk a drop during the race. Another noteworthy Salazar performance was in the 1978 Falmouth, Massachusetts road race, where, after finishing 10th in 33:04, he collapsed with a temperature of 107 degrees Fahrenheit (41.7°C) and was read his last rites prematurely.

Bob Ward, the conditioning/strength coach for the Dallas Cowboys football team, invited us out to their training facility to undertake fitness testing on the players. The size of these men was impressive — 6 ft 2 in to 6 ft 6 in (1.87 to 1.98 m) and weighing 250–350 lbs (113–158 kg). The nature of American football emphasises speed, strength and power. Endurance is not necessary because the game is a series of short plays lasting less than 10 seconds followed by at least a 30-second rest (more if it is time for a TV commercial). When a player feels 'tired' he can take himself out of the game for a breather. Consequently, there is little incentive on the player's part to develop endurance.

Bengt Saltin is probably the best-known exercise physiologist in the world and in 2002 received the IOC Olympic Prize for his pioneering research in sports medicine. Through his regular collaboration with Bengt at the August Krogh Insttitute in Copenhagen, Jere worked with anaesthesiologist Niels Secher, a former world single sculls rowing champion. In order to understand more about the effect of muscle fibre recruitment on cardiovascular responses, Niels would administer controlled doses of the Amazon Indian arrow poison curare, which paralyses slow-twitch red muscle fibres and, because these fibres make up the diaphragm, kills people through suffocation. As long as the subjects are on a ventilator there is no problem.

The world athletics championships were held in Rome towards the end of 1987, which was also the 75th anniversary of the International Amateur Athletic Federation. They had produced a book to mark the occasion — *One Hundred Golden Moments* — and all those who made the book were invited, all expenses paid, to this event. I was the only New Zealander included.

It was quite an occasion. People like Fanny Blankers-Koen, Gaston Roelants, Emil Zatopek, Lasse Viren and Peka Vasala — and the Russian runner, Tatyana Kazankina, winner of three Olympic gold medals and setter of seven world records (who Miki described as very attractive in her post-running years) — were in attendance. Kazankina stood only 1.61 metres tall and weighed 48 kilograms. Fanny Blankers-Koen must have been in her 70s but was still a sprightly woman. Emil Zatopek was interesting. I sat next to him at one stage and had to introduce myself, although it was the second time I had met him. We had both been at the Rome Olympics. But it was an honour to be among that group and included in the *One Hundred Golden Moments*.

We all stayed in the same hotel on the outskirts of Rome, which was a bit of a pain because the transport wasn't very good and the facilities at the hotel weren't that great either. The events were not particularly memorable, either, except for the women's 10,000 metres walk. This was held on a cloudy day and it was so humid that the women had heat problems. It was similar to that Los Angeles marathon when the Swiss runner, Gabriel Anderssen-Scheiss, was weaving all over the track — the walkers were weaving as they came into the stadium, and the crowd, which didn't understand what was happening, thought it was funny. But it was far from it. I saw one woman fall into one of the flower boxes alongside the track. A lot them didn't finish — they'd gone nearly 10,000 metres, into the final lap, and weren't able to finish because they were in such distress.

This amazed me because this was not a marathon taking just over two hours but a 10,000 metres walk and it created problems. The damaging thing about high humidity is that sweat doesn't evaporate so you don't get a cooling effect but you lose a lot of sweat and become dehydrated. The combination was devastating and a good lesson to me to understand how important it is to keep hydrated.

In 1988 a senior medical student, Maggie Reilly-Hagan, who was a professional tennis player before deciding to go to medical school, teamed up with me and we looked at the forearm blood flow in tennis players. Many years earlier, a doctor in Auckland had done x-rays of the forearms of professional tennis players participating in the big annual event at the Stanley Street stadium. He observed that not only was the musculature much bigger in the dominant forearms of Rod Laver, Roy Emerson and others, but also the width and density of the ulna bone.

I reasoned that the exercise of playing tennis would stimulate the vascular growth in the tennis-playing arm and this was the hypothesis of the study. To our surprise, there was no difference between the dominant and non-dominant forearms for maximal blood flow. In thinking about the possible reasons for this finding, Maggie and I felt that, in tennis, the racquet was gripped firmly in a static contraction and that this was more like resistance training than true aerobic training. We know that resistance or weight training does not produce vascular growth and so this seemed a reasonable conclusion.

An interesting sidelight to this study involved a postdoctoral fellow in Jere Mitchell's group, Tim Musch, who had finished his fellowship and moved to the medical school at Hershey, Pennsylvania. Tim had obviously talked to the Hershey cardiologist, who was interested in this field, and within a year they had done the same study and published the findings in the *Journal of Applied Physiology*. Unfortunately, their inexperience with the technique led them to the wrong conclusions. They reported an increased blood flow to the tennis-playing forearm. It turned out that Tim was the chairman of the session in which I presented our conflicting findings, and he had the task of trying to explain why they had already published findings which were different from those which I presented. It didn't help that he took our ideas and scooped us for publication.

Also at this meeting in Dallas, research was presented by a new colleague, Ed Balaban, who was a Doctor of Osteopathy (DO) and a haematologist. He had been working with Robert Vaughan and me on introducing a new technique for assessing iron deficiency in runners. Low iron stores lead to low haemoglobin levels and anaemia, which impairs blood oxygen-carrying capacity. Therefore, being able to predict the level of iron stores is a useful tool for the athlete, who can take corrective dietary action. The standard way to assess these iron stores is to measure the plasma level of a protein known as ferritin, which is correlated to bone marrow iron stores. Dr Balaban was able to measure the level of ferritin in red cells — known as tissue ferritin — and felt that low levels in the presence of normal plasma ferritin would define a subgroup of athletes at risk for developing anaemia.

Various studies continued to be presented at annual ACSM meetings through to the 1990s. It was at this time that a hospital across town which had built a very nice sports medicine facility approached us with an offer of laboratory facilities and funding better than we were receiving at St Paul. This development represented a parting of the ways for Jim and myself. Jim decided to accept the offer, from Baylor Hospital at the new Tom Landry Sports Medicine and Research Center, named after the legendary Cowboys coach Tom Landry. However, I indicated to the administrators at St Paul that I would be interested in staying at the laboratory, recruiting staff and continuing research.

This made sense because, in my role of Wellness Coordinator,

I was involved in delivering the required fitness testing, body fat assessment, lipid profile and exercise advice for our faculty and staff joining the St Paul Fitness Centre. This saved them the $50 initiation fee for the testing that would normally be done by the Fitness Centre staff. With Jim relocated across town, I settled in to recruit staff, selecting a cyclist with a Bachelor's degree in physical eduation, Phil Wyrick, and Sue Bryant, a nutritionist wanting to do exercise research. Robert Vaughan continued to bring in his elite women distance runners for testing.

We were the fortunate recipients of two special cycle ergometers to test on behalf of the manufacturer, Diamond Back, better known for their racing bikes. These ergometers interfaced with the transmitters used by Polar heart rate monitors, which just about every exercise lab was using. It was possible to dial in an exercise heart rate and the bike would automatically increase resistance and power requirements until the HR was reached, adjusting resistance up or down as necessary. The other important feature was that the power output (wattage) was independent of the pedalling rate, so that, if the rider slowed down, the resistance would increase commensurately.

These bikes immediately gave me ideas for further studies. We would be able to accurately compare the effect of different exercise intensity, based on heart rate, while holding the total caloric expenditure constant. In other words, provide an answer to the question: Is it better to work a higher relative workload for a shorter time than a lower workload for a longer time? In reality, it would be like comparing runners. Is it better to run five miles at seven minutes a mile than eight minutes a mile? However, calories burned on a bike are the same for everyone, whereas in running the energy expenditure is weight-dependent.

The other study addressed a common practical question fuelled by marketing claims: What is the best aerobic exercise? Is it cross-country skiing, running, walking, rowing, cycling or what? The approach to this question was to exercise volunteers for five minutes on each type (modality) of exercise at three levels — easy, moderate and hard. The oxygen consumption was measured to provide an accurate caloric expenditure for each five-minute exercise bout. With the energy expenditure and heart rate information, we were able to discern which exercise gave a greater energy production for a given heart rate. Results of both studies were presented by Phil and Sue at the annual ACSM meeting in Dallas in 1992.

Nevertheless, after two years, the hospital was experiencing a financial crisis and our operation was targeted. We were considered a drain on the hospital resources and, as I had not been able to secure outside grant funding or provide adequately reimbursable services, the lab was closed down and I found myself back in Gunnar's Space Medicine lab. But there was hope on the horizon.

CHAPTER FIFTEEN

Triple breakthrough

My first stroke of luck came when the lab group across the corridor from Dr Blomqvist moved to another location and I was given the space to establish exercise physiology. The second was that the Parkland Hospital diabetes clinic director, Phil Raskin, received funding to do a drug study, which required an accurate measure of body fat — there was space in my new lab and a state-of-the-art underwater weighing facility was constructed. This proved useful for other purposes too. For example, the resident epidemiologist, Dr Bob Haley, was working on unravelling the puzzle of soldiers who fought in the first Gulf War and suffered a variety of neurological and other ailments, which became known as Gulf War Syndrome. Most of them put on weight and Dr Haley wanted this quantified.

The third major break came in 1997, when the National Heart, Lung and Blood Institute (NHLBI), a division of the government funding agency the National Institutes of Health (NIH), circulated a request for proposals to address the public health issue of insufficient participation in regular physical exercise. The NHLBI scientists observed that there was sufficient research on the benefits of exercise including what type, how much, how hard and how often, but that surveys consistently revealed that very few people were getting adequate, if any, regular exercise. What, they asked, was the best way to motivate people to actually make the commitment to exercise and stick with it? In essence, this would be a clinical trial testing interventions designed to encourage sedentary people to become active.

Ben Levine, who had developed a laboratory funded by Presbyterian Hospital and known as the Institute for Environmental and Exercise Science, while maintaining his faculty appointment as a cardiologist at Southwestern, sat down with me and we decided we should prepare a proposal for the NHLBI. The problem for us was that one of the main parts of the study would be to design and implement the behavioural interventions. Ben and I were exercise physiologists and inexperienced in this area.

Across town at the Cooper Aerobics Center, their research director, Dr Steve Blair, was also working on a proposal. His team had already undertaken a study to encourage people to exercise and therefore had a 'track record' of success — important when funding agencies are investing a lot of research dollars. Steve's institution probably could have handled the complete study, but he recognised the advantage of building a coalition with UT Southwestern Medical Center and invited us to partner with him. Eventually, Ben and I had a meeting with Steve and his colleague Dr Andrea Dunn, a psychologist, and agreed that we would be responsible for the laboratory testing. Steve Blair was the principle investigator (PI), Ben was the Co-PI, and I was the clinical director for the Dallas site.

Our group was one of three chosen from the proposals submitted. The other two were Standford University, near San Francisco, and the University of Tennessee. A fourth group from the Bowman Grey School of Medicine was selected as the co-ordinating centre responsible for designing how the data would be collected, setting up the database and performing data analysis. Standford University, incidentally, was established as a non-traditional, non-campus university to provide distance learning, online or e-learning programmes for mature students worldwide to advance their career and academic qualifications.

The plan was that each clinical centre would enrol, from local doctors' clinics, 350 sedentary subjects, male and female and of varied ethnicity, free of major diseases such as diabetes, heart disease and cancer, and ranging in age from 35 to 70 years. They would be randomised to either a top-level intervention, an intervention with less contact and encouragement, or a control group, who would receive a brief encouragement to exercise from their doctor and be sent home with an American Heart Association pamphlet about the importance of regular exercise. Each participant would be followed for two years and be tested at entry (baseline), six months, 12 months and 24 months. It was expected that four years would be required to recruit the patients and complete the study and a further six months to analyse the results.

Once the centres had been selected, a period of six months of planning meetings was undertaken, usually at Washington DC, to refine protocols and procedures. The flow chart below describes the organisation for major clinical trials starting with screening candidates, baseline testing, randomisation and follow-up.

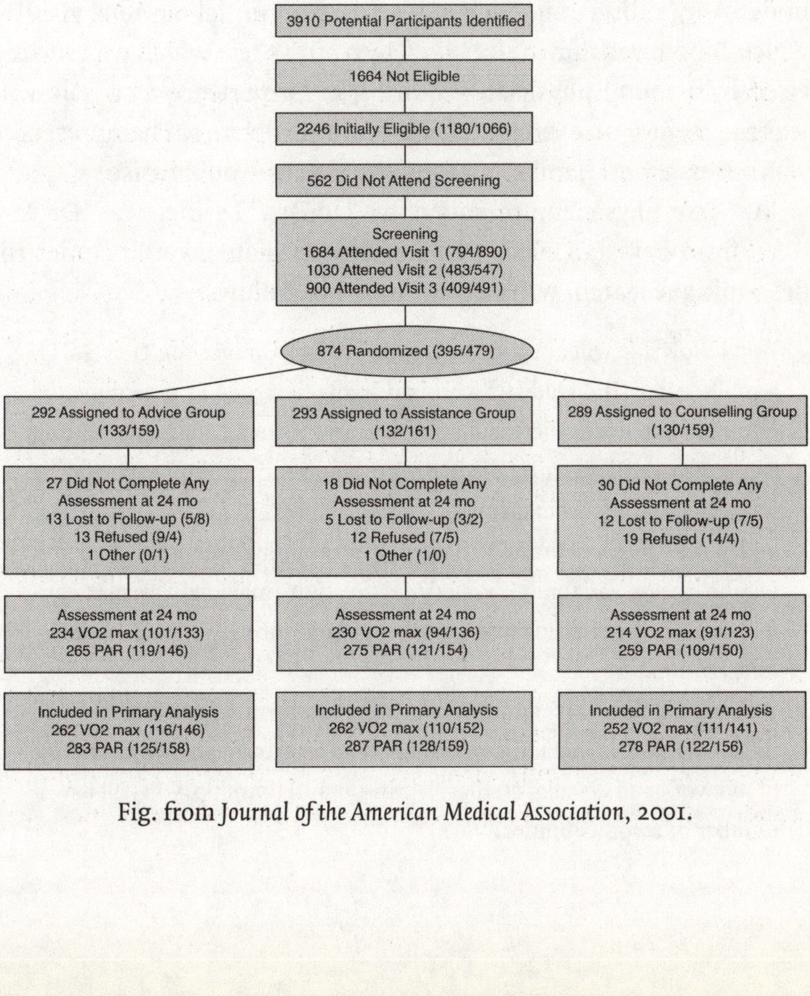

Fig. from *Journal of the American Medical Association*, 2001.

The budget for the Dallas clinical centre covered 50 per cent of my salary and included a new state-of-the-art system for the measurement of oxygen consumption and a treadmill. In addition, I had the funding to hire a laboratory assistant. Among the candidates interviewed was a 26-year-old who had just completed her Master's under an exercise physiologist specialising in immunology at the University of North Carolina. Amy Strasner turned out to a great choice. After a rocky early start we worked together well. Amy was a hard and conscientious worker, often having to be ready to see subjects in the lab at 7 a.m. She was hopelessly hooked on the fortunes of the football team of her undergraduate alma mater, the University of Florida — the Florida Gators.

As the study got under way, the Aerobic Center provided us with a regular supply of 'interns' — unpaid labour to help out in the lab under Amy's direction. Each subject had an initial baseline visit in which blood was drawn, followed by a stress test which was supervised by a young physician acquiring lab experience as a fellow. I was the mentor on exercise testing for these doctors. Their presence was necessary for liability reasons should any trouble arise.

My first physician, recruited by Dr Ben Levine, was Dr Jay Revi, from Pakistan. Ben, who is very articulate when it comes to describing research, wrote to Jay in part as follows:

> Your fellowship will be sponsored by the Activity Counseling Trial (ACT), a multicenter NIH study which is primarily designed to determine the optimal strategy for increasing physical activity in a community setting to prevent cardiovascular disease. Our laboratory group is specifically interested in the mechanisms of the cardioprotective effect of exercise, and in the context of the ACT trial, we are examining autonomic function (via heart rate variability), vascular regulation (maximal vascular conductance and arterial stiffness), and coagulation after two years of activity intervention.
>
> Over the next six months, we must perform approximately 200 follow-up studies including maximal exercise tests, heart rate variability, blood work and vascular studies. During your fellowship, you will have a number of responsibilities:

> 1) To assist an experienced technical and professional staff in the performance of the exercise testing procedures, including the measurement of maximal oxygen uptake and the interpretation of the exercise electrocardiogram. You will be primarily responsible for providing medical back-up in case of emergencies. In this context, you will be directly responsible to Dr Peter Snell, Co-PI and director of the Human Performance Laboratory, and Ms Amy Strasner, project manager for ACT, and will become expert in exercise testing procedures.

After a year, in mid-1999, Jay was replaced by Chris Coleflesh. Chris later changed his name to Chris Cole, when he began seeing patients privately after our study was completed and he headed off to Cleveland. (One of our top faculty scientists is Clive Slaughter. Privately, I wondered, if he ever considered surgery as a career, how that name might have gone down with patients.)

After the baseline testing of the subjects, we met with Aerobic Center staff who were responsible for delivering the intervention — different levels of advice and encouragement to exercise based on the extensive research and experience from the cadre of investigators and advisors associated with the study. The behavioural scientists outnumbered the exercise scientists by at least two to one.

Incidentally, the selection of the name, Activity Counseling Trial or ACT, gained its proposer, Dr Jim Sallis from San Diego, a bottle of champagne at our first meeting in Washington DC. My own submission was close (Physical Activity Counseling Trial or PACT). It's all about the acronym!

At one of these early planning meetings, we were discussing the pros and cons of including a measure of heart rate variability in the protocol. After the meeting, Paul Ribisl, the Chair of the PE department at Wake Forest University, part of the Bowman Grey co-ordinating centre, and I were presented with certificates, which were inscribed, in large type:

> **Noble Prize in Medicine presented to Paul Ribisl and Peter Snell for including heart rate variability in ACT.**

The certificates came complete with signatures and an impressive-looking seal. I duly put the certificate in my office and when the Pakistani physician arrived and visited me, he spotted the certificate and suddenly became very respectful and said, 'It will be a great honour for me to work with such a great scientist.' I burst out laughing as it was apparent that Dr Revi thought I was a Nobel Laureate. At least I was old enough to be one but that's about where it stopped. I pointed out that the certificate was a gag from my colleagues and that the English word 'noble' was not *Nobel*.

Several publications were derived from ACT, the major one being the primary results paper *Effects of Physical Activity Counseling in Primary Care: The Activity Counseling Trial: A Randomized Controlled Trial*, which appeared in the *Journal of the American Medical Association* in 2001. The success of this clinical trial is debatable. There were no differences in fitness or physical activity among the men across the three interventions. Only women in the group receiving the most encouragement and support improved physical activity and fitness. Although the behaviouralists may have been disappointed that their best shot didn't work, the good news is that a physician's advice is effective. This is a positive message for the New Zealand Green Prescriptions programme, which unfortunately is not supported by enough GPs, according to SPARC's Dianne O'Neil, who supervises the programme.

After four years, the funding for ACT came to an end. Amy decided to head off to Penn State to pursue a PhD. Her mother died too young of breast cancer and Amy became passionate about dedicating her career to understanding more about this terrible disease. Chris Coleflesh left for the Cleveland clinic to undertake a cardiology fellowship. However, the NIH allowed me to keep the equipment on the understanding that I would be using it in NIH-funded research. So, following ACT, I made a conscious decision to partner with physicians undertaking research where my expertise in exercise, metabolism and body composition would be helpful. This decision coincided with a marked upsurge of interest in exercise to treat various metabolic diseases.

Chief among these was the work being done on lipodystrophy by Abhimanyu Garg and Nicola Abate (an Italian) and his wife, Manisha Chandalia (an Indian), who were studying the genetics of insulin resistance in Chinese and Asian Indian populations. One of the groups that develop lipodystrophy are HIV-positive patients treated with highly active antiretroviral therapy (HAART) to prevent the onset of AIDS. The side effects of protease inhibitor drugs are abnormal fat distribution (it comes off the limbs, backside and face, while accumulating on the upper back and sometimes neck), elevated plasma triglycerides and insulin resistance. Exercise has been shown repeatedly to improve insulin sensitivity and lower triglycerides in normal populations and therefore was included as part of the therapeutic approaches employed by Dr Garg.

Our library invited me to give a talk on fitness at a 'brown bag' luncheon meeting of the staff. From the interest and enthusiasm displayed by this group, I decided to set up a little study to test my ideas about defining the exercise dose so that everyone would do the same amount of exercise — the fitter ones would accumulate their required caloric expenditure faster than the less fit. The exercise was walking the medical school corridors, on a course whose distance I had determined with a measuring wheel. Eight laps of the corridors were required for a mile. A baseline treadmill test was done and a follow-up after eight weeks. There was a nice improvement across the board and I felt confident that the exercise dose of 5 kcal/kg performed three times a week at 75 per cent of VO_2max was effective. It is always gratifying when someone involved in a study like this is motivated to continue. The guardian of the photocopying operation, Beverly Hayes, was one such person. She is still exercising regularly after eight years.

This sort of activity filled some gaps after ACT, and other collaborations evolved as physicians became increasingly aware of the powerful effects of exercise on gene expression and metabolism. Among these was Kevin Oeffinger, a family practice physician specialising in cancer. He recruited my help in studying 118 young adult survivors of childhood leukaemia or technically acute lymphoblastic leukaemia. The consequences of the chemotherapy and, in some cases, cranial radiation produced some side effects, including elevated risk factors for heart disease, and balance and gait abnormalities. The study was to test the effects of a 12-months' lifestyle intervention, which was administered by the Cooper Aerobics Center. My role was to conduct the pre-and post-treadmill testing.

CHAPTER SIXTEEN

Good, bad, sad

Meantime, on the home front, I had agreed to become patron of the New Zealand Parkinson's Society. My brother Jack had suffered from the disease for a long time and I wanted to do something to raise the awareness of Parkinson's in New Zealand. I also wound up meeting the new Governor-General, Dame Silvia Cartwright, in Government House in Wellington at a function organised by the Arthritis Foundation at which she and I presented medals to arthritis sufferers.

Early in January 1992, I received word from Jack that my mother was seriously ill from lung cancer. She was never a smoker, but Dad smoked a lot and this was probably a result of second-hand smoke. I was already scheduled to visit New Zealand because Wanganui was organising a 30th anniversary re-run of the first New Zealand four-minute mile in 1962. The chosen date was 27 January.

I called Jack and said I could come over but asked if he thought Mum could hang on a while until I came over for the re-run. Jack reckoned that was reasonable, although he had thought she was close to dying. However, Air New Zealand allowed me to catch an earlier flight on the basis of a family medical crisis, but not Miki, who came on the regular flight a day later. A short time out from Honolulu, her aircraft had engine problems and the flight was delayed by another day, by which time Mum had died. Miki called us from her Honolulu hotel room and spoke to Mum a few hours before she passed away. Miki got on well with my mother, who appreciated her insistence that I put my family before the demands of the New Zealand public.

Meantime, I arrived in Wanganui for the week-long race re-run preparations and during that time raced up to Pukekohe and spent time with Mum, who seemed fine. We played crib, had a walk around the garden and it was a nice visit. That evening, she had to go into the hospice in Pukekohe, and died later that night. Since then, I have always thought that in some cases people are able to control when they're going to die. My mother knew I was coming home and decided to wait, but she also knew that, with the pain of the cancer, she could not carry on after that. So she waited, I had the visit, and then she let go.

So, in one week, amazingly, I was able to join all the participants in the 1962 race back in Wanganui, visit my mother and then attend her funeral. It wasn't easy after her death to go down and do what I had to do in Wanganui — I had to get up and make a speech and it was very difficult — but the event at Cook's Gardens was a lot of fun. We tried to do the race in two laps inside four minutes to keep pace with the original race commentary as it was played over the loudspeaker system. Then I went back to Auckland for the funeral.

Sadly, just six months earlier, Miki's mother, who had been suffering from diabetes for many years, died at the age of 76. She had a wonderful sense of humour and, just as Miki did with my own mother, I had good rapport with her. Later in 1996, Miki's grandmother, Rachael, died at the age of 103. Her grandfather lived into his 90s. This would suggest that Miki has good longevity genes as long as she can avoid diabetes. Finally, Miki's Dad, Ralph, who was suffering from heart disease, died two years later.

CHAPTER SEVENTEEN

This was my life

The turn of the century and the years since have been both frantic and fruitful and packed with New Zealand-based activities.

The Halberg Trust celebrated the new millennium by making a special award in February for New Zealand's Sports Champion of the Century at their annual Sportsman of the Year ceremonial dinner. A huge marquee was set up in the Auckland Domain for the occasion.

The procedure for determining who was to be the champion was to select first a winner from each decade from the beginning of the century. The early selections were tricky because New Zealand's defining Sportsman of the Year awards did not begin until the *Truth* weekly newspaper established the concept, possibly in the 1940s, which became a Halberg Trust property some 40 years ago. But the system meant that the sports writers and journalists had a relatively small number to pick from. All the potential candidates and all the other winners of various awards were assembled in this marquee and the Governor-General at the time, Sir Michael Hardie-Boyes, made the announcement.

I had previously met Hardie-Boyes at the world veterans orienteering championships, which were being held in Wanganui over the Christmas–New Year period, and where I was part of the official opening ceremony conducted by Sir Michael. He and I saw the new millennium in at Feilding, where I officially started a midnight orienteering event. This was all at the beginning of a particularly busy period in my life as far as New Zealand was concerned.

In September 2001 I was in New Zealand for a Peter Snell Institute of Sport fundraising dinner when I was told I would be going to an Air New Zealand function at Mt Albert Grammar. That morning, for some reason, I had a visit from some Air New Zealand executives and remarked that I would be seeing them again that evening. They acted surprised and said they knew nothing about it. At the time, I thought that was strange — but not strange enough to be suspicious. The last thing I would have dreamt of was that I would be in a *This Is Your Life* show. Everybody else was in on it: Miki knew, and so did my daughters and all my other family members. This may have been one of the things that made Opunake feel that it was important in my life, because the chairperson of the Egmont District Council, Jean Roach, was the person who arranged for my sister's nephew to play me as a youngster running around Opunake, which appeared in some of the film footage shown in the show.

On the afternoon of the function, I had a fairly gruelling round of visits in the company of Colin Kay, visiting potential sponsors for the Institute of Sport. By the time I was dropped off by him, I was feeling in need of a rest, but this Air New Zealand 'do' lay immediately ahead. A limo arrived to take Miki and I to Mt Albert Grammar but the driver seemed to get lost. I said, 'Look, I know exactly where it is. I can direct you', but the driver didn't seem interested and took us on a tiki tour which at one time took us into Epsom. What was happening was that the timing with the TV channel wasn't quite right for my arrival.

I was finally taken to my old school grounds, we walked into the school hall, I looked around and saw a few people I knew and, all of a sudden, Paul Holmes sticks a microphone in my face and asks a silly question: 'Excuse me, sir, are you the man who as a boy was the Te Aroha primary school tennis champion?' It then became apparent what I had been conned into!

However, I must say that it's a very nice honour to have a programme like that laid on for you, and it was great meeting all the guests who came from various parts of my life. It was also wonderful seeing my daughters all dolled up for the occasion — I don't think I'd ever seen them like that before. And it was particularly special that Roger Moens and George Kerr had travelled down for the show. My only disappointment was the way Paul had his book of notes and it seemed that following along with what was on the script was more important than letting interesting conversations flow.

After the show was over, I had to wait around for a while. I was anxious to spend some more time with Moens and Kerr, but when we got to their hotel there was nothing organised, I was unable to find out where they were, and I ended up not seeing them again. Incidentally, what the Air New Zealand people had been to see me for was to invite Miki and I to be their guest at the Sydney Olympics, which was a wonderful gesture.

Various other things occupied us at the time. In no particular order: I collected some unexpected accolades; my daughter Jacqui had been studying for a Master's in Asian studies at Auckland University and graduated in 2000; and it was also the year of the Sydney Olympics and I was invited back to take part in the Olympic Torch Relay round New Zealand. It came to me by helicopter at the top of the Coronet Peak chairlift near Queenstown and was lit there for its run around the country. I walked it over to Annelise Coberger, the Olympic skier, who skied off down the mountain with it. I actually got to carry it again when it reached Auckland. Murray Halberg was scheduled to carry it for a lap but he was unable to do it and I carried it for him near to the Auckland Domain, where I handed it over to John Walker to light the overnight flame.

Murray and I were together in Wellington and the South Island for fundraising luncheons for the Halberg Trust. Then, in September, thanks to Air New Zealand's generosity, Miki and I were in Sydney for the Olympic Games opening. I hadn't seen the Games since Munich, when I decided it wasn't much fun just sitting in the stands watching. But by 2000 I was old enough not to feel that I was missing being out competing. I really enjoyed the Games and thought the Aussies did a great job in hosting an excellent Olympics.

Around this time — and this was Miki's idea — I had nominated John Landy for induction into the International Scholar-Athlete Hall of Fame. She felt that John was a Renaissance man of many talents, having written several beautifully illustrated books on Australian natural history using his own photography. This was in addition to his stellar athletic career. The trustees of the Hall of Fame liked the idea and he was eventually inducted at Rhode Island in June 2001. I attended to see that happen. This is, in part, what the Hall of Fame now says of John Landy:

> World record-holding miler, naturalist, agricultural scientist, photographer, author, environmentalist and governor of the state of Victoria in his native Australia, John Landy epitomised the multi-dimensional sportsman.
>
> But perhaps John's most memorable race, also in Melbourne, was at the Australian National Championships in 1954. Running in the mile race at Olympic Park, he was on a record-setting pace after half a mile when another great miler, Ron Clarke, fell after another runner's spikes clipped his heel. John, after vaulting over Clarke, stopped and helped Clarke to his feet and then, although 60 yards behind the rest of the field when he resumed running, caught up with and overtook the leaders to win the race in 4 minutes and 4 seconds. Almost a half century later, John's gesture of stopping and helping Clarke to his feet was voted the Australian Sporting Moment of the Century.

In August, the world track and field championships were held in Edmonton, Canada, and a lot of gold medallists were invited to take part in Legends of Gold activities. Sebastian Coe, John Walker, Parry O'Brien, Al Oeter and I were among a stellar group who attended the championships and made some of the presentations. I presented the medals for the 800 metres.

The same month, New Zealand hosted an international physiology conference in Christchurch. My mentor Jere Mitchell was a guest speaker and I was asked to introduce him. So Miki and I were back in New Zealand and we took the chance to make my first visit to Akaroa. We also travelled to the West Coast with the Mitchells and spent a night on a sheep station, where we were looked after in luxurious accommodation. We also spent time there in bed and breakfast places and taking in the sights.

CHAPTER EIGHTEEN

Institutionalised

Colin Kay had headed up an organisation that was involved in supporting athletes and coaching, and in 2000 he approached me with the idea of renaming it the Peter Snell Institute of Sport and putting together a group of trustees he had worked with. Colin had been not only Auckland mayor and Regional Authority chairman but was also an Auckland representative athlete and overall team manager of the New Zealand team at the Commonwealth Games in Perth in 1962, which Murray and I were part of. He was a man I had some respect for and I knew he was a good organiser with a good idea worth supporting. It also allowed me to promote some of my ideas on things such an organisation could do in the area of talent identification.

My position was that I was rather lucky to have been involved in athletics, based on my rather unnoticeable performances as a teenager, and it was only chance circumstances when I was 19 that led me to give running a try. I met Arthur Lydiard and within two or three years ended up with an Olympic gold medal. That would never have been predicted on my performances at Mt Albert Grammar. So I realised that there was a lot of good talent going unrecognised, because if you go only on competitive results then the well-trained, better-prepared individuals, particularly among teenagers, would beat those who hadn't had the same opportunities. In my case, my running was based pretty much on my fitness as a rugby player, a tennis player and all the other sports I was interested in.

My intention with the Institute was to promote the idea of doing some testing of the physical qualities and skills of individuals who might be perfectly suited to sports they hadn't even thought of — for example, rowing or cycling. The other angle was that there is so much sports assistance being doled out by the government — at that time through the Sports Foundation and later through SPARC — that it seemed to me that volunteer organisations and not just waiting for a government handout were also important. Without volunteerism, a lot of good work would not be produced. So I liked the idea that what Colin envisaged would not be part of a government entity — I saw that as being only a good thing.

Over the years, I think the Institute has done a good job in being supportive of athletes, although its resources are nowhere near those of the government. But, unlike the government, the bureaucracy is minimal and efficient and I believe athletes have appreciated being assisted in areas such as coaching and achieving competition overseas. However, one of the problems with an organisation such as this is that it always comes down to trying to raise enough money to be able to assist athletes. I don't see myself as a fundraiser and I've been happy to leave that aspect to others.

In 2001 — a long time ago, it seems now — Garth Gilmour and I started on our second book together, *Use It or Lose It*. It was finally published in 2006, after five years in the making. It was a collaborative effort with Garth which has given me a lot of pleasure because essentially it reflects what I have been dedicating myself to for the last 25 years or so — delivering advice and programmes that improve the wellness of individuals and encouraging people to take a preventive approach to their health.

For example, I believe that people should know what their cholesterol levels are, and what their blood pressure is. Men should have a regular test that helps to detect prostate cancer. Women should have mammograms regularly. Middle-aged people should have colonoscopies to detect the presence of any cancer in the colon. Many diseases can be detected early and treatments can be initiated. I feel that my friend and colleague John Davies died of melanoma which could have been picked early enough to save him. These are all fairly simple strategies that everyone should be doing but probably don't, and this forms a large part of the focus of *Use It or Lose It*.

The book allowed me to put out there in published form the knowledge that I have accumulated in this area and represents exactly the work that I do. I am very proud of the book and I believe that if a lot more people read it they could all be a lot healthier. The title was selected with the idea that if you don't use your *muscles* regularly through exercise they will decline in function; similarly, if you don't use your *brain* regularly, you won't be able to think as well and your memory won't be so good. In fact, just about any body function you can think of will deteriorate and lose its function if you don't use it as it was designed to be used.

Back in New Zealand, in May 2002, I was a guest at a Peter Snell Institute of Sport function organised by Colin Kay, at which I received from the Governor-General Dame Silvia Cartwright the DCNZM (Distinguished Companion of the New Zealand Order of Merit) I had been awarded in the New Year Honours.

During this time, I was invited to a sports physiology meeting in Jyvaskyla in Finland. The interesting thing was that this was where Murray Halberg set his world two-mile record in 1961 on that very successful trip around Europe and Scandinavia that four of us had with Arthur. I managed to find a photograph of Murray running that race and put that up on screen in the introduction to my talk. I also got involved in an orienteering race in the old city of Turku, where I had won an 800 metres race in 1961.

The expectations of the local press for my orienteering were high and they were greatly disappointed when I took a long time to get back. Finally, I visited an overweight-looking Pekka Vasala (1972 Olympic Games 1500 metres champion) at a well-known sports camp called Vierumaki, which was where Arthur had given a number of talks when he was coaching in Finland and where he met Evira, who was to become his second wife and who unfortunately died prematurely of cancer.

CHAPTER NINETEEN

Running around again

Miki and I have never lost our competitive urges. We have toyed at various times with triathlons and cycling before, in 1982, we caught the orienteering bug. That year, an orienteering event was organised in the city of McKinney, not far from Dallas, by the local recreation officer (who didn't know much about orienteering), but Miki spotted it and decided she would like to give it a go. I had tried it in New Zealand in my late twenties, when Gordon Pirie and Ralph King invited me out to Woodhill Forest. That time, I was frustrated by not being a very good navigator and felt that my physical abilities were not much use without the ability to find my way around. But in McKinney, I was the only one who had done anything before. It was a very primitive event and I won it, with Miki finishing third.

She was immediately hooked, so when the opportunity came up to do it again we found out, just by chance, that there was a club in Dallas. The woman who organised that club had called me on a professional level and during a meeting mentioned orienteering. So it wasn't long before we were involved pretty heavily in events in and around Dallas. By 1990, we had made some larger trips, but our first really big international event was in the Asian Pacific orienteering championships which were held mainly in Canada but with some events in Washington State as well. I was able to go back and visit Pullman and meet some New Zealand orienteers, including Robbie Robinson, who was a very good orienteer, as were his wife Val and daughter Tania.

Later that year, Norm Harris, a former fellow journalist in Auckland with Garth, who was now writing for the *Sunday Times* in London and was the organiser of a huge public fun run in Hyde Park, invited us to be the run's special guests for that year and we were delighted to do that. Then we attended our first US orienteering championships which were held in Harriman State Park, a beautiful big park up the Hudson River valley and quite close to New York City. By this time, we were deeply into the sport and in order to make a contribution to orienteering in our local area, we had bought some software that allowed us to make maps of forests and parks in the Dallas region. For the next 16 years, we participated in every US championships, including one held in Alaska. Miki was five times her age group winner and medalled in all but two. I managed two US championships.

My first chance to orienteer back in New Zealand came in 1992 when I was at a conference which was recognising Professor Jack Sinclair's retirement. Jack, a former New Zealand mile record-holder and 1950 Empire Games representative, was a co-founder of the Physiological Society of New Zealand — and another former Mt Albert Grammar pupil. I gave a presentation of my research interests at that function and later went down with Miki to do an event on the slopes of Mt Taranaki.

In 1995 we were invited to a big event in southern Sweden, in an area called Skane. It attracted some 13,000 participants, whereas a typical US championship might have three or four hundred. It explains why the Scandinavians are so good. The meeting involved five days of competitions. Robbie and Val Robinson were there again and did really well. Their daughter Tania has competed with distinction for many years on the New Zealand team.

The first world veterans' championships we competed in were held in Tasmania near Launceston. The United States later hosted this event in some beautiful forest country in northern Minnesota, which we also attended. Neither of us did very well and we came to appreciate how particularly good the Scandinavians were. New Zealand was particularly conspicuous among the top finishers.

The first really big event we participated in down in New Zealand was very significant because this was in 2000, on the eve of the new millenium, and we actually had a race which started at midnight around the streets of Feilding. The rest of the event was staged in some very nice pine forests on sand dune-type terrain just south of Wanganui.

It has been a sport which has given us both a great deal of satisfaction and has helped to keep us fit and healthy.

In 2006 my brother Jack died in Pukekohe after spending the last 15 of his 79 years coping with Parkinson's disease. His death, from a fall, was particularly unfortunate. The house he and his wife Daphne had lived in for many years was not suitable for someone with Parkinson's — there were a lot of steps and stairs, with concrete steps both back and front and down to the garage. So they built a new place which was just single storey, with no steps, and very safe.

They lived there for a short period while they were selling the old house. The day Jack fell, the sale had been completed and Daphne and Jack had returned there to hand over the keys. Jack decided to get out of the car, go up the steps and give them to the new owner. To Daphne's horror, as he went up the steps, he teetered and fell backwards, hitting the back of his head on the concrete. He comatosed, went into Middlemore Hospital and picked up pneumonia, as is often the case with hospitals, and, after several weeks, he died.

CHAPTER TWENTY

From gold to bronze

In late 2005 I had received a letter from a retired New Plymouth surgeon, Fridtjof Hanson, who had become a passionate student of sculpting in clay. He said that following a visit with his mentor, well-known Wanganui sculptor Joan Morrell, he was working on a larger-than-life-size figure of me running. He said that he had no plans for the statue and no one had asked him to produce such a sculpture.

I replied expressing interest in his project and asked him to email me photos of the work in progress. Then I received a letter from Heather Cormack, writing on behalf of the Egmont Community Arts Council. She informed me that her council wished to do something to recognise my birth in Opunake in 1938 and asked if I had any ideas for some permanent feature such as a plaque. I immediately thought of Dr Hanson, who probably would be delighted to have his work on display, and mentioned to Heather that a statue of me running was in existence. The Egmont Arts group visited Dr Hanson's New Plymouth studio, liked what they saw and set in motion plans to raise money to have the clay model cast in bronze. Heather remembers receiving mixed responses when she mentioned the statue possibility at various Christmas parties, so it is a testament to their persistence that this small coastal Taranaki community raised the $40,000 required for the project and were able to have the work completed by Ross Wilson by April 2007. The impact on me was profound and I felt very proud to receive such recognition. One's place of birth is important, and I believe the nine years I spent in

Opunake before moving to Te Aroha played an important part in shaping my development as a person.

The unveiling of the seven-foot tall statue coincided with my visit to Massey University in Palmerston North as a visiting research fellow and to receive an honorary Doctor of Science degree and deliver the graduation address. A few days after the Massey graduation, Miki and I travelled to Opunake and headed up the mountain to the beautiful Dawson Falls lodge for an evening reception to meet members of the Arts Council, whose effort had made the statue project possible. The chair of the Council was Jean Roach, sister-in-law of Janica, who was in my class at Opunake Primary School. We stayed in a nice cottage close to the cliffs leading down to the beloved beach of my childhood.

The unveiling took place on a beautiful sunny Saturday morning. Shops had created welcome home signs and running scenes in their front windows. The statue was mounted on a stone pedestal on a corner in front of the Taranaki Savings Bank, a major contributor. After the ceremony, attended by a large crowd, including my sister Marie and Jack's widow Daphne, a Highland pipe band led Miki, myself and a group of children a block towards the beach. We turned and walked past my old house, paused for a group photo, and continued on to the recreation centre for a reception and reunion with many of my old classmates and my standard three teacher, Bruce Telford, now aged 85. Opunake's population is only about 1200 and it seemed that just about every one of them was there.

In 2006 I had been contacted by Massey University to see if I would have any interest in participating in some collaborative research under which I would visit New Zealand for a period and engage in research projects at Massey. I thought it was a good idea in principle because it would allow me to do some things in New Zealand in the area of adult-onset diabetes in the Maori and Polynesian population, who have four times the risk of developing this disease compared with Pakeha.

So, in October of that year, I made a two-week exploratory visit and had meetings with Massey scientists at their three campuses at

Palmerston North, Wellington, and at Albany in Auckland. They have a strong exercise science group in each centre but no co-ordinating professor for the discipline. I think Massey was interested in seeing if I could fulfil that role, but unfortunately my work in Dallas involves a considerable number of research projects and it really wasn't possible for me to even entertain the idea of spending time in New Zealand at the expense of my Dallas career. In Dallas, my salary depends on funding from research grants, and if I was not in Dallas doing that work that would present a problem.

However, we agreed that I would come back in May of 2007. Massey had also decided to award me an honorary Doctor of Science degree. This was a significant honour because it represented the first serious recognition in New Zealand that I had more to offer than an athletic career which was now 40 to 45 years in the past. I felt that they were acknowledging the fact that I had accomplished some important scientific goals. As I mentioned earlier, I received the degree in Palmerston North just a few days before I visited Opunake for my statue unveiling.

Some serious work is being done at Massey. We have laid the foundation and set out the protocols for collaborative research into arthritis and adult-onset diabetes. The intervention — by which I mean the treatment which we hope will have a positive effect — is, in the arthritis case, aerobic exercise. One group, in addition to anaerobic exercise, would do resistance or strength training, while another group would take fish oil for the important omega-3 fatty acids which have been shown to have some efficacy in alleviating arthritis pain and helping prevent the damage done by certain substances.

Arthritis is not caused just by mechanical damage — such as a runner's knees going bad — because even sedentary individuals get arthritis. It is a result of an out-of-control inflammatory response. The body's immune system is designed to protect the body against invaders but sometimes loses control and the body's normal tissues can be attacked. We make use of the anti-inflammatory properties of omega-3 fatty acids to counter that.

With adult-onset diabetes, we know that diet and exercise help. Adding fibre to the diet is what we are trying to encourage and helping reduce obesity is also effective. Exercise improves insulin sensitivity. But the challenge is how to achieve a change of behaviour and have participants in a study sustain that for a reasonable time — say, for example, 12 months. This will be an ongoing project in which I am taking a great deal of interest.

CHAPTER TWENTY-ONE

Where to now?

So, what is the future for Peter Snell? This is 2007 and I am 68 years old. The goals for myself would be to maintain a physically active lifestyle, to be able to avoid medications unless absolutely necessary — other than maybe an occasional painkiller for arthritic pains (though less so since increasing my marine omega-3 fat consumption) — and to choose foods wisely to make these things happen. With Miki, I hope to continue being active and enjoying life at home, as well as travelling to new places. For physical activities, I will continue cycling, orienteering fairly regularly, walking, biking and playing racquetball, the American equivalent of squash, once or twice a week.

As far as work is concerned, I will continue for a few more years yet. Professionally, the Massey connection is important because this will allow collaborative research activities involving Massey to be undertaken in Dallas. Periodically, I will be able to spend some time in New Zealand under this arrangement.

That's my goal. I don't look beyond helping to continue the promotion of principles of prevention and healthy living so that we can all age more successfully than we do at present. I hope that achieving that objective will have a big impact in reducing health costs and taking better care of people who, as they age, cannot take care of themselves. This has got to be a huge and growing burden on the economy unless something is done about it.

EPILOGUE

Lydiard knew that

One of my objectives in studying physiology and biochemistry has been to try to understand why Arthur Lydiard's training methods worked so well, and I am frequently asked: 'Now that you understand the science of running, what parts of the Lydiard training system would you change?' The fascinating aspect of finding out exactly what was happening to me during training and racing all those years ago is that, typically, my answer is that I would not change anything. Arthur knew exactly what he and his disciples were doing and why we were doing it so successfully.

My education has enabled me to understand the physiological effects of Arthur's training. In simple terms, the formula is that two years are spent acquiring an endurance base through aerobic distance running and, once this is achieved, the athlete works towards a large volume of training at race pace, with some work on developing leg strength, through uphill training, and leg speed, which can be enhanced during the downhill phase of hill training.

Arthur was not just a coach. He was a scientist. True, he did not follow the recognised scientific method of testing hypotheses by comparing experimental groups with 'controls' and then analysing the differences in performance variables with statistical tools. What he did, though, was read avidly — particularly the writings of British coach Francis Webster, who argued that endurance was an important component of speed. This reading, coupled with his experience as a marathon runner, led him to test different variations of training mileage and pace, initially on himself, and make careful observations — just like a scientist. When he finally found the mix of pace and mileage that produced the best results for him, he tested the training out on other athletes.

Certainly, there has been some new understanding of issues such as glycogen depletion and the overtraining syndrome that plagues many elite athletes. However, my contention, when I talk to coaches about Lydiard training, is that a good distance training base protects the athlete from the effects of overtraining. Arthur knew this.

Does science really help? Not much. When scientists begin to think they are coaches, the result can be a disaster. I cannot think of a single successful training innovation proposed by a scientist. Their contribution has been to follow along and explain why particular training methods or ethnic groups, such as the Kenyans, are successful. Lance Armstrong, for example, has benefited from carbon-fibre technique and wind tunnel experiments to minimise air resistance through body position, clothing and helmet design, but his superior endurance is attributed to his exceptional ability to utilise oxygen. At least scientists don't make inane comments such as 'athletic success occurs in cycles', which tells us nothing about *why* and *how* top runners develop.

Trial and error methods, used carefully, are effective, and Arthur Lydiard created the physiological rationale to support his. I remember doing his famous 22-mile (35.4 km) course with Murray Halberg and feeling tired and wanting to take advantage of the offer of a car ride home at the 15-mile mark. Murray killed that idea with the comment that the real benefit of the run was the last seven miles so I made it on my feet. Years later, I was able to confirm the physiological reason behind this astute observation. Research in Sweden by my PhD supervisor, Dr Phil Gollnick, showed that during exercise of moderate intensity the depletion of muscle glycogen occurs first in slow-twitch fibres and then, after an hour, in fast-twitch fibres as well. According to Henneman's size principle, the slow-twitch muscle fibres, which are connected to small motor neurons, are activated first. As the exercise intensity increases, fast-twitch fibres connected to large motor neurons are recruited to provide the additional force.

Gollnick's finding indicated that, as slow-twitch fibres became depleted of their glycogen and were unable to continue to contract, fast-twitch fibres took over. On the assumption that the adaptation of individual muscles fibres in muscle occurs only if the fibre is used, moderate-pace running over an extended duration of one and a half hours or more results in a training effect on the fast-twitch fibres.

The other method of training fast-twitch fibres is to run at a fast pace, for 30 seconds to two minutes, followed by one to two minutes of recovery — interval training. Often, this is done at race pace, so a four-minute miler might do a series of 10 x 400 m in 60 seconds, with a two-minute easy jog between, or perhaps 15–20 x 200 m at slightly under 30 seconds with a one-minute jog between. There are many permutations and combinations of interval training as long as it bears some relationship to race pace. The downside is that the high intensity of this training causes metabolic and mechanical stress that can lead to overtraining. Lydiard knew this — his system eliminates the risk.

As I say, I am constantly defending the value of long-distance training for middle-distance runners. Some coaches and most 'sports' scientists still claim that it violates the law of specificity — that running that is substantially slower than race pace will induce slow movement patterns in the athlete. This reasoning is understandable, because most of them have never known what it is like to do marathon-type training and experience the 'tireless state' touted by Lydiard. The coaches' negativity can be described only as stubborn refusal to try a method that may not make sense to them but which has yielded phenomenal results. Some coaches have even said: 'We tried Lydiard's stuff and it didn't work.' That is hard to respect. There is no argument that when an athlete runs long distances at six to seven minutes a mile, the body 'learns' a slower movement pattern and may be less efficient at race pace running, but this is quickly remedied with the combination of two or three weeks of speed training coupled with race-pace repetitions. Again, Lydiard knew this.

The slow running we in the Lydiard school refer to is running at 40 to 59 per cent slower than race pace. It is relative to the event. For example, seven minutes a mile is a useful pace on which to build a base. It is about 50 per cent slower than the race pace of a 1:50 800-metre runner but only 30 per cent slower than a 30-minute 10 k runner's race pace. Slow running does not mean plodding — it means running at a pace just below the anaerobic threshold, about 70 to 75 per cent of VO_2max. The inability to run a mile in four minutes is not because the athlete does not possess sufficient speed or muscle mass to generate the force but because the energy requirements of the pace cannot be met aerobically and fatigue arises from the effects of anaerobic metabolism.

The important issues in distance training today include understanding the exercise dose and response required for maximum development of the oxygen delivery system; the intensity and duration relationship on muscle fibre adaptation; and early indications of maladaptation to training — the overtraining syndrome. Arthur Lydiard knew all about this more than half a century ago. His successes in New Zealand in the 1960s and Finland in the 1970s influenced many coaches to try his methods, which emphasised several months of conditioning with a running volume of 160 kilometres a week before undertaking a four-week transition phase of hill work, which preceded eight to 10 weeks of interval training and speed development on the track.

The physiological implications of a high volume of training at moderate speed have not been well understood by many scientifically oriented coaches. They question how running at a relatively slow pace can be beneficial for an event such as the 1500 metres, other than by providing a base on which to build a heavy programme of race-pace related interval training. But athletes and coaches who used the programme properly knew it worked — the best performances in my career were immediately preceded by a thorough programme of long-distance running. I ran a marathon not long before breaking the world mile, half-mile and 800 metres records on grass tracks.

The muscle fibres used in racing characteristically adapt by an enhanced perfusion of blood through increased capillary density and the activity of oxidative enzymes. For this to happen in a specific population of muscle fibres, they must be made to contract for prolonged periods. I have explained the two methods which can be used for this purpose and why the one, marathon-type training followed by hill work and speed training, is better than the other, race-pace interval training. Another important issue is the question of recovery between hard intervals. Sessions of hard 400- or 200-metre runs may be very demanding if the athlete is allowed only a short recovery, say, of one or two minutes. If the purpose of the intervals is to train the muscle fibres required for the level of work involved in racing, what is the purpose of the short recovery? The only explanation I have ever heard is that the athlete is becoming accustomed to fatigue and developing his/her 'buffering system'. This is simplistic and may be the major reason for the lack of success of many athletes who excessively use fast intervals with limited recovery.

Consider the consequences of this type of training physiologically. There are two conditions which inhibit muscle fibre contraction: lack of fuel — muscle glycogen; and low intramuscular pH. During long-distance running, some degree of glycogen depletion produces a desirable effect, as outlined above. But, during hard interval training, the accumulation of lactate, and its associated hydrogen ion, inhibits the activity of the key glycolytic enzyme phosphofructokinase and the binding of actin and myosin filaments. This situation reduces contractility and impairs muscle performance and the total volume of training that can be accomplished. In addition, this level of training intensity causes short-term damage to mitochondrial membranes and induces the secretion of cortisol, which is a proteolytic hormone. There is no good evidence or reasoning that training with high levels of lactic acid, as is the case with hard intervals and short recoveries, has any beneficial effect that cannot be acquired from early-season competition. Indeed, there is much anecdotal evidence that such training leads to the development of the overtraining syndromes, overuse injuries and less than optimal performance.

The correct use of intervals is to maximise the amount of fast running up to race pace. This can be accomplished only by taking enough time between the effort phase to allow the clearance of lactate and the recovery of muscle pH. Many runners have found that heart rate recovery to 120 to 130 beats a minute is a useful guide. And athletes who are well conditioned with several months of distance running are better able to tolerate the effects of high-intensity training. This points to the fact that the intensity and duration of interval training should be individualised to the athlete's level of conditioning.

As I have said, we now know that when muscles fibres become depleted of oxygen, they are no longer able to contract and other adjacent fibres in the muscle take up the slack. But for this to happen, the moderate-pace running must be for an hour or preferably more so that the slow twitchers have all been depleted and the fast twitch fibres are activated. So it is all about depleting the glycogen stores in muscles to enhance the training effect. This explains how 'slow' running, if done long enough at around seven minutes a mile, improves resistance to fatigue and also your speed at the end of a race. Runners who feel that they are doing distance training by running six or eight miles with an occasional 20-miler thrown in will get some cardiovascular benefit but will not achieve the same muscle adaptation as those who run 12 to 15 miles with the occasional 20-miler added to the mix. And it is well established that maximal cardiovascular conditioning occurs after about 12 months but that muscle and circulatory changes may take years. This accounts for the maturity of most marathon runners.

Interval running, incidentally, was popularised as a training method in the 1930s by the German 800-metre world record-holder Rudolf Harbig. The original method, introduced by coach Gerschler and cardiologist Reindell, called for effort ranging from 30 to 70 seconds at an intensity that elevated the heart rate to about 180 beats a minute. This was followed by enough recovery time to return the heart to 120. The method had instant appeal for athletes because it was race-specific training and allowed the performance of a large amount of work. It also appealed to armchair coaches and scientists.

Contemporary interval training involves a wide range of effort periods, distinguished by the terms short- and long-intervals. It should not be confused with another form of training involving repeated effort and better described as high-intensity training. This aims to develop speed and anaerobic capacity. A six-week programme of intense, intermittent hill running using endurance-trained Canadian athletes produced impressive improvements in an intensive treadmill run test (17 per cent), peak blood lactate (14 per cent) and high energy phosphates in muscles (15 per cent), but VO_2max, anaerobic power and muscle fibre showed no change. McMaster University in Canada gave cyclists six sprint interval training sessions over two weeks. Each session consisted of four to seven all-out sprints on a cycle ergometer separated by four minutes of recovery. The finding was that while VO_2max was unchanged, their cycling endurance performance improved from 26 to 51 minutes at the same work rate (80 per cent of their VO_2max measured before training). While studies of this type may seem compelling, my experience has been that excessive high-intensity training, especially without a good endurance base, ultimately leads to impaired performance.

At a recent gathering of American coaches, I produced a paper which I entitled *What is wrong with American middle and distance runners (marathon excluded)?* and aimed at suggesting why they were not winning their share of Olympic medals and offering changes that might be helpful. The main problem I identified was too much racing under the college scholarship system — a problem that I first observed when visiting California in 1961. (New Zealand's 2006 Commonwealth Games 1500 metres champion, Nick Willis, is fortunate that his own coach at the University of Michigan, Ron Warhurst, is nurturing Nick's long-term future.) America has a large talent pool — including some of the best teenage runners in the world — a high standard of living, the best sport science, college scholarships, the latest equipment, knowledgeable coaches and competitive opportunities. So I questioned why they were not winning at the same level as US sprinters, jumpers and throwers.

There are compelling reasons why the best runners are from countries in Africa and not the States — and it is NOT because of the altitude of East Africa, Ethiopia or Morocco or because they possess some inherent genetic advantage. In US high schools, the best natural talent is often exposed to fast interval running, excessive competition and other forms of speed work. This regimen may be appropriate for events up to 400 metres and, in the short term, yield quick results for middle-distance runners, for whom this work should be done only after developing an endurance base. But the emphasis on results and bragging rights may encourage coaches to look for short-term results for the school rather than considering the athletes' long-term development. Consequently, much of the training is high-intensity, with short-recovery intervals mainly over 200 to 400 metres. This produces peak form relatively quickly but carries a high risk of overuse injuries, lowered resistance to infections, and the lethargy associated with overtraining. Thus, while the cream from their high schools is very good — indeed, much better than most other countries — after four years of college, the rest of the world leaves the US behind.

It is my belief that the college scholarship system and its emphasis on winning is inherently disastrous for middle-distance runners. The runner is often asked, in a single meeting, to double at 800 and 1500 metres and then run another 800 in anchoring the medley relay. Furthermore, with competitive cross-country and indoor seasons, there is little time to develop a good endurance base. Finally, on graduation after four years, the 22-year-old athlete has little place to go — no coach, no training partners, no structure and, without a shoe contract, no means of support. The results speak for themselves: no US Olympic medals in middle-distance running since Dave Wottle won gold — and that was 35 years ago. At Athens, the US marathoners produced two medals (men's silver and women's bronze), which showed that the programmes of non-college coaches Bob Larson and Joe Vigil are paying off.

Traditionally, 1500-metre races have been tactical affairs with the field bunched going into the last lap (Athens was a notable exception, when it became a two-man race between El Guerrouj and Lagat). In these races, US athletes have been consistently outclassed in the final 400 metres, which was mistakenly interpreted by some as a lack of speed. But the 1500 is not a speed event — the ability to use one's speed at the end of the race depends on that person's endurance.

An understanding of the physiology of adaptation to stress helps in identifying the problem of excessive high-intensity training and competition. Sprinting, throwing and jumping are explosive activities requiring strength and speed. Athletes in these events thrive on competition. Strength is determined not only by muscle size but also by an important neural component, which is the athlete's ability to recruit muscle fibres. We have all heard of great feats of strength performed under emergency conditions. For example, the woman who was changing a tyre when her baby crawled under the car and the jack slipped. The woman lifted the car to protect her baby and held it up until the child crawled out to safety. That's a graphic demonstration of the neural component, which may well be enhanced by competition.

For middle-distance runners, competition is a two-edged sword. Unlike short, explosive activities, sustained high-intensity exercise comes with a metabolic price — high lactic acid and low muscle pH; high levels of the catabolic hormone cortisol and an increased risk of overuse injuries and the overtraining syndrome. So, what are the practical answers to the college problem?

- The US needs to nurture and develop its talent, not exploit it for short-term results for the glory of interscholastic and collegiate competition — and the prestige and profit of the coach.

- High school coaches should place more emphasis on off-season endurance training in which athletes regularly run for up to an hour at a comfortable pace — around seven to eight minutes a mile. At the college level, these runs should be up to 15 miles at six to seven minutes a mile.

- Exhausting workouts should be avoided and competition limited to six to eight races a season over the specialty distance with a goal of peaking for two or three major races. For 800-metre runners, additional under-distance races (200 and 400 metres) can be used for speed sharpening.
- The coach should know how to recognise signs and symptoms of overtraining syndrome and the potential for overuse injuries such as stress fractures.
- At universities, coaches should respect the future possibilities of athletes with high talent and the goal should be improving them, not getting as many races as possible out of them in four years.
- Talented athletes out of high school might consider the possibilities of attending a college which does not have a scholarship programme or participating as a 'walk on'.
- A structure of regular state meets is needed to provide competition for athletes who have graduated from college and athletes not on college scholarship. A practical solution would be for colleges to include events for former students.

In 1961 our group of Lydiard, Halberg, Philpott, Magee and I, on the way to Europe, stopped off at Palo Alto, California, for warm weather tune-up races. Arthur talked at length with high school coach Forest Jameson and Stanford senior middle-distance runner Robin Ruble, among others, and essentially came to the conclusions outlined above. While some understanding of the special needs of middle-distance runners has been achieved, it seems that the US will continue to squander much of its talent.

Index

USE IT OR LOSE IT
Be Fit, Live Well

Garth Gilmour and Peter Snell

Use It Or Lose It is the former great Olympic champion Peter Snell's challenge to us all as we contemplate health and fitness in old age. After researching this subject as a scientist for many years, Snell has written a book for the general reader.

There is a crisis all over the world, asserts Snell, in the mounting health problems associated with poor exercise and worse eating habits. For the first time, life expectancy is on the verge of shrinking. Now a world expert on the relationship between ageing, physical fitness and health, Snell has strong views on what we can all do to keep fit, eat well and be happy.

You'll enjoy life longer, claims Peter Snell, if you take on board the messages in this book. *Use It Or Lose It* contains a wide range of suggested activities and exercises and sound dietary information to enable us to take control of our lives.

'This easy-to-digest book offers comprehensive and insightful directions towards a number of issues relating to the physiology of ageing: how and why exercise can improve wellbeing as we age, and more importantly, the type and amount of exercise and recreational activity one needs to partake in to support successful longevity . . . the content is both highly credible and achievable.'

— Wendy Sweet, *Fitness Life Magazine*